The Economic Value of Higher Education

THE ECONOMIC VALUE OF HIGHER EDUCATION

Larry L. Leslie
Paul T. Brinkman

AMERICAN COUNCIL ON EDUCATION
MACMILLAN PUBLISHING COMPANY
NEW YORK

Collier Macmillan Publishers
LONDON

The American Council on Education/Macmillan Series in Higher Education

Macmillan Publishing Company
866 Third Avenue, New York, N.Y. 10022

Collier Macmillan Canada, Inc.

Library of Congress Catalog Card Number: 87-22085

Printed in the United States of America

printing number
1 2 3 4 5 6 7 8 9 10

Library of Congress Cataloging in Publication Data

Leslie, Larry L.
The economic value of higher education.

(American Council on Education/Macmillan series in higher education)
Bibliography: p.
Includes index.
1. Education, Higher—Economic aspects—United States. 2. Education, Higher—Social aspects—United States. 3. Higher education and state—United States. I. Brinkman, Paul, 1942- . II. Title. III. Series.
LC67.62.L47 1988 338.4'737873 87-22085
ISBN 0-02-918601-3

To our parents
Doris Whitehead Leslie and Allen Edward Leslie
Rita J. Brinkman and Arnold L. Brinkman

Contents

List of Figures and Tables

Figures

Tables

Preface

This book concerns policy. It concerns private policy, as it relates to investing in higher education by private individuals and less directly by private individuals and their families. It concerns also public policy, first regarding the public or social investment in higher education, then regarding the degree to which contemporary higher education financing schemes serve the emergent social goals of promoting social equity and opportunity.

As such, the book addresses the policymaker, both private and public, at all levels. When individuals make college attendance decisions, in considerable part they are making private investment decisions. Public policymakers face conceptually the same decisions in deploying public funds. Governments must decide how much to spend, where to spend it (for example, in 2-year or 4-year institutions, public or private), and in what form (for example, institutional or student aid). Higher education administrators and other institutional policymakers are very much involved, too, for they must administer those policies plus set some policies of their own, such as how high tuition should be and how student aid should be targeted.

This book is unique in two important respects. First, it examines critically, and subsequently extends far beyond, conventional methods of assessing the value of higher education. Thus, a great deal of new knowledge is gained—knowledge that sometimes contrasts sharply with what is presumed to be true.

Second, the unique analytical methods employed offer conclusive evidence as to what is known about the economic value of higher education. Employing methods that carefully synthesize essentially all existing empirical evidence, definitive results are obtained concerning such questions as the magnitude of the rates of return to higher education, the contributions of education to the national economy, the economic impacts of colleges on their local communities, the effects of higher tuitions upon enrollments, the equity effects of the combination of higher education financing and enrollment patterns, and the effects of student aid.

While this book is aimed primarily at those who set policy for, or invest in, higher education, it will also serve as a valuable resource for those who conduct research on the economics of higher education. The extensive bibliography and especially the appendices, which describe systemically the characteristics of literally hundreds of studies, will make it possible for the researcher to quickly assess progress in an area of study and find the questions that remain unanswered.

We owe a special debt to Tullisse Murdock for letting us incorporate in Chapter 8 the results of her dissertation on the effect of student aid on persistence in college. The comments of the anonymous reviewers were also helpful. The responsibility for any errors of fact or judgment is ours alone.

We wish to acknowledge gratefully the expert technical asistance of Dr. Kenneth Brown and, in the preparation of the manuscript, the assistance of Cara Summerfield, Alice Stilwell, and Kathy Bolton.

PART I

Summary and Stage Setting

1

Introduction and Summary

By the mid-1980s the United States was spending roughly $109 billion on higher education. Including indirect costs, the figure was close to $170 billion. The former figure alone represented 2.6 percent of the Gross National Product (GNP).

Is higher education a good investment?

This issue is what this book is about. Specifically, the book addresses the following critical policy questions:

- What is the economic payoff of a college education for a private citizen?
- What is the economic payoff of higher education for society?
- How successful is contemporary public policy in meeting the goals assigned to higher education, particularly in regard to social equity?
- Are the costs and benefits of higher education distributed fairly among different income groups?
- How effective are pricing policies as public policy instruments? Specifically, how sensitive are students to the price of enrolling in higher education?
- How effective is student financial aid in promoting educational opportunity?

Two aspects of the way in which the questions are addressed in this book are particularly noteworthy: Answers are gained through an integrative synthesis of the research that has been done on these questions, and the focus throughout is on the "hard data" of rigorous economic and financial analysis.

The first two of the critical policy questions are perennial, and in some form have been asked from the beginning of higher education in this country. The third question and those following it date from a more recent, socially conscious time. Nonetheless, in all cases there exists a body of research that, when properly synthesized, provides clear information to policy- and decision-makers at both the social and private, or individual, levels. However, the body of existing research studies is anything but a set of neat, tidy packages that easily lends itself to synthesis. A hallmark of this book is its rigorous employment of a set of meta-analytic techniques that we specifically designed to facilitate integrative synthesis of research findings, and that enable the policy information to emerge from a background of much noise and confusion in the research literature.

In focusing on the economic and financial aspects of these critical policy questions, the book necessarily leaves much unsaid. As the elements of Figure 1.1 suggest, the overall aims and purposes of higher education in the United States extend far beyond those that can be measured readily in pecuniary or

FIGURE 1.1 The Aims and Purposes of American Higher Education

Promoting Educational Opportunity

Promoting Growth and Economic Productivity

Supplying Trained Men and Women

Achieving Specific Social Objectives

Developing an Educated Citizenry

Creating Knowledge and Stimulating Learning

dollar terms. Many of these aims or purposes are difficult, if not impossible, to measure, and economic and financial analysis has addressed only a few of the more obvious, pecuniary ones. By generally ignoring the nonpecuniary or otherwise nonmeasurable aspects of the payoff of higher education, we by no means wish to imply that these aspects are unimportant. Quite the contrary. Indeed, we mention the nonpecuniary purposes of higher education here at the outset because they are crucial and because one of our fundamental positions in this book is that existing research is incomplete in this regard. We chose the narrower, pecuniary focus in order to write a book of manageable proportions, in order to speak to the conventional, albeit limited, criteria for evaluating higher education in the United States, and because the nonpecuniary dimensions have already been well treated elsewhere, especially in Bowen (1977) and in Feldman and Newcomb (1969). The more measurable economic and financial aspects, in contrast, have not yet been synthesized in a manner appropriate to their importance and potential for policy analysis insights.

A Historical Note

Formally, economics arrived on the education scene only a relatively few years ago. Although Adam Smith (1776) identified "the skill, dexterity, and judgment" of labor as one of the two great determinants of "the wealth of nations" and Alfred Marshall (1927) connected "skill formation" in labor to "societal concerns," the field of economics was little more than an occasional and irregular visitor to education and education policymaking until about the late 1950s. The public influence of economics probably peaked during the Kennedy years, but the field still remains a major force in education policymaking today.

The entrance of economics into public policymaking and ultimately into higher education policy in the United States can be traced to the establishment of the Bureau of Agricultural Economics in the Department of Agriculture in 1922 and to newly created statistical services in the Departments of Labor and Commerce soon thereafter (Barber, 1981). Though far removed from the centers of power, and showing little advancement during the Great Depression when New Deal politics were greatly at odds with prevailing economic orthodoxies, economics finally "arrived" in 1940, when Lauchlin Currie was appointed as the first economic adviser to the President (Barber, 1981). But it was in the person of the liberal Leon Keyserling, who became Chairman of President Truman's Council of Economic Advisers in 1950, that economists and economics truly came into their own in the public policy arena (Hambry, 1973, pp. 293–300). Keyserling was enormously influential in formulating Fair Deal policies, relying as he did upon voluntarism, faith in education, and the notion that an expanded economy would offer prosperity to all.

After Eisenhower's less active presidency, Kennedy was elected on the promise to "get the country moving again." To meet this promise, he gathered together an advisory group calling themselves The New Economists, who at a time when deficits were rising proposed the largest tax cut in American history. The economic boom resulting from passage of the tax cut probably surpassed the expectations of even the most optimistic advisers, and raised the standing of economics to an all-time high. Writing a few years later, Walter Heller (1966, pp. 1–3), Chairman of President Kennedy's Council of Economic Advisers, pronounced:

> Economics has come of age in the 1960's . . . the Federal government has an overarching responsibility for the nation's economic stability and growth. And we have at last unleashed fiscal and monetary policy for the aggressive pursuit of those objectives . . . Interwoven with the growing political and popular belief that modern economics can, after all, deliver the goods . . .

Economists and economic thought soon began to enter into all branches and aspects of government. Education was no exception.

The vehicle upon which economics rode to prominence in education policymaking was appropriately labeled "human capital" theory. The human capital concept arose out of the inability of conventional economic analysis to account for differences in national income growth between rich and poor countries. Because these differences could not be explained by variations in the employment of traditional factors of production—labor and physical capital—it was reasoned that variation in *quality,* specifically in labor quality, must account for the missing variation (Denison, 1964; McPherson, 1982).

The idea of human capital is that the personal decision to spend scarce, private resources on education is an investment decision. Individuals choose from among alternative investments, selecting education when the expected stream of resulting lifetime earnings exceeds the stream of anticipated educational costs by a margin sufficient to yield a rate of return greater than anticipated returns from alternatives. Educated workers possess a stock of human capital not unlike the stocks of machines and other producer goods possessed by firms; these education stocks are depleted over the working lifetime just as inventories are depleted and equipment is depreciated; education stocks contribute to production and thus to economic growth conceptually in the same way as do the components of physical capital.

Theodore Schultz (1960) often is credited with developing the human capital idea and its application to education, although about the same time Jacob Mincer (1958) published a paper titled "Investment in Human Capital and Personal Income Distribution," and much earlier J.R. Walsh (1935) had written "The Capital Concept Applied to Man." Of course, enlightened public policymakers had favored investment in education long before economic and human capital rationales had been well articulated, but the primary government motive for educational spending previously had been to promote social equity (Carnevale, 1982, p. 112). In any case, as Blaug (1968, p. 11) observed, there was no literature in the field and no one had even used the term "economics of education" until about 1960.

Scarcely a decade later a rich literature existed and a few economists were specializing in the economics of education. By 1972, when the Education Amendments were passed, such specialists had become instrumental to federal and state education policymaking. Economists were teaching economics of education courses on college campuses, testifying before congressional postsecondary committees, serving in the federal Office of Education, and discussing the economic value of higher education on morning news programs.

Today, though still influential in governmental policymaking, the economics of education seems to have passed its zenith. Writing almost 2 decades after his seminal text, *The Economics of Education,* first appeared, Blaug (1985) concluded that the heyday of the economics of education had been reached in about 1970, culminating a "golden decade . . . when no self-respecting Minister of Education would have dreamed of making educational decisions without an economist sitting at his right hand."

Nonetheless, most of the empirical higher education finance work, and a particularly large portion of the seemingly valid research (with respect to its internal validity, at least) is still found in the economic literature. It also is true that this is the literature generally credited with being the most influential in the public policy arena. Higher education leaders at One Dupont Circle in Washington, D.C., for example, where a substantial share of national-level higher education political interventions originate, take very seriously reports by economists that "we are overinvesting in higher education" and that "student aid contributes very little to equalizing opportunity," to mention only a few reported conclusions of the recent past.

Of course, it may well be that higher education leaders exaggerate the importance of such results. Perhaps policymakers pay less attention to economic research than the education leadership believes or, at least, fears.

Perhaps, for instance, the federal effort in support of higher education would have declined even without negative reports by some economists on the value of higher education; perhaps higher education shares of state support would have declined regardless of the reports, too. Perhaps the declines are no more than statistical artifacts resulting from emerging and more pressing national and state needs. Perhaps it is not that higher education has been reduced in public favor as much as it is that requirements for national defense, health care, care of the aged, and the needs of the penal system have increased dramatically. It is entirely possible that economic and financial research results have very little or no effect on public financing policy toward higher education. But, again, even if we knew these speculations were true, those individuals who have been disturbed, or for that matter elated, at the research reports doubtless would continue to worry about research impacts in case someday someone in power began to take them seriously, too.

Researchers, for their part, rarely know whether their work will impact policy, though often that is their aim. Even if they knew and the results were not encouraging, no doubt they still would seek to advance knowledge. Such is their lot, their role.

With the foregoing in mind, in Part II we turn to the evidence at hand regarding the value of higher education. We examine first, in Chapter 4, the evidence concerning the yield to the individual on his or her investment in a college education. The hard evidence here is severely limited in quality, though often cited. We strongly emphasize the importance of details in reaching conclusions, and that a great deal may be learned from nonpecuniary considerations. In Chapter 5, we examine similar yields for society and, again, the importance of missing information. The analysis here regards society in general as well as the states and communities. Again, the caveats are many. We utilize a good deal of our available space in describing the limitations of the information, yet we show in both Chapters 4 and 5 that definite conclusions can be reached.

In Part III we focus on contemporary financing policy issues. We address the matter of higher education opportunity, the newest goal, knowing that incremental, or new, money will tend to be targeted on incremental (new or added) goals. We take this line of inquiry because where new money is being directed is where most of the current policy issues will be found. Specifically, we ask, is the higher education opportunity goal being served and are the selected forms of financing effectively targeting that goal? In Chapter 6, we explore whether past and present systems of higher education financing, coupled with enrollment patterns by income group, result in a direct transfer of wealth to the rich or the poor. In Chapter 7, an estimation is made of the extent to which students respond to higher education prices, thereby demonstrating the likely success of financial subsidies in promoting educational opportunity; that is, if enrollments are affected by college costs, then student subsidies that reduce costs should increase enrollments of targeted students. Evaluated in Chapter 8 is student aid, the presently favored technique for achieving enrollment goals.

Results of the Integrative Reviews

THE PRIVATE CALCULUS

Our integrative reviews/meta-analyses demonstrate the following conclusions, with regard to the questions stated at the outset of this book:

- College does pay off, in most cases, for the individual who invests in higher education. The payoff typically is quite handsome and is a good deal more handsome than most observers perceive.

Conventionally measured, the internal rate of return[1] on the private investment in an undergraduate degree is of the order of 11.8–13.4 percent. The return on investment in graduate education probably is of the order of 8 percent for 1 year of graduate study and is about 7.2 percent and 6.6 percent for the master's and doctor of philosophy degrees, respectively. Further, although the private rate of return on the baccalaureate degree probably declined in the mid-1970s, the decline almost certainly was not as great as publicized and since that time almost certainly has returned to near-historic rates.

- Private rates of return reflect primarily variations in costs, not earnings. If deemed to be too low, private rates of return to higher education may be increased merely by raising public support levels.

The popular perception is at odds with realities. When we speak about high or low rates of return or state that rates are declining, most persons assume that the financial *benefits* are what is primarily at issue. The facts, however, differ. Rate of return studies are considerably more sensitive to costs than they are to earnings, and thus say more about what things cost than what they are worth. This is best seen through the example of a simple and oft-cited finding reported in the rate of return literature: It is widely known that rates of return on elementary schooling are highest of all levels of education, and that rates decrease as the educational ladder is ascended to the baccalaureate and graduate degrees. What is generally not known is that the high rate of return for elementary school derives from the fact that the private costs of elementary school are at or near zero, due to child labor laws and free public education. In contrast, college students forego substantial earnings in order to attend college, and they, proportionately, pay the highest share of direct costs of any educational level. As a result, their rates of return are relatively low, even though their relative benefits are often greater than the relative benefits enjoyed by individuals who do not attend college. Private rates of return vary primarily because costs vary so much, proportionately, by educational level, not because earnings vary proportionately. The economic orthodoxy related to economic efficiency has been that more public support should be directed to educational levels where rates of return are highest—the elementary and secondary schools. The *cost-sensitivity principle* of rate of return calculations points clearly in the opposite direction. Greater public subsidies will only drive rates of return higher; hence, if rates of return at a particular level are judged to be too low, prudent public policy is to raise public subsidies at that educational level. Social subsidies that are too low may lead to economic inefficiency due to underinvestment. Hence,

[1]The internal rate of return is the annualized lifetime yield on the investment in higher education. Conceptually, the rate is no different from an annual rate paid on a savings account or a bond. See Chapter 4 for the technical definition.

the results of rate of return studies argue for greater public support of undergraduate and especially graduate study, not for less—at least on this criterion.

- Costs of college usually are overstated in rate of return calculations, resulting in private rate of return results that are inaccurately low.

Researchers typically employ cost estimates originating in the institutions themselves. Due in part to government student aid regulations, institutions have an incentive to overstate these costs. Further, only rarely do researchers appropriately reduce published cost figures to reflect government aid and other student subsidies. The size of this error and the resulting error in the rate of return estimate often is large. As one example, Rogers (1969) has shown that typical subsidies to Ph.D. students reduce their direct costs by 50 percent, which raises the Ph.D. rate of return, in Rogers's data, from *1 or 2* percent to *8 to 10* percent.

- Rate of return methods are conceptually faulty, resulting in an additional, major understatement of private rates of return.

The problem is seen most clearly when one examines the sources of student expenditures. Again, as guides for individual college attendance decisions, only the student's actual costs should be reflected. In 1980, college freshmen paid 18 percent of the direct costs that were ascribed to them for rate of return calculations. Parents and governments made up most of the remainder. Therefore, the *student's* net private rate of return obviously was much higher than reported.

Further, though all or nearly all costs are considered in conventional rate of return analyses, only the monetary earnings of college graduates are included on the benefits side. Thus, rate of return estimates from conventional methods are inherently biased downward. If the "consumption" values, such as the pleasures of learning and collegiate social and cultural activities are included, the private returns increase still more. If the nonmonetary investment benefits such as greater fringe benefits and superior working conditions, better health and longer life, and more astute savings and spending habits are considered, private rates of return accelerate even more.

THE SOCIAL CALCULUS

The social benefits of higher education are examined in three ways: through social rates of return, the contributions of higher education to the national economy, and the economic impacts of collegiate institutions upon their communities. These are not mutually exclusive categories, yet each assesses somewhat different aspects of economic contribution to society and each does so from a different perspective. The various levels of government must view their investment in higher education in light of their own costs and benefits while recognizing that public investments employed and benefits received by larger political subdivisions spill over to lower levels as well.

Social Rates of Return

- As measured by social rates of return, society receives a positive payoff on its investment in higher education. Again, the return is very handsome and is higher than is commonly perceived.

As conventionally measured, the rate of return on the public investment in undergraduate education very likely falls between 11.6 and 12.1 percent. Each method of calculation yields an estimate a few tenths of a percentage point smaller than the comparable estimate of private rates of return and clearly higher than benchmark rates traditionally employed to judge social investments. Social rates of return have been quite stable since 1939; the limited evidence available suggests an upturn in recent years.

- Conventional social rate of return calculations understate true social rates of return. The understatement results from conceptual errors and practical, analytical problems.

Conventional approaches to social rate of return analysis essentially consider only three of the four parts of the cost–benefit equation. Both private and social costs are considered ("social" costs conventionally are considered to be private plus social costs), but on the benefits side, only pretax returns to private individuals are included. Purely social benefits are almost entirely excluded due to practical difficulties in estimation. With full costs but only partial benefits considered, published social rate of return estimates are incorrectly low. The only *social* benefit included is the marginal pretax earnings of college graduates. Such taxes are small in comparison to public support of higher education, and for this reason and this reason only, social rates of return are consistently lower than private rates of return. By implication, conventional analyses make the assumption that incomes of all other citizens are unaffected by the activities of American colleges and universities; in other words, except for the graduates themselves, society would be unaffected by the disappearance of all the nation's colleges and their graduates.

Because social rate of return calculations reflect both social *and* private costs, the points made previously regarding overestimates of private costs pertain here also. Further, social cost estimates often are overstated, too, by the adding on of research and public service costs, even though measured benefits are connected directly only to the activity of instruction. The seriousness of these errors is emphasized once again by reference to the *cost-sensitivity principle:* Rates of return are primarily sensitive to educational costs rather than to the differential earnings of college versus high school graduates.

- Higher education yields to society important nonmonetary benefits.

In addition to the substantial, though understated, 11.6–12.1 percent social rates of return obtained from conventional estimation methods, higher education provides important nonmonetary benefits as well. These benefits may be classified as consumption benefits to students (e.g., fraternity/sorority membership, attendance at cultural and athletic events, the pleasure of learning) and nonstudents (e.g., cultural and athletic events, educational television), and as investment benefits (such as lower welfare and crime rates, community leadership and volunteer work of graduates, productivity gains and furtherance of research and development). Primitive estimates suggest that the magnitude of the nonmonetary social benefits may be roughly equivalent to the value of the monetary ones, thus, by implication, roughly doubling effective social rates of return.

CONTRIBUTIONS TO THE NATIONAL ECONOMY

An alternative approach to the social rate of return calculation is estimation of the portion of national income gain that is attributable to higher education. Although based on the same data as rate of return formulations, the "growth accounting" approach is a more inclusive one because all growth is accounted for and is apportioned out to the various factors of production—land, labor, and capital—with education being viewed as an improvement in labor.

- Education is a major contributor to economic growth in the United States.

Education, overall, tends to explain directly about 15–20 percent of growth in national income, and higher education accounts for about one-fourth of the direct total for education. Another 20–40 percent of national income growth, generally, though not universally, is ascribed to improvements in knowledge and its application. Higher education, along with research and development in industry, contributes importantly to knowledge and knowledge application. Knowing that economic growth originates in (1) land additions or improvements, which have been very small in this century; (2) capital increases, which are specified with relative ease; or (3) labor growth and improvements (education or on-the-job training), a reasonably accurate estimate of the contribution of education and of higher education is possible—and the estimate is substantial. Nevertheless, it is observed that the strength of the "growth accounting" or economic contribution studies is in their inclusiveness rather than in their precision.

CONTRIBUTION TO THE COMMUNITY ECONOMY

"Economic impact" studies, which assess the economic contributions of colleges to their communities, are testimony to the fact that conventional rate of return studies do omit important external benefits. Economic impact studies focus on the benefits captured by individuals other than college graduates, such as the community members who profit from spillovers from academic institutions. Further, these studies make a case for community support of local colleges and universities *independent* of the case that can be made at higher political levels.

- The existence of a local collegiate institution adds considerable wealth and employment to the community.

Colleges and universities bring external financial resources to their communities. Some of these resources are spent locally by the institution's employees and students and by the institution itself, and are again respent until each dollar finally leaves the community as a nonlocal expenditure. Thus, collegiate institutions not only employ local individuals themselves, but also create jobs in community business and governmental enterprises through related expenditures. The best estimates of the local economic contributions are for community colleges, where estimating is least problematic. For each dollar in a college's annual operating budget (educational and general expenditures plus auxiliaries), on average, approximately $1.50–$1.60 of local business volume is created. For each $1 million (1985–1986), on average, about 59 jobs are created. A typical small, public college with a $10 million budget will add about $15–$16 million to the local economy and provide, directly or indirectly, roughly 590 jobs. A typical large, public institution with a $100 million budget will add about 10 times these amounts. These are figures that best pertain to public institutions; the contributions by private institutions may be greater (1) to the extent that they utilize fewer public funds and (2) attract more nonlocal students.

Whereas the preceding considerations represent traditional expectations of higher education, contemporary, additional expectations are primarily of an "equity" or "equal opportunity" nature. Colleges and universities are expected to contribute to improving economic conditions of the poor, many of whom are members of minority groups. Does higher education in the United States contribute to or detract from this goal? Do financing policies possess the potential to advance economic opportunity?

WEALTH REDISTRIBUTION

The first test of the preceding questions is a simple, albeit limited one. Since publication of "The Distribution of Costs and Direct Benefits of Higher Education: The Case of California" by Lee Hansen and Burton Weisbrod (1969), it has been perceived widely that tax and enrollment patterns in the United States act to cause the poor to subsidize the higher education of the rich. This perception is based upon the assumptions that taxes used to support public higher education tend to be regressive and that the probability of college attendance advances as wealth increases, thereby resulting in a condition whereby the poor pay more than their fair share and the rich enjoy the metaphorical fruits of the former's labor. The integrative review reaches an opposite conclusion.

- Generally, higher education in the United States acts to redistribute wealth from richer to poorer, although the degree to which this is true varies considerably across states.

Consideration of pertinent tax systems and enrollment patterns suggests that higher education has acted progressively rather than regressively in most states whose tax/enrollment patterns have been examined by researchers. Adopting procedures to standardize study methods and decision rules used to reach conclusions, the integrative review reveals that with one exception, higher education acts to redistribute wealth from richer to poorer or, at worst and infrequently, from the poor to the middle class, but not from the poor to the rich. Where the middle class benefits, the redistribution from the wealthy usually is greater than it is from the poor. The middle class does appear to be the largest beneficiary of prevalent state tax/attendance patterns. Second-generation studies—those that employ improved analytical methods—demonstrate consistent and stronger conclusions of progressivity.

Relative progressivity is a function of relative state conditions, primarily in two areas: tax progressivity and public/private enrollment mix. Progressivity is relatively strong where state taxes are most progressive and where a large private sector attracts students from wealthier families, leaving proportionally more lower-income youth in the public sector. Examples of such states, where wealth redistribution studies have been reported, are New York and, to a lesser degree, California.

Most of the literature regarding what is known as the wealth redistribution studies is somewhat dated. Therefore, the integrative review reflects largely what was true in the late 1960s and early 1970s, rather than conditions today. For example, in estimating cost burdens by income class, only one or two of the reviewed studies took into account the billions now spent on need-based student aid programs. Inclusion would, of course, improve equity and add to progressivity.

STUDENT RESPONSE TO PRICE

Politically acceptable public interventions in the United States are found almost exclusively in the form of financial incentives and disincentives. The question is, how great is the potential for money to achieve equal opportunity goals? Once this is known, we may proceed to an assessment of specific financing strategies for improving opportunity in higher education.

- Higher education students do respond to prices. Enrollments vary with prices charged; hence, subsidies that reduce net prices should effectively increase enrollment levels for targeted students.

Every study examining the effect of higher education prices on enrollments has concluded that enrollments decline as prices rise and enrollments rise as prices decline. The best estimate is that, on average and all else equal, first-time enrollment rates for 18–24-year-olds will decline .6 percentage points for every $100 price increase, when expressed in 1982–1983 dollars. This means that given a participation rate of approximately .33 (only about one-third of the age group is enrolled), actual enrollments of first-time students should decrease by about 1.8 percent if nothing else were to change (.6 × 3 because the *rate* applies to all, not only to those enrolled). Because our interest here is in appraising the potential policy effect of reducing net prices, the estimate meets our need.

- Student response to price seems to decline with family wealth and institutional prices and selectivity; therefore, response is greatest among low-income students in public community colleges and is least among the wealthier students who enroll in private colleges.

Studies of national samples tend to observe enrollment rate declines of .5–.8 percentage points per $100 price increase, all else equal. Rate declines of .6 or .7 points are likely for public 4-year schools, depending upon selectivity, and for public community colleges a rate decline of .9 percentage points is a good estimate. On average, for private institutions, where students tend to be somewhat more able academically, where a $100 increase is smaller relative to total price, and where family wealth tends to be greater, declines of .2–.5 percentage points might be expected. All of these effects are for the *ceteris paribus* case (i.e., all other factors equal). These predicted enrollment effects have not been observed directly in recent years because other demand elements (income, competitor's price, and taste or preference) have been working in the opposite direction. Most notable among these elements are changing tastes or preferences for higher education among women and older students.

STUDENT AID AND EQUAL OPPORTUNITY

Student financial aid can have several purposes, including rewarding academic achievement, but most aid monies are spent in an effort to equalize educational opportunity. Targeted on individuals from low-income families, most aid is designed to allow these individuals to participate in higher education, attend relatively costly and prestigious institutions, or remain in school at persistence rates comparable to those of students from more affluent families.

- Student aid does increase access. It is estimated that grant aid is responsible, in part, for the enrollment of more than a million full-time low- and middle-income students.

Studies of the impact of student aid on access take the form of econometric analyses, student opinion surveys, and participation rate calculations. All of the findings in the analyses and the surveys indicate that student aid helps equalize access to higher education. Results from the econometric studies suggest that grant aid had enabled 20–40 percent of current low-income students to attend college. In the opinion surveys, typically 40–50 percent of aid recipients say they could not remain in school without student aid. The results of participation rate calculations, which reflect numerous socioeconomic developments, are not unanimous, but in most studies the data indicate that some progress has been made. However, the targeted low-income population still does not participate in higher education at anywhere near the levels for middle- and high-income populations.

- Student aid does promote choice. Because of aid, additional low-income students are able to attend relatively costly 4-year and private institutions.

Studies of the impact of student aid on choice take the same three forms as they do for access. Some of the econometric analyses focus on the effect of aid in situations in which students have been accepted for admission by two or more institutions. The results of these studies are clear: Student enrollment choices are influenced by aid awards, particularly in the form of grants. Other econometric studies specifically examine the impact of the federal Pell Grant program. The results are conflicting, as some but not all studies agree that Pell Grants are effective in helping low-income students enroll in relatively high-cost institutions. There is greater certainty that state student aid programs are effective in promoting choice. Data from student opinion surveys indicate that many aid recipients believe that student aid has enabled them to attend the institution of their choice. The results of participation rate calculations are ambiguous. There were significant college choice gains early in the student aid era, but low-income and nonwhite individuals remain underrepresented in relatively costly and prestigious institutions.

- Student aid allows aid recipients to persist in college about as well as nonrecipients. Given that large numbers of aid recipients are from low-income families, this can be taken as a positive result.

Numerous studies roughly comparable in form have been done on the effects of student aid on persistence. In comparisons of the persistence of aid recipients to that of nonrecipients, effect sizes associated with student aid typically are quite small. Across all studies, aid recipients appear to have a slightly better persistence record, but neither group has an advantage in studies that control for academic ability. Aid effects differ somewhat by the measure of persistence, the amount of aid, and the form of aid. Nonwhite aid recipients do not persist as well as white aid recipients.

In summary, going to college pays off handsomely, both for the individual and society. Individual rates of return on the higher education investment, even when measured conservatively, exceed those of benchmark investments. Social benefits as measured by rates of return are only slightly lower than individual rates; like the latter, they probably understate substantially the true benefits. Higher education contributes to national growth and productivity, and higher education institutions make a significant contribution to the economies of the communities and states in which they are located. The contribution of higher education to emerging social goals is less definitive. Wealth transfer through higher education is probably progressive in most states, but the margins appear to be modest. Students are shown to be responsive to the price of higher education, which allows subsidies in the form of low tuition or student aid to have an effect on access, choice, and persistence. Student aid does have a positive and sizable impact on students from low-income families. Nonetheless, despite the many billions of dollars spent on aid, those students remain underrepresented in higher education generally and especially in certain types of institutions. In the face of rising costs in higher education and unsatisfactory conditions in many of our homes and primary and secondary schools, it seems as though we have had to run hard just to remain in place.

2

Method—Integrative Review of Higher Education Financing Research

In one sense there is nothing new in this book; in another sense everything is new. The evidence brought to bear on the issues addressed is not original; yet the manner in which that evidence is marshaled is entirely new, at least to higher education financing policy research. Attempted for the first time is an integrative review and a meta-analysis of that research.

Jackson (1980), who wrote the seminal paper on integrative reviews, describes their use as "inferring generalizations about substantive issues from a set of studies directly bearing on those issues" (p. 438). He defined the analysis portion of integrative reviewing as "The process by which the reviewer makes inferences from the primary studies" (p. 446). In his paper Jackson devoted considerable space to meta-analysis, an integrative review technique in which statistical procedures are used to transform findings of the individual studies into a common metric.

Meta-analysis, in particular, was developed largely in response to criticism that social scientists never seem to be able to agree about what their research has shown. Since its inception, social science research has been characterized by conflicting results and indecision. As a result, the influence of that research in affecting public policy has been quite limited. Policymaker frustration with social science research and researchers is poignantly illustrated by the following statement by former congressman James G. O'Hara, who chaired the U.S.

House of Representatives Subcommittee on Postsecondary Education. "Why can't you academics ever agree on anything? A few days ago we heard someone from Brookings testify that student aid has a negative effect; a day later someone else said aid doesn't matter one way or the other; and now you are telling us that it promotes student opportunity. What are we to believe?" (personal communication during hearings—June 13, 1974).

The major problem in obtaining consistent social science research results is a soluble one. What is needed is an approach that standardizes results and exercises great care in evaluating evidence. The process of integrative reviewing, particularly meta-analysis, is such an approach.

Why the Discrepancies

After reviewing hundreds of empirical works on questions addressed in this book, it is our judgment that the primary reason social scientists report conflicting evidence is simple lack of adequate care in formulating conclusions. Specifically, the problem arises when researchers overgeneralize from their own work and fail to examine carefully the samples, methods, and findings of others—in short, the explanations of why results vary. Further, social scientists demonstrate a predilection for focusing on generalizable findings, often to the exclusion of study idiosyncrasies, as well as, perhaps, the human tendency to wish to report something new or different.

Results of individual studies on social science questions differ primarily because the studies themselves differ, not because answers are lacking. Results may vary due to sampling error, methodological approaches taken, or differences in the phenomenon studied (Jackson, 1980). In the absence of these or other differences or errors, the direction of results of very similar studies can differ only when the effects studied are very modest or nonexistent.

Historically, reviews of the research literature have not reached their full potential in clarifying what is known because review procedures have been poorly designed. When conducting reviews, otherwise careful social scientists, for some unknown reason, commonly set aside even the most rudimentary scientific methods and attitudes. As a result, these reviews typically are lacking in results standardization, in adequate descriptions of key elements of research design, and in effort to reach conclusions through reconciliation of differences in results.

Admittedly, these are most burdensome and time-consuming tasks. Our own efforts as described herein, though we are deeply conscious of what must be striven for, are far from perfect. Yet, with some expenditure of effort we have been able to make considerable progress over previous reviews. We are confident that our efforts have resulted in at least the accurate identification of direction of effects, where these effects exist in any strength, and in most cases we have succeeded in achieving what we believe are valid and reliable estimates of the magnitude of effects as well.

Another problem for the social scientist and for the reviewer is the ever-present intrusion of personal values, which constantly impede the exercise of the scientific attitude. We remember always Maslow's admonition that in the end all the social sciences are value laden. Few social science researchers lack interest in what their results show, and their conclusions, if not their findings, often reflect personal biases. In composing reviews, it is easy to ignore the facts through selective omission, aggrandizement, and disparagement: The reviewer may ignore or criticize studies yielding results unfavorable to his or her personal values. Integrative reviews, especially meta-analysis, reduce the role of personal values, especially when the analysis is complete. Of course, the meta-analyst may interpret results erroneously, as in any empirical work, but such errors and value biases tend to be relatively evident.

That reviewers of scientific studies usually fail to employ scientific methods may come as a surprise to some readers. To others, the veracity of this point may be obvious. Most reviews of scientific studies often include whatever published works the reviewer has come across, and merely posit who found what and when, with perhaps a sentence or two or at best a long paragraph seeming to describe randomly the characteristics of each study reviewed.

These facts obviously struck Jackson long before they occurred to us. Writing in 1978 and in 1980, Jackson described the common failings of review articles and how scientific reviews should be conducted. He identified reviews that merely listed any factor found to affect a given dependent variable and others that cited only the evidence in support of a particular viewpoint.

Meta-Analysis: Concept and Approach

The principles articulated by G. B. Jackson (1978, 1980) are fundamental to the meta-analysis techniques articulated by Glass, McGaw, and Smith (1981) and later added to by Hunter, Schmidt, and Jackson (1982). Complete meta-analysis is the logical conclusion to calls for application of rules of scientific evidence to social science reviews. Meta-analysis applies scientific principles of integrative reviewing not only to sampling and research design, but also to statistical analysis. Indeed, the statistical approach of meta-analysis is a useful point of departure for describing meta-analysis, because it is the particularly unique element of this method and illustrates the model upon which the entire meta-analysis process is based.

In preface, the form of the statistical estimate, as classically defined by Glass, McGaw, and Smith (1981), applies to experimental situations in which there is at least one experimental and one control group. The simplest meta-analytic statistical test is the "sign" test, which considers only the direction of results: Do studies show positive, negative, or neutral effects and is the preponderance of results statistically significant? Having determined the direction of results, if any, what is the magnitude of the effects? For this, Glass and associates introduce the "Delta" or D-statistic, which is calculated as "The mean difference between experimental and control groups divided by within-group standard deviation" (p. 102). The division standardizes differences in mean values.

Unfortunately, there are very few experimental studies in higher education finance, and very few variance terms are reported in the finance literature. These omissions, however, may not be serious for our integrative reviews and meta-analyses of higher education finance, as we shall now see.

In simple terms, the statistical approach of meta-analysis conceptually is the same as that applied in well-designed empirical studies. In meta-analysis the estimates or results of the several studies reviewed serve as observations in the same way as do, for example, posttreatment test scores of subjects in the classical learning experiments that are common in the educational research literature. Just as effects will vary by subject (individual) in an experiment, so do the generalized study estimates that compose a meta-analysis. Further, just as the external validity (generalizability) of a single study is limited by the characteristics of the subjects, so is the generalization that may be made from a meta-analysis, which will be composed of results from studies of varying traits.

In the case of an educational research study, if the subjects sampled, for example, are atypically able and are all from upper-socioeconomic-status families, results may not apply to less able subjects from less privileged homes. Similarly, a meta-analysis of results obtained at selective, private liberal arts colleges may not apply to public community colleges that are "open door." In either case the policymaker must exercise care in applying results. The meta-analyst may aid the policymaker in this effort. Like the generalizations made from a discrete experiment, in meta-analysis generalizations may be only as broad as the studies reviewed; and the single, summative estimate of effects must be evaluated based upon the particular mix of study conditions represented.

Critics of meta-analysis seem to fail to see the parallel of integrating results from different studies with integrating results from different subjects or cases, as is done in any traditional research. Any traditional study "averages" results for disparate subjects or cases just as meta-analysis averages results of disparate studies. Conceptually, there is no difference. Just as we are interested in how a treatment affects a heterogeneous group of subjects (students?), we are interested, in meta-analysis, in the aggregation of results from different studies, each study itself being based on results for a number of different subjects.

Hence, the aim of meta-analysis is not only to derive a single quantitative estimate, or a single set of estimates; the larger purpose is to provide systematic analysis of unbiased samples of completed studies. Central to this is the meta-analysis matrix, which is a summary representation of each study analyzed, including descriptions of sampling, design, analysis, results, and any special conditions. The matrix is the core of meta-analysis—the content; the synthesized quantitative estimate or estimates described above may, at times, be secondary. Classical meta-analysis, which terminates in statistical estimation of variable effects, normally is the ideal end to be sought after in integrative reviewing, subject to study conditions and resources. The meta-analysis matrix, however, is indispensable.

Review methods employed for this book implement these integrative review and meta-analysis principles. In most cases some sort of meta-analytic calculation is made; in all cases integrative review and meta-analysis principles and procedures are taken as far as our purposes, resources, and the conditions of the reviewed studies allow. We go farther on some questions than others because of relative differences in the form and substance of available research: Some research topics simply are more conducive to meta-analysis than are others. Also, some questions are more central to the purposes of the book; we allocate our time and resources accordingly.

SOME PRACTICAL DIFFICULTIES

It will be informative here to state some of the practical problems in performing higher education financing policy meta-analysis. First, pertinent studies often are modest in number; this limitation, of course, reduces our confidence in the quantitative estimates made. Second, it follows that the breadth of study conditions sampled often will be limited, thus reducing generalizability.

The relative importance of these variations in study conditions to the meta-analysis and ultimately to public policymaking may be great. To illustrate, let us consider an issue addressed later in the book. Student response to higher education prices is shown to be a function of many factors, such as family or student income, ability, motivation, peer influence, and characteristics of the college attended. Thus, for example, pricing policies that may apply well to community colleges and their students may not fit the conditions of private research universities or liberal arts colleges very well at all. Because the aggregate meta-analysis estimate of price response is a function of the populations of the studies sampled, this estimate clearly is affected by the mix of these populations. Policy applications to specific cases must reflect an awareness of this mix.

By far the largest task in higher education finance meta-analysis is study standardization. The degree of variation in higher education research methods and statistical analyses is extraordinarily large; by comparison, in the traditional social science disciplines, design and analysis homogeneity is the rule. The magnitude of the standardization problem cannot be overstated. The authors of this book spent much of their time on standardization efforts that would not even be necessary in most social science disciplines. Standardization in one representative, complete meta-analysis of 25 cases consumed about 3 months' time.

Another problem is a technical one that arises because most researchers in higher education fail to report measures of variance—that is, deviation from the mean value—usually making it impossible to weight individual study results as suggested by some theorists in the formal meta-analysis literature. Of course, one would expect greater accuracy in an estimate from consistent data than from highly disparate data; however, the issue and its implications are not clear cut.

Insights into the utility and proper use of variance terms may be gained by referring again to the analogy of the classical experimental study. The first thing suggested by highly consistent data (e.g., very similar student scores) probably is homogeneity in the population studied. If subjects are greatly different, one would anticipate variations in the magnitude if not direction of effects on study participants, as it is known that subject performance on many measures will vary by such factors as age, sex, maturation, and ability. Hence, consistency in subject scores for a given study may be reassuring for considerations of internal validity (accuracy), but the implications for external validity (generalizability) may be less favorable. Not only is variation in "scores" for different types of students expected, this variation in subjects may be a virtue because the treatment thus may be generalizable to broader populations.

What is true for the individual students' scores is true for the grouped averages of these scores in the meta-analysis: Large variance terms for individual studies may not be a bad thing. Using again the example of student price response, we would expect from theory considerable variation in student response to, say, tuition increases because students vary in regard to such factors as family income, personal motivation to attend college, alternative price (i.e., university) choices, and so forth. Thus, low variances for individual studies probably reflect sample homogeneity and limited generalizability, whereas a large variance term suggests a broad sample and high generalizability. It follows that in meta-analysis the mean estimates from studies of similar populations should be quite consistent and that the mean estimates from a number of studies of different populations should be quite inconsistent. One would expect, for example, that the mean estimates of price response from a number of studies of broad national samples would be quite reliable (consistent), though internally (among individuals) highly variable, while a number of separate mean estimates taken at community colleges, public universities, and private colleges would vary considerably across the institutions, even though responses by students within each college type would be relatively consistent.

Perhaps the usual omission of variance estimates in higher education studies is not all bad because there may be a potential for misuse of this data. The case for weighting more heavily studies with low variance terms is debatable. It is somewhat puzzling how one would adjust policy to reflect these variance differences if they were known; that is, would it make sense to attach greater quantitative weights to low-variance estimates obtained from homogeneous groups? Perhaps weighting makes sense in the meta-analysis of experiments because sample homogeneity is common; however, in the studies examined herein, sample heterogeneity typically is great, thus rendering such weighting problematic.

The final problem or issue to be discussed here is whether some quality control should be exercised in selecting studies for the meta-analysis. Simply put, does meta-analysis, in its focus on averages and in essentially treating all studies equally, yield less than optimally valid estimates? Some of the critics of meta-analysis argue that the natural order of events in scientific research is such that better and better studies are produced over time, so that later works in a field of inquiry tend to yield more valid results than earlier ones. If this is so, a single study correcting for all earlier design errors should yield a result superior in accuracy to the average of all such works over time.

Proponents of meta-analysis tend to hold that this is an inaccurate portrayal of reality. First of all, the notion of constantly improving research designs is probably largely a myth. Usually, there are only *different* designs, each vigorously defended as superior to previous approaches, but all of which tend to possess merely advantages and disadvantages, in contrast with the alternatives.

Another argument in this connection is that in their variety of methodological and statistical approaches and in their breadth of populations studied, the works analyzed in meta-analysis provide a richness of context that is highly useful in assessing the value of study results to specific applications, that is, cases.

A common way to resolve the problem of potentially flawed studies is to combine results in at least two ways: one meta-analysis in which all studies are included and one in which questionable studies are deleted. This has been our general approach. Our experience has shown, however, that usually the more poorly controlled studies or those of questionable designs yield results consistent with those that are not obviously flawed (a provocative finding in itself). In other cases the results of flawed studies often are balanced out by other flawed studies that yield results at the other extreme. When this balance fails to occur, the preferred procedure is to point out the probable reason for the disparate findings, but still offer both sets of results. Jackson (1980) suggests that the meta-analysis should contain at least a modest number of well-designed studies if one is to evaluate the effects of seemingly flawed studies.

Conclusion

In the following chapters, the integrative review and meta-analysis is taken as far as possible on the central questions related to the value of higher education. In these cases, synthesized estimates are made of what the empirical research has shown. The numbers of studies available generally are adequate to lend considerable confidence to the overall estimate of effects; however, for subpopulations numbers often are small and generalizations, therefore, must be viewed as more tentative. After traditional questions of the value of higher education are addressed in Chapters 4 and 5, the analysis turns to assessments of achievements in the area that has drawn the major policy attention in recent years: equality of higher education opportunity. In order to accomplish this assessment, first (Chapter 6), higher education sources of support and enrollment patterns are examined by income class. Here, the assessment is more integrative review than meta-analysis. Next (Chapter 7), employing a generally complete meta-analysis, the potential of financing as a public policy instrument is evaluated through examination of the student demand studies, which address the relationship between higher education prices and the student's enrollment decision. In the final content chapter (8), integrative review techniques are adhered to and the meta-analysis is taken as far as possible.

3

Approaching the Assessment of Higher Education Financing Policy

The financial analyst's standard approach to decision making in policy analysis is simple and straightforward. Does the policy option represent a prudent investment of resources? Specifically, how does the investment opportunity compare to alternatives? If the comparison is favorable, what is the optimum level of investment? That is, at what point of investment in one option does an alternative become more desirable? After the option is selected and the activity is begun, periodic reevaluation is necessary to determine whether the option continues to be a superior investment in comparison to old and new choices. Assuming that the option should continue, at least at some level, then allocation decisions must be made: Is the amount of the investment too great or too small? As new resources become available for investment, where would they be put to best use? In this simple decision-making paradigm, the analyst needs to know at the outset only the relative cost of alternatives and relative benefits. In this standard approach, the choice with the greatest yield on investment is the correct one. Reevaluations require recalculations of total costs and total benefits over time to reidentify best yields and optimum allocations.

Although this decision model is very simple, applications for policymaking are very difficult. Often, problems arise in specifying costs; usually there are problems in specifying benefits. As a result, the analyst often oversimplifies the analysis, assessing what is easily measured. Though often elegant mathematically, such limited quantitative analyses seldom are of much practical value. The paradigm still has great value, however, in providing a framework for policymaking, an ideal model to work toward, even though the goal will be seldom if ever achieved. With this constraint in mind, let us turn to policy analysis in higher education financing.

The financial analyst's paradigm or model poses two basic questions for higher education financing policy analysis:

- Should investments be made in higher education?
- If so, how large should the investments be?

A Historical Policy Sketch

In answering the first of these questions, one can imagine the choices faced by the earliest settlers in what is now the United States. Beginning for convenience where formal higher education began, in the Massachusetts Bay Colony, it is not surprising that obtaining food and shelter took precedence over higher learning during the first years after 1620. Very scarce resources had to be invested in providing the most basic of benefits necessary for sustenance and survival. The policy alternative of starting a college was not a viable one. No formal cost–benefit analysis was required, nor was much thought even needed, as the margins of the correct choices were very large.

By 1636, however, the calculus apparently had changed. Basic necessities had been provided, though not in great abundance; the colonists now could get by. Another need, a spiritual one, became a high priority. From where would come the clergy required to meet spiritual needs, especially in the long run? One can conceive of a growing concern for things spiritual, as the most fundamental needs began to be met. One easily can conceive also of serious doubts as to how so fledgling a colony could possibly afford a college. Doubtless, the college would have been delayed longer had not John Harvard's gift greatly reduced the cost to the colony and had there not been some confidence that Mother England could be relied upon to aid greatly in financing the ongoing operation of the college. In any case, Harvard was founded to prepare clergymen, and the factors leading to its founding in the particular year of 1636 illustrate rational policymaking in the best cost–benefit sense. It is worth noting in passing and for future reference, however, that normative twentieth century financial analysis probably would not have supported the decision to start the college because the quantifiable financial benefits would not have justified the costs to either the students or the larger citizenry. The analyst's paradigm works, in principle; it does not work in practice, for example, when intangible benefits such as spiritual ones are involved.[1]

We could speculate with great confidence that the decision to continue Harvard College in 1637 (the decision actually was probably not to discontinue it) was made with relative ease. The initial large investment had been made, and the incremental cost of the second year of operation likely was relatively small; but further, the College no doubt already had a political constituency and even a self-interest on the part of the single professor, the builder, the materials suppliers, and so forth. In practice, just as there were few serious challenges to Harvard once it was established, there rarely are challenges to any public or quasi-public organization once it is founded. Over time, organizations develop an inertia that is almost impossible to arrest, as numerous interests are vested in the continuation of the enterprise. Some of these vested-interest groups are the employees; those who buy from and sell to the enterprise, including in this case the students and their families; former clients, such as alumni; and those who somehow perceive indirect enrichment of themselves, such as those who believe that a college contributes to the general welfare.

Establishment of colleges was an early priority in most of the colonies even though the quantifiable economic benefits, though probably not the costs, were small. Apparently, the "return" on investment, when compared to other possible expenditures, was judged to be high. Policymakers as well as students placed a high value on religion and on a classical education that could be transformed directly into little else than the ministry, although society was judged also to benefit indirectly through the education of the men who would become public leaders.

Almost certainly, the colonists were not of one mind in this. Surely there were those who argued for delays in starting colleges until life and limb were more secure; surely there were those with less enthusiasm for paying for more ministers; and surely there were those who questioned whether higher education truly contributed to better public leadership. Undoubtedly, the skeptics were sometimes correct, if not in judging on economic criteria whether a college should be started, certainly in taking exception to the size of the investment. But these "correct" views were overridden, and this case would not be the first nor the last time that policymakers would base their decisions on other than solely economic criteria.

The earliest colleges technically were private ones, even though their support, at times, had public dimensions. Somewhat later, colleges of a distinctly public bent were created, and gradually additional purposes of the colleges evolved,

[1]Although much work has been done in attempting to quantify such values in cost–benefit studies, the results rarely if ever are added to those benefits that can be directly assigned a dollar value.

although large, new responsibilities almost always were merely add-ons rather than replacements for older ones. Public officials and lay boards of private institutions began to perceive a new role for colleges as preparers of specific types of public servants. The accompanying change in curriculum was quickened when businessmen and financiers began to replace clergymen on boards of trustees in an attempt to overcome the loss of public support at private colleges. Eventually, though not without considerable opposition by the colleges, these institutions began to prepare professionals—engineers, army officers, and physicians. The notion that the colleges produced important social benefits was greatly expanded. Financial benefits to students became evident too. Another change was that the distribution of costs had been altered considerably. Costs that had been heavily the burden of donor groups, especially religious ones, had become somewhat more public in nature. The private value of higher education to the student was still seen to be relatively small, and the student was asked to pay only small tuitions, although he was expected to donate his own time and effort.

The next major change bearing on our discussion was the dawning of Jacksonian Democracy and, several decades later, the creation of the land grant college. The new public expectation was for colleges to expand opportunity and to be the source and transmitter of practical knowledge. Although colleges in the United States had been largely elitist and most remained so, some of them began to change noticeably. This became the age of the A & Ms, the colleges for the sons and even an occasional daughter of the farmers and mechanics, of agriculture experiment stations and cooperative extension, of home economics, and of normal schools and later teachers' colleges. For these institutions, financing was heavily public, with private support minimal and student tuition very nominal or nonexistent. As always, the student contributed his or her own time and usually paid associated living expenses.

The latter half of the nineteenth century was also the time when many students had to travel to the Continent in order to partake of real graduate-level education. They brought that vision back with them, and by the end of the century the pantheon of university goals included being a source of new knowledge, especially the kind that flows from basic research.

The Great Depression witnessed the arrival of another new role for higher education: agent for dispensation of the general welfare and for economic salvation. The colleges enrolled large numbers of unemployed youth and were compensated for their efforts. They also housed and fed those involved in federal programs such as the Civilian Conservation Corps (CCC) and National Youth Administration (NYA). By now a pattern had emerged: The nation would turn to its colleges for help in meeting emergent social problems.

The lesson learned was quickly applied with the entry of the United States into World War II. Now the colleges and universities were asked to prepare great numbers of selected military leaders and to provide technical, defense-related training. The magnitude of this role, of course, was greatly reduced immediately after the war, but a related one was not. This was the role of conducting government-sponsored research, which was largely defense related during the war but expanded greatly into other areas thereafter.

After World War II the immediate challenge for colleges in the United States was again to provide opportunity, this time for the millions of veterans whose normal college years already had passed by. Eventually, the veterans passed through the system, although veterans from new wars would follow.

Provision of opportunity for yet another group would soon emerge, and the scale of the task would be of previously unheard-of dimensions. The new initiative was the National Defense Education Act and the stimuli were Sputnik and opportunity for low-income youth. By the mid-1970s the new educational opportunity venture would be in full swing. This time the primary target would be those previously left out or largely ignored as targets of higher education policy—the members of minority groups.

Evolution of Mission

Even this very incomplete historical sketch tells us that higher education in the United States today serves several broad purposes, some public and some private, and that efforts to assess benefits must be broad based too. Higher education in the United States began with the preparation of clergymen not because large economic gains would result, but because of an intangible social need. In the following years investments in higher education continued and grew because new college-related utilities were identified. There was a sense that society benefited through better informed leadership; individuals believed that higher education promised personal growth and development. It was many decades before direct connections were made or even were contemplated between higher education and personal financial gains. Eventually, colleges did begin to prepare professional and, much later, technical and kindred workers; then the personal, financial rewards from college became more evident. Of course, society's aim in providing the necessary resources had little to do with enhancing the personal wealth of students, except as that wealth would contribute to the general welfare. A similar statement can be made in regard to higher education as enhancer of opportunity. Public leaders eventually identified colleges and universities as vehicles for gaining a more equitable distribution of wealth and greater social mobility. Obviously, higher education must result in higher incomes for the target population if this situation is to occur; therefore, a private benefit must accompany achievement of the social aim. Other benefits of higher education suggested in the historical sketch include the creation and advancement of knowledge through research and the creation of wealth for the society overall. Of all these goals and benefits, only the more equal distribution of wealth is aimed directly at enhancing incomes, and then only for selected individuals. All other goals result in greater wealth for individuals only incidentally. The fact that individuals do benefit economically is fortuitous for society, because private individuals therefore are more willing to share in the substantial costs.

Thus, the goals and hence the benefits of higher education that exist late in the twentieth century are numerous and broad, having been added, one by one, over the centuries. Some of the benefits conceivably can be measured quite directly, others, satisfactorily only with difficulty, if at all.

Numerous formal goal sets have been composed in recent years; the following is representative. It was derived by the Committee for Economic Development (1973) from several existing goal statements in the literature. The last goal was added by the Committee as it addressed a perceived crisis in higher education finance in the early 1970s and as it reflected upon emerging priorities.

1. *Knowledge and the stimulation of learning.* The primary function of a college or university undergraduate program is teaching–learning. It is the generation and dissemination of knowledge and the discipline of the intellect. It entails induction into the uses of reason, the cultivation of critical intelligence, and the stimulation of a continuing desire to learn. The full development of the individual also requires the refinement of the moral and aesthetic sensitivities and the cultivation of a concern for human values.

2. *An educated citizenry.* We believe that the strength of democracy in the nation depends to an important degree on an educated citizenry. Elementary and secondary schools provide the basic literacy and communication skills essential to good citizenship. But the development of public policy, the conduct of public affairs, and the cultivation of the discriminating intelligence essential to civic leadership depend generally on more advanced education.

3. *Education for the achievement of specific social objectives.* The many important goals sought by society allow great leeway for an individual institution in determining the particular area or areas of knowledge and skills on which it can most effectively concentrate. Other institutions will find that their capabilities move them in other directions, and they will attract a different group of scholars and students. No single institution can do all that higher education must accomplish.

4. *Supplying trained men and women.* Although we commonly think of professional education as graduate education, the majority of undergraduate degrees granted are in effect professional degrees. Obvious examples are degrees in engineering, education, business, and the fine arts. Thus, even at the undergraduate level, the training of professional workers is an important goal of colleges and universities. A major educational development of recent years is the trend toward the preparation of paraprofessionals, many of whom are trained at the undergraduate level. The human-services occupations are burgeoning, especially in allied health fields and social services. Community colleges, technical colleges, and proprietary schools train many of these paraprofessionals, but traditional four-year colleges are assuming a larger role in their education.

5. *Economic growth and productivity.* The contribution of higher education to economic growth and productivity comes about especially through the education of technical and professional people and managerial leaders and through the creation of new knowledge and the development of its practical uses. Although the creation of knowledge occurs largely in graduate research activities rather than undergraduate education, the two are mutually involved, and it is difficult to separate them completely.

6. *Equality of opportunity.* Education beyond high school is often an important factor in determining an individual's chances of achieving economic success and of attaining the life-style to which he or she may aspire. Equality of postsecondary educational opportunity, therefore, is essential to providing each person a fair chance to move into and along the mainstream of socioeconomic life. But individuals from higher socioeconomic backgrounds currently attend colleges and universities at rates that exceed by as much as nine to one those of individuals from the least-advantaged backgrounds. Our recommendations on financing higher education are designed to diminish this disparity. (pp. 19–21)

Goals are required to assess the success or value of any enterprise. This goals framework is a thoughtful one and is probably as good as any as a reference point in our effort to assess the value of higher education. In order to conduct a valid appraisal, one would need to assess accomplishment of all goals, that is, assess all the benefits desired. Deciding whether to support higher education or how much to invest requires reference to more than a single criterion (degree of goal achievement). Less than a full assessment may result in counterproductive decisions and almost certainly in greater or lesser investment than is optimum. Hence, we are returned again to the practical difficulty of identifying and quantifying the wide range of benefits and even costs of higher education.

Policy Formulation in Practice

Although at first glance the problems and difficulties in composing a valid assessment of the value of higher education appear almost incapacitating, policymaking can and must proceed in the absence of complete and wholly accurate information. First, the basic decision whether to support a collegiate system, like the Pilgrims' decision to raise cabins and plant corn, usually is so obvious that measurement of benefits would be superfluous. Few could imagine a postindustrial society existing without colleges and universities. Similarly, there is no question that professional men and women, research, an informed electorate, and so forth, are necessary and desirable. Apparently, the margins by which these outcomes represent good investments are so great as not to require benefits estimation.

Clearly, the issue becomes not whether the investment should be made but how large it should be. More particularly, in practice the actual question almost always is how large the annual increase should be. This is because public financing tends strongly to be incremental in nature; that is, the assumption is made by resource allocators that last year's budget represents appropriate allocations in the past and that all that is necessary now is dividing up any new money to achieve new goals or expand old ones.

Another question that arises in practice is the form that the public subsidy should take. From an efficiency standpoint it may be that certain forms of support are more successful in achieving desired ends, per dollar invested. Further, particular approaches may induce other parties to increase their share of costs. Thus, for example, it is now common to find in legislative halls annual debates regarding the optimum proportional allocation of state subsidies for higher education among general institutional support, categorical aid, and student aid, as well as regarding how high student tuition and fees should be. Overall, for governments at least, the financing policy issues tend to be how large the incremental subsidy shall be and how it shall be allocated.

To the prospective student formulating personal higher education decisions, the practical choices are quite different, however. In contrast with the public choices, the most fundamental question for the individual will be whether to invest in higher education at all. Given the potential student's value system, the private policy question will be whether higher education compares favorably to alternative investments. Again, both costs and benefits must be considered. What will be the individual's costs? What do the benefits promise to be? And what are the costs and benefits of alternatives? If an affirmative college attendance decision is reached, then a specific investment vehicle—an institution—must be selected. Also, unlike the public's choice, the individual's periodic reevaluation will be more than an exercise. Have the investment dynamics changed significantly? How much have costs risen? How much already is invested? What new information is available regarding likely benefits? How have conditions of alternatives, such as labor markets, changed? Of course, for some students these personal policy decisions will be parallel to those for society: Higher education will represent such a favorable investment that little if any thought need be given either to initial or continued attendance, although selecting the specific investment form, the college, usually will require some consideration. In this another parallel exists. How much should the individual invest, not only as is reflected in the selection of a particular college, but in deciding what the final certificate or degree goal should be?

Conclusion

In this chapter we have sought to establish a framework or a way of viewing higher education financing policy decisions, both for individuals and for society.

We have hinted strongly that the decision model of the financial analyst, as it is typically employed, is likely to be inadequate and inappropriate as a basis for making those decisions because it leaves much unsaid. Yet the fault is not in the concept of the model, but in the application. We have shown that the goals and benefits of higher education are many and that they have been added incrementally, and we have suggested that in practice measurement may be very elusive.

Although, as normatively employed, the analyst's classical model may yield inappropriate or inadequate public policy, policy analysis is still mandatory. What is called for is better analysis, not rejection of a conceptually sound instrument. Policy decisions must continue to be made, with or without adequate and appropriate information. To aid in those decisions, certain information will be sought out and supplied. It may be that once the self-evident or accepted truths are added to what is strongly suspected and to what is known, we may have obtained most of what will be needed for adequately informed policymaking.

In the following chapters, we examine a good deal of the information used in making higher education financing policy. We attempt to alert the reader when this information is questionable, either in factualness or suitability. Nevertheless, we try to be realistic. Our position is that because policymakers must make decisions, we should provide the most valid information available. We will add our own observations, as appropriate, so that an informed and broad-based policy may be possible.

PART II

The Economic Value of Higher Education: The Classical Tests

HIGHER EDUCATION BENEFITS accrue privately and collectively. Private individuals who participate in higher education may benefit monetarily and nonmonetarily. They may realize higher earnings, invest more wisely, and make more prudent purchases, to mention only a few of the possible monetary benefits. Students also may enjoy certain nonmonetary consumption benefits associated with the collegiate experience, such as attendance at college events and the joys of learning. They also may benefit later in matters of consumption, for example, from participation in cultural events and enjoyment of leisure reading. Finally, college graduates may transfer certain benefits to their children by adopting more effective child-rearing practices and, in turn, providing greater encouragement of college attendance, thus completing the cycle.

By convention, the collective or social benefits of higher education include the gains to college graduates plus those that "spill over" to society at large. Conventionally, in social benefit terms the gains to college graduates are defined as the associated increases in (pretax) marginal earnings; the spillovers are the benefits that are "external" to the individual, that is, that accrue to society rather than to the individual college graduate. Again, each of these types of benefits may be monetary or nonmonetary.

In Part II, as throughout this book, our focus is on those benefits that have been quantified through economic and financial analysis. We perceive it is the "hard" rather than the "soft" evidence that is most persuasive to policymakers, and for this reason we have concentrated on quantitative estimations of effects, which primarily are the monetary benefits. Further, we could add little to the nonquantitative treatments of others and could not hope to rival the eloquence of authors, such as Howard Bowen (1977) and Kern Alexander (1976), who have written on this subject.

4

Higher Education as Private Investment

One of the elder statesmen of higher education in the United States once remarked that the financing of higher education is primarily an act of faith. Our initial reaction was one of incredulity. Those who toil in disciplines with relatively high degrees of "knowing" probably would share our initial disbelief. In our own case the proven wisdom of this man caused us to contemplate his meaning. What he meant, of course, was that, in conventional scientific and quantitative terms, we are incapable of proving higher education to be worthy of any particular amount of public support.

From the tone of his remarks, it was clear that this eminent man judged the implicit question to be not even a very good one. In his view, society had long ago decided that the value of higher education—though implicit rather than explicit—was patently obvious, that the margin of the value of higher education over that of most alternatives was so great as to render the spending of any conceivable amount of public expenditures a good investment. This conversation took place almost 20 years ago.

The common perception today, and one that likely will persist into the

An earlier version of this chapter appeared in *Higher Education: Handbook of Theory and Practice*, vol. 2, edited by John C. Smart, pp. 207–234.

twenty-first century, is that the dynamics have changed considerably. As more and more people have been educated, the economic value of a college education seemingly has declined. How can anything so common be of great economic value?

Correct or not, the perception is a reality worth evaluating. Higher education constantly is under increasing pressure to justify itself, to show why it requires ever higher financial support when there exist reported oversupplies of highly educated workers in the labor force.

From where do these perceptions come? First, they come from evidence all around us: from the observations that our own or our neighbors' sons and daughters after 4 years of college cannot find work, at least at the level perceived to be commensurate with their education; from our own direct knowledge of extraordinarily long applicant lists for almost any professional-level opening; and from media reports of oversupplies of most professionals—lawyers, business graduates, ministers, and even physicians. These perceptions are reinforced by popular writings and by "hard evidence" from respected economists, who report on morning and evening news programs of the "declining rates of return on the college investment." Personal impressions are one thing, hard scientific evidence quite another.

One of the themes of this chapter is that in making personal college attendance decisions, individuals need to possess accurate information about the economic value of a college education. True, there are other values of higher education, but individuals do base their attendance decisions in considerable part upon financial expectations. Leslie, Johnson, and Carlson (1977) found, for example, that economic motives were listed as a basis for college attendance about 3½ times more frequently than noneconomic motives by a sample of high school seniors within a few months of graduation. More recent evidence indicates that the dynamics have not changed. In the 1985 national survey of college freshmen, 83 percent listed "get a better job" and 70 percent listed "make more money" as "very important" reasons for attending college. Fully 71.8 percent agreed that "The chief benefit of a college education is that it increases one's earning power" (Astin, Green, Korn, and Schalit, 1985, p. 47). Mattila (1982) demonstrated that individuals alter their attendance decisions when (internal) rates of return (IRR) to schooling are known. His estimate was that male college enrollments declined by 15–32 percent from what they would have been, as a result of the alleged and publicized IRR decline in the 1970s. Knowing the economic value of a college education, the potential student can factor in other, nonmonetary benefits and reach a better informed college attendance decision.

Research has been quite helpful in providing some of the information necessary to private investors, at least in an aggregated or "average" form. Researchers have offered several information alternatives to the potential student-consumer, some simple and straightforward, others more complex and more difficult to understand. The vehicle chosen for the meta-analysis is the internal rate of return approach; however, some attention will be given first to other major ways of viewing the important question of whether higher education represents a good private investment.

Chapter Overview

There are three major ways to estimate the monetary yields of a college education: (1) *Earnings differentials* of young men favored college graduates over high school graduates by more than $6,000 per year in 1983, although approximately 21 percent of this difference may be accounted for by inherent (noncollege) differences between the two groups. (2) Estimate of the *Net Present Value* of a college education—that is, the present value of a college education after costs are subtracted and corrections are made to adjust for the changing value of money, over time—ranged in 1979 from $60,000 to $329,000 for men and from $44,000 to $142,000 for women, depending upon varying discount and productivity rates employed. (3) Traditionally calculated *private rates of return* for the undergraduate degree are estimated at 11.8–13.4 percent, for 1 year of graduate work at 8 percent, for the master's degree at about 7.2 percent, and for the Ph.D. at about 6.6 percent. Private rates of return probably declined in the mid-1970s, but since have returned to historic rates.

Private rates of return are more sensitive to cost than to benefit fluctuations. Rates can be increased merely by increasing public subsidies to students, thereby reducing private costs.

Traditional rate of return estimates tend to be understated because costs are overstated. The size of the understatement typically is large. Few students pay full costs; accurate calculations for individuals must reflect subtractions for subsidies provided by others.

Traditional rate of return calculations include only the direct monetary benefits. Other benefits may roughly equal the monetary ones, causing true rates of return to be much higher than stated in this overview.

Earnings Differentials

Probably the first approach to estimating the pecuniary value of a college education was calculation of an earnings differential. Put simply, how much on average does a college graduate earn in comparison to how much those with less education earn?

The beauty of this measure is its simplicity. It is easy to understand, and it is easy to calculate from readily available census statistics. Earnings differentials generally are less contentious than more complex measures, which possess the added liability of often showing disparate results.

Simplicity is also the earnings differentials' greatest limitation. On average, one would expect higher earnings by those who attend college compared to those who do not, simply because the former are known to possess higher average ability and motivation. Also, the earnings differential identifies only benefits; it says nothing of costs. If the potential student wishes to compare the expected average yield on an investment in higher education to yields on alternative investments, as would the professional policy analyst, this measure is of little value. Nevertheless, for many potential students the earnings differential may be adequate. Further, measures that include average costs may be inappropriate to individual circumstances.

One can conceive of many types of students with many different costs and many different likely or expected benefits. There may be truly "average" students who pay their own full costs and who are average in background and ability. These students will benefit from knowledge of full, average cost–benefit information. A student equal in ability but whose parents are willing and able to pay all the direct costs, however, may find the earnings differential more useful. This student need only place a rough value on her or his investment in time (earnings foregone), make an appraisal of the personal enjoyment and satisfaction gained from student life versus likely alternatives, view the earnings differential, assess the importance of family preferences, and reach a college attendance decision. The decision may be made with difficulty or with ease, but knowing the yields for "average" students who pay average full costs probably will help very little.

These are only two student types; there are many others. There is the government-aided student whose direct costs also may be low or nonexistent, the student who may pay full costs but opt for a low-cost college, one who expects relatively high earnings from pursuing a high-paying occupation, the student who is ambivalent about financial rewards and plans a service-oriented career, and many others. All of these, in making the personal investment decision, may find the earnings differential or some other measure equal or superior to measures that include average costs.

Often, in comparing earnings differentials, only the separate earnings of men are considered because data for males are more available over time and because female work patterns have changed greatly in recent years. For younger men (ages 25–34), the median income of college graduates, at $21,988, was more than $6,000 greater than the median income of high school graduates ($15,789) in 1983, compared to about $1300 greater in 1958 and $400 in 1950 (Table 4.1). The ratio of median college to high school graduate earnings was 1.13 in 1950, 1.27 in 1958, and declined to 1.23 in 1965 and again in 1979 before increasing again thereafter. It stood at 1.39 in 1983. The ratio for high school graduate to nongraduate income has changed even more, also being 1.13 in 1950 but reaching 1.47 in 1983, and growing more regularly than the college to high school ratio. For men the value of education by income differential measures seems clear.

In 1960, college graduates overall (men and women) earned 65 percent more than high school graduates; in 1980 the gap was 58 percent. Among inexperienced males, relative earnings were 65 percent higher for college graduates overall in 1960, 55 percent higher in 1970, and 53 percent higher in

Table 4.1

MEDIAN INCOME OF MALE COLLEGE GRADUATES, MALE HIGH SCHOOL GRADUATES, AND THOSE WITH SOME HIGH SCHOOL, 25–34-YEARS-OLD, WITH INCOME DURING THE YEAR: 1950–1983*

Year	College Graduates (1)	High School Graduates (2)	Some High School (3)	Ratio (1)/(2) (4)	Ratio (2)/(3) (5)
1950	3,510	3,095	2,735	1.13	1.13
1958	5,970	4,688	4,275	1.27	1.10
1961	6,640	5,175	4,425	1.28	1.17
1963	6,947	5,612	4,903	1.24	1.14
1965	7,474	6,151	5,254	1.21	1.17
1967	8,282	6,882	5,922	1.27	1.16
1969	10,228	8,008	6,693	1.28	1.20
1971	10,908	8,556	7,331	1.27	1.17
1973	12,349	10,153	8,448	1.22	1.20
1975	13,232	10,767	8,241	1.23	1.31
1979	17,345	14,280	10,983	1.23	1.30
1981	20,589	15,393	11,173	1.34	1.38
1982	21,149	15,298	10,948	1.38	1.40
1983	21,988	15,789	10,711	1.39	1.47

Source. 1950 Census of Population, Special Reports, *Educational Attainment,* table 12; 1958–1982, U. S. Bureau of the Census, Current Population Reports, Series P-60 *Income of Families and Persons in the U. S.* various issues, 1983 from forthcoming P-60 report.

*Figures in current dollars.

1980; for inexperienced females relative earnings were 54 percent higher in 1960, 67 percent higher in 1970, and 72 percent higher in 1980 (Rumberger, 1984). The premiums paid for a college education have declined for men but increased for women.

Alpha Factors

The alpha factor was constructed in an effort to correct one of the limitations of earnings differentials, their lack of adjustment for preexisting differences between college attenders and nonattenders. Alpha values, which are expressed as decimals less than 1.0, conventionally are multiplied by earnings differentials to adjust for such possible differences as ability; parents' education, income, and occupation; marital status; family size; health; religion; and region of the country. These adjustments can be seen in some of the rate of return studies in the meta-analysis.

Our search uncovered 13 studies that reported alpha values for the baccalaureate degree; the simple average was .79. In other words, if one wishes to adjust for differences between college attenders and nonattenders, one may correct for these differences by multiplying the earnings differentials by 79 percent. This figure tells the potential higher education investor how much more the average college graduate will earn over the average high school graduate after the gap is reduced by earnings due simply to ability and background differences.

Based upon results from 17 studies, alpha values appear to increase with educational level. The values are smallest for schooling levels below high school, increase for high school graduates, and are still higher for 2-year and technical degrees, before reaching .79 for B.A. holders. The average for the graduate level is .90. The importance of innate and inherent personal advantages to earnings apparently decreases as one advances educationally.

Our own assessment after studying the existing literature for almost 2 years is that the .79 value may be too low. We have observed from this literature that higher education interacts with many of the variables listed in the previous paragraph and that holding these variables constant understates the true earnings effects of education. For example, the family culture that accompanies middle- and high-socioeconomic status enhances the gains to be realized from education, and to remove this contribution from earnings estimates biases the earnings effect downward. Another, somewhat different point can be made in regard to other variables, such as occupation. Because higher education is a prerequisite or nearly so for many occupations, controlling for this variable, too, biases estimates downward. Holding occupation constant eliminates the earnings variance due to earnings/occupation interaction—surely a major source of income differentials. All in all, we lean toward the view of those who believe that adjustments are too large. For example, Psacharopoulos (1975) and Griliches (1979) have found that ability does not add much to variations in college and high school graduate earnings. Fairly consistent results are obtained at about a 12 percent addition to college versus high school graduate earnings. Hines, Tweeten, and Redfern (1970) have done perhaps the most complete analysis of the factors thought to affect the college–high-school earnings gap and found that effects largely cancel out. Most importantly, impacts of ability are almost offset by productivity gains over time (secular growth). Their overall result is that unadjusted private rates of return are 13.6 percent and fully adjusted private rates 13.2 percent; their unadjusted and adjusted social rates are each 9.7 percent.

Net Present Values (NPVs)

Even though earnings differentials and alpha factors may be quite useful to potential students, measures employed by professional analysts almost always have included consideration of cost, too. One such measure is the Net Present Value (NPV), which literally is an estimate of the present value of a college education after costs are subtracted from benefits, each figure—cost and benefit—adjusted to reflect changing values of dollars over time. That is, a dollar spent today to purchase higher education is worth more, considering foregone interest, than one to be earned at some later date.

The problem with NPVs, in addition to those implied in the earnings differential section, is the difficulty in selecting an appropriate interest rate for calculating NPVs (Cohn, 1972). The decision maker selects an interest rate, depending upon her or his own view of the economic future, and reads a dollar value in a table. This figure is the pecuniary value of the education, expressed in current dollars. The figure is extremely sensitive to the interest rate selection, especially over long time periods.

Although our in-depth analysis of the returns to higher education is contained in the next section on rates of return, an example of an NPV formulation is available from Cohn and Geske (1986). Using 1979 Bureau of Census lifetime earnings data for men and women by years of schooling completed, Cohn and Geske calculate several NPV estimates of the earnings of college graduates over high school graduates, at various combinations of discount (interest) and productivity rates. The NPV earnings difference estimates for male college graduates range from $60,000 at a 5 percent discount rate and no productivity rate increase to $329,000 at no discount and no productivity rate increase. For female graduates the range of NPV earnings differences is $44,000–142,000. Cohn and Geske then (1) select one of the earnings differentials (the lowest one); (2) calculate, at the same rate of discount, the present value of the costs of college; and (3) subtract (2) from (1) to obtain an NPV figure of $23,000 for men and $7,000 for women. These values reflect a 62 percent greater benefit than cost value for male college graduates and a 19 percent greater benefit than cost figure for females. For the next highest NPV earnings differences, but the same cost values, the figures for the benefit excess over cost are 311 percent and 119 percent, respectively, for men and women. Each of these are only illustrative data that derive from particular assumptions about discount and productivity rates. Also, the values do not take into account differences such as student abilities. The difficulty in reaching private investment decisions from NPV studies is evident from these disparate results under varying assumptions, which are problematic, to say the least.

Internal Rates of Return (IRR)

Conceptually, the internal rate of return (IRR) is the NPV in reverse. In calculating an IRR, conventionally, the analyst estimates from workers' earnings profiles the expected stream of lifetime earnings for graduates and nongraduates, and from college cost data estimates, the costs of attendance. After costs are corrected to current dollars through compounding, the analyst calculates the interest or discount rate that would set the earnings value equal to the cost value. This rate is the IRR. A simple alternative is to consider the rate of return to be the relative increment of earnings associated with a given increment of education (Mincer, 1974).

This value, the IRR, is easy to compare to other potential yields. The implicit rule is that one should invest in higher education so long as the IRR exceeds market interest rates. Of course, this value changes; the IRR literature generally compares IRR estimates to 10 percent, which is a common benchmark figure for the rate of return on investment in the equities (stock) market.

We selected the IRR as the basis for composing the most thorough and complete estimate of the direct financial value of higher education for males.[1] Table 4.2 contains four methods or ways of grouping the results.

First note, however, that all midpoint estimates are positive; that is, a college education does yield benefits in excess of costs when each is properly adjusted. The overall pattern of principal findings, as Jackson (1980) reminds us, is critically important and should never be omitted in integrative reviews.

In Method 1 all 43 estimates from the meta-analysis are combined, including multiple estimates for different years by some authors (Table 4.2). Occasionally, the original work contained more estimates than are presented in the tables here; where estimates exceeded 4 or 5 in number, we selected estimates for those years common to most studies. Therefore, although there is some heavier weighting of the results of certain researchers because we included more than one estimate from a few studies, the values are not unduly weighted by the results of any particular researcher. Finally, for studies that report only a results range, Method 1 (as do all methods) employs the mean IRR estimate.

For the 43 estimates in Method 1, the mean private internal rate of return for undergraduate education—usually the undergraduate degree—was 12.4 percent, with a standard error of 1.0 percentage points. The median estimate was lower, 11.5 percent. The range of estimates was from 5.0 to 21.4 percent. Emphasizing traditional statistical approaches, our best estimate of the true, private, internal rate of return, as normatively calculated by researchers, is 12.4 percent; and we may be 95 percent certain that the true rate ranges between roughly 11.4 and 13.4 percent.

Method 2 eliminates the weighting effect where multiple estimates are provided for a single study and therefore reduces the importance of any particular

[1]These are adjusted or controlled values as opposed to unadjusted or uncontrolled, where both are offered. They include one estimate for "some college," one for a 2-year technical school, and one for "4 or more years" of college. Data for the unemployed are included in the case where the choice is offered; value of leisure and other nonpecuniary benefits are excluded.

For consistency, "males" or "white males" data are used where possible. All but five studies essentially are (estimates) for men or white men only. Bureau of Census earnings/income data are available for women only since 1963, and females' decision-making processes are more complex (Mattila, 1982).

Table 4.2.

SUMMARY OF PRIVATE RATES OF RETURN TO HIGHER EDUCATION—UNDERGRADUATE

		IRR	(*N*)*
Method 1	Mean	12.4	(43)
	(S. E.)	(1.0)	
	Median	11.5	
Method 2	Mean	11.8	(26)
	(S. E.)	(1.5)	
	Median	11.4	
Method 3	Mean	13.4	(6)
	(S. E.)	(2.4)	
Method 4	Mean	12.2	(14)
	(S. E.)	(1.5)	
	Median	11.4	
By Year	Means		
1939		15.0	(3)
1949		11.6	(5)
1959		12.3	(12)
1969		13.0	(10)
1973		11.7	(6)
1980		16.5	(1)

Source. Appendix Table 1.

**N* = Number of estimates represented in the mean estimate.

research design or assumptions. A single, mean estimate was substituted for multiple estimates. Otherwise, Method 2 is the same as Method 1.

The mean results of Method 2 are slightly lower. For 26 estimates the mean IRR is 11.8 percent, and the median is 11.4 percent. The range of estimates is from 5.0 to 20.0 percent and the standard error is 1.5 percent, suggesting a 95 percent confidence interval of 10.3 to 13.3. Of course, our best estimate

FIGURE 4.1 Private Rate of Return Estimates in the Literature

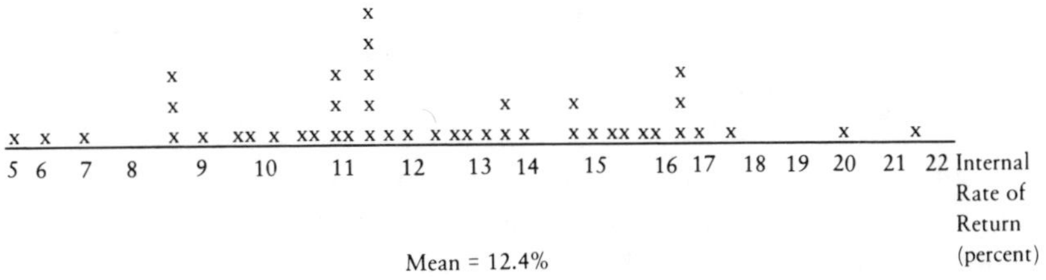

```
                                   x
                                   x
                x                x x                                 x
                x                x x               x      x          x
x  x  x         x  x  xx x  xx  xx x x x  x xx x x x      x x xx xx  x x  x        x      x
-------------------------------------------------------------------------------------------
5  6   7   8      9     10       11      12      13  14     15      16  17  18  19  20  21  22 Internal
                                                                                               Rate of
                                                                                               Return
                              Mean = 12.4%                                                     (percent)
```

of the true IRR from this method is 11.8 percent, with probabilities of the true IRR, as always, decreasing as the 10.3 and 13.3 percent ends of the range of likely true values are approached (due to the shape of the normal curve).

Method 3 is a refinement of Method 2, in that consistently *and* particularly well-designed studies are singled out for inclusion. The six studies of Method 3 employed broadly representative samples, were in our judgment neither over- nor undercontrolled, employed good cost specifications and income data, and were limited to the results of 4 years of college. The six studies were numbers 03, 07, 10, 17, 24, and 27 in the meta-analysis matrix (Appendix Table 1). The mean for these six studies was 13.4 and the range was a more narrow one of 11.0 to 16.9; the standard error was 2.4, larger than in other methods.

In method 4 the least compatible studies were eliminated; then Method 2 was employed. Studies were omitted if they were of special samples, lacked controls, or were missing key evaluative information, or if the earnings or income measure was inconsistent with those of other studies. Studies deleted in Method 4 were numbers 05, 08, 09, 18, 20, 22, 23, 25, 26, 28, 29, 30, and 33 (Appendix Table 1). For the 14 studies of Method 4, the mean was 12.2 percent, the median was 11.4 percent, the range was 8.5 to 16.9 percent, and the standard error was 1.5 percentage points, yielding a 95 percent confidence interval of 10.7 to 13.7 percent. Not surprisingly, the variation in results was smaller in Methods 3 and 4, in which study comparability was emphasized in making selections.

The 43 estimates reported in the meta-analysis matrix cover many different years. Of course, rates of return may vary with time. The final entries in the table show private, internal rates of return for each census year from 1939 to 1969, for 1973—a year of particular interest, as we shall see later—and for 1980. The reader should note the small number of studies (*N*s) for several years. The results by year shall be placed in context in a later section of this chapter.

Depending upon the method employed, the mean estimates from the four methods ranged from 11.8 to 13.4 percent, although the higher figure was for only six studies. If one were to omit the highest "grand mean," which reflects only six estimates, the range would be narrowed to 11.8 to 12.4 percent, a fairly "tight" range of mean estimates. We are not inclined to narrow the range further, as we do not believe there is a strong basis for favoring one of the methods over another. We are at the stage where trade-offs begin in meta-analysis.

METHODOLOGICAL ISSUES

By trade-offs, we mean that one could argue for exclusion of particular studies due to inferior designs, and to some extent we have done that in Method 4, although some of the excluded studies were merely incompatible with those included. The trouble with making exclusions is that (1) what is often involved is frequently more personal opinion than anything else, and (2) such exclusions can detract from the richness of the meta-analysis.

On the first point, with few exceptions we are impressed with the general quality and consistency of rate of return studies, particularly in the internal validity sense. (Our departures from the IRR studies, which we will discuss in this chapter, have little to do with their internal validity.) Where study designs vary, and there *are* major differences, authors almost invariably are able to defend their positions well. Only occasionally have researchers reached a general consensus on which of two or more methodological tactics or approaches is superior, but even then issues remain.

As to the second point, a principal strength of the meta-analysis method is in the external validity sense. A broad meta-analysis, sampling disparate populations and analyzing results in varying ways, adds greatly to the generalizability of meta-analysis findings. Thus, omitting studies only because they are different may be shortsighted. Of course, if a study is obviously flawed or is highly suspect, deletion may be wise.

Let us consider just two examples. Hunt's (1963) study of those who responded to a *Time* magazine survey of readers in 1947 perhaps should be eliminated on the sole ground that the sample was not representative. One properly may ask whether an income bias is not likely in the data, not only because of the unrepresentativeness of the *Time* readership but also because high-earning *Time* readers might be more likely to respond to the request for earnings data than would the readership at large. In this case, even though Hunt's analysis was careful and generally thorough, the study probably should be excluded. This decision is supported by the fact that Hunt's results in the adjusted form are roughly 100 percent at odds with the mean values in Table 4.2. On the other hand, Rogers's (1969) study of New England junior high school students whose earnings were followed for many years should not be omitted merely because the sample is limited and the analysis was not as well controlled as most. The sample adds richness to the meta-analysis as the study is one of the very few to employ longitudinal data, thus overcoming one of the major shortcomings of typical IRR studies: the necessity to generalize lifetime earnings patterns from earnings profiles taken at one point in time.

There remains, of course, the possibility that one particular study has overcome the shortcomings of all others and has reported the only truly valid result. We do not believe such a study exists, or if it did, that it would be broadly recognized as such. For these reasons, we prefer the mean estimates resulting from synthesis of many works (the meta-analysis), which represent the collective wisdom of many experts.

The major factor that affects results in the studies reviewed is degree of control over variables (besides education) that also are related to earnings or income. As noted we utilized the most highly controlled results where alternatives were available; this produces the most conservative findings. Yet the matter of proper control or adjustment remains open. We note only that multiple regression or earnings function approaches generally achieve lower IRR estimates, principally because they usually control for more variables but also because they usually separate the effect of education from learning via on-the-job-training (OJT) (Mincer, 1974, p. 131). Conventional IRR analyses that do not correct for or control variables tend to reach findings that are somewhat higher. The same conventional analyses that apply an alpha coefficient to correct the IRR may report high results if the correction is small or low results if it is large. The evidence that might help to sort all this out is mixed. Our own leaning after reviewing the evidence is toward making small alpha corrections of the order of 12 percent.

In any case, it does seem to us that thoroughly controlled or heavily corrected methods go too far. Most regression analyses fail to include interaction terms and in holding all else constant, ignore the shared contribution to earnings by variables that are correlated with education. Controlling or correcting fully for such variables as socioeconomic status and occupation seems to us shortsighted. As stated by Douglass (1977), socioeconomic status (SES) is itself a product of the education of an earlier generation (p. 376). Indeed, mother's or father's education generally is considered to be the best proxy for SES. Clearly, the encouragement, early experiences, and general family milieu of a middle- or high-SES family contribute greatly to the decision to attend college and to college selection. SES itself is to a considerable extent a function of educational level; it is, conceptually at least, one of the "benefits" in IRR cost–benefit analysis for previous generations. Controlling or correcting for occupation seems to us to make almost no sense at all. Since many occupations essentially require college-level preparation, removing the effects of education biases the effect of education downward. Hanoch (1967), whose IRR research is among the most highly regarded, observes that "There is a real question" regarding "the meaning of 'holding constant' variables in a regression analysis." In regard to the illustrative case of controlling for occupation, Hanoch notes:

> If, on the one hand, occupation and industry are to be excluded from the analysis, the elements of ability, nonpecuniary returns, and motivations associated with these classifications will be lost. On the other hand, a high degree of mobility exists among occupations and among industries, and this mobility depends strongly on schooling and on age. Thus, "holding constant" the occupation or the industry allows only for intragroup differentials of earnings. It eliminates the effects of schooling and age on interoccupational or interindustry differentials. . . . As a result, it was decided to exclude occupation and industry variables from the equations and thus avoid serious biases in the estimated coefficients of schooling which, after all, are the target estimates of this analysis.

At the same time, such a control can adjust for the so-called screening effect, whereby, it is said, a college education tends merely to "screen" individuals for employment. This point seems to us a moot one, because the policy question is, What are the effects of college? not, What explains those effects? (For one of the most recent treatments of the "screening hypothesis" see Blaug, 1985.)

Probably most controversial of all is the proper correction for ability; suggested corrections range from 0 to as much as 35 percent of the IRR (Taubman and Wales, 1974, p. 77). In earlier IRR work, it was assumed that a substantial ability correction should be made because higher ability persons are more likely to enroll in higher education. Later, it was reasoned that ability is little more than a proxy for achievement, which is precisely the variable through which higher education acts (Griliches, 1970; Eckaus, El Safty, and Norman, 1974; Psacharopoulos, 1975, Chapter 3). Again the issue is one of interaction: Is not education, to a considerable extent, the process through which ability bears fruit? Mincer (1974, pp. 139–140) discusses how the inclusion of ability in regression analyses obfuscates the effect of education.

Other corrections are noteworthy, though probably less troublesome. Most everyone agrees that earnings differentials should be corrected for certain more objective factors, most of which result from employing earnings profiles taken at a point in time, rather than from longitudinal earnings data. Examples are adjustments for mortality, unemployment, and secular growth (naturally occurring earnings growth over time resulting from productivity increases). Another example is correcting for varying taxes paid at various earnings levels and for hours worked. The latter issue is embodied in the selection of earnings versus income as the appropriate benefits measure. Theoretically, there is general agreement that hourly or weekly earnings is the superior benefits measure primarily because these measures control for the trade-off between work and leisure (Griliches, 1977). Further, some income measures include returns to physical assets. Practically, however, the choice is not one-sided. First, the ability to trade off leisure for work is not consistent across occupations having varying educational qualification requirements. In short, the opportunity to work more hours may be viewed as one of the payoffs to college. Second, returns on some physical assets appropriately may be considered as returns on education because the greater wage earnings may lead to greater capital investment. Returns on inherited wealth probably should be excluded, however. In any case, the need for an "hours worked" correction is, at most, modest, regardless of how one decides the issue, because the impact on rates of return apparently is quite small. Using 1969 census data, Carnoy and Marenbach (1975), for example, find a 15.4 percent IRR on income and a 16.2 IRR on earnings.

Although the need for these corrections is generally accepted, the overall effects are small because individual impacts are minor or largely cancel each other out. By adding in the corrections one by one, Hines et al. (1970) show that the downward effect on private rates of return is only .4 percentage points, from 13.6 to 13.2 percent, even when ability is included. In the case of social rates of return, the corrections completely balance out.

A final comment concerning the mean values from the IRR meta-analysis is that the findings of the component studies ideally should be, but cannot be, standardized in the IRR studies. How standardization may be done can be seen in a later chapter in which studies of student response to tuition increases are examined. In the case of the rate of return studies, the issues of standardization are quite different, and the task is unmanageable, if not impossible.[2]

OTHER LEVELS OF HIGHER EDUCATION

Although results are somewhat mixed, it appears that the return on less than 4 years of college also is a favorable one, while returns on graduate education generally are substantially less. Returns on "some college," which would include associate degree holders and graduates of vocational-technical programs as well as dropouts from baccalaureate programs, average about 10 percent, compared to the 11.8–13.4 percent mean estimates for the baccalaureate. The numbers of such studies, however, are fewer, and seldom is there differentiation below the B.A. Of course, the less time one spends in college, the lower are the costs; therefore, earnings differentials must be less too.

Private rates of return for graduate study appear to decrease slightly by degree level, being about 8 percent for the seventeenth year of education, 7.2 percent for the M.A., and 6.6 percent for the Ph.D. in the studies reviewed, when midpoint estimates are used to construct means. (See Table 4.3.) However, there are fewer studies on which to base these conclusions, and because the mean estimates are not far apart, we cannot rule out the possibility that the true rates do not differ by graduate level.

A major reason for our necessary ambivalence is that the anomalies of graduate IRR studies are many and important. Most such studies are of special groups, rather than of broad samples of graduate degree holders. It is not surprising, therefore, that IRR estimates vary tremendously, ranging from a negative value obtained from an oversampling of education students at a nonprestigious midwestern university (Maxwell, 1970) to as high as 20 percent for particular students in specific regions of the country (Curtis and Campbell, 1978).

[2]First is the matter of which controls to exercise. This is itself very much at issue. Second, if agreement on this issue could be reached, how would one remove the effects of inappropriate controls already exercised? Clearly, the original data sets would be required. One of the major, persistent problems of meta-analysis of higher education research is the absence of published information sufficient for standardization. We briefly considered solving the problem by building the "perfect model," by incorporating all of the best thinking of some 25 years of IRR research and applying the principles to constructing a current, complete set of census earnings data and to the best cost data available. To this we would have substituted the data from other studies. Of course, we quickly realized that the result of our effort would be just one more IRR study that would claim to be the best.

Table 4.3

SUMMARY OF PRIVATE RATES OF RETURN TO HIGHER EDUCATION—GRADUATE

ID No.	Author, Year	Year 17	Private M. A.	Private Ph. D.
01	Ashenfelter and Mooney, 1968		6.5	8.8
02	Bailey and Schotta, 1972			neg. to 20.3, .8*
09	Danielson, 1969–1970		6.2	8.5
11	Eckaus, 1973	4.0		
15	Hanoch, 1967	7.0		
23	McMahon and Wagner, 1982		−.7 to 12.7	−1.8 to 19.3
25	Mincer, 1974	12.2		
28	Rogers, 1969		1 to 2, 8 to 10**	
30	Taubman and Wales, 1973		8	4
31	Tomaske, 1974	≅9		
33	Weiss, 1971		10.6	8.7
			12.9***	8.9***

Note. I. D. numbers are from meta-analysis matrix. See Appendix Table 1.

*Authors' best estimate.

**Including 50 percent subsidy.

***Completion of degree in prescribed (expected) time.

The major explanation for this broad range of IRR estimates is wide cost variations, which have a disproportionate effect on IRR results. IRR for Woodrow Wilson fellows were relatively high (Ashenfelter and Mooney, 1968) because fellows received student stipends, and perhaps because they were highly able (Siegfried, 1972–1973) or, more likely, better educated. Bailey and Schotta (1972) estimated returns at only .8 percent for academics after long periods of (and thus costly) study. Weiss (1971) calculated that finishing a Ph.D. in the prescribed time has about the same effect on the IRR as does inclusion of student earnings: Each about doubles the private return rate. By showing that the costs of Ph.D. study in English and sociology are less than half those in physics and zoology, Butter (1966, p. 38) demonstrates the flaw in applying average cost data to Ph.D. IRR analysis. Within every graduate field and level, returns are higher for persons who pursue careers in private industry than for those who accept academic employment (Weiss, 1971). Curtis and Campbell (1978) found that the range could be from .04 to 20 percent. What seems safe to conclude is that financial rewards are relatively limited for future academics and are quite high for others who participate in graduate education. More importantly, it would seem that a wise graduate school attendance decision demands cost and earnings information specific to individual circumstances.

IRR OVER TIME

Historic rates of return, of course, may bear little relationship to realities at any given time. Perceptions that higher education may represent a poor investment are of relatively recent origin. It was not until the mid-1970s that the value of a college degree came into public question. Caroline Bird published her popularized book, *The Case against College,* in 1975, the same year Richard Freeman's landmark paper, "Overinvestment in College Training," appeared in *The Journal of Human Resources* (1975). Both publications questioned the economic value of a college education, and both were quickly sensationalized in the media. As is often the case, however, newsworthy events may belie reality.

Freeman's work (1975 and 1976) generally followed conventional research designs and was sufficiently detailed to permit careful evaluation. It now appears clear that a decline in rates of return did occur between 1969 and 1974, as Freeman held, but that rates were not as low as he suggested. Because Freeman used a consistent method in calculating annual rates, reduced IRR in 1974 over 1969 seems evident; however, his atypically low estimates can be explained in considerable part by anomalies in his method. To illustrate, Freeman analyzed only males in their early employment years. Rumberger (1984) has since shown that relative earnings for females and males moved in opposite directions between 1960 and 1980. Earnings for male college graduates did decline relative to high school graduates, but the opposite was true for females. Witmer's (1980) IRR combined results for both men and women support Rumberger's conclusions. Regarding the use of early employment data, Freeman made the assumption that low initial earnings mean low earnings throughout the working lifetime. Psacharopoulos (1981) has pointed out that the use of earnings profiles for inexperienced workers understates the returns to college graduates because these individuals are more likely to be involved in the job search process. Smith and Welch (1978) demonstrated convincingly that Freeman's two-point decline was really only 1 point because he compared persons of the same age rather than persons of the same experience. Freeman's method does not vary from most others in some of these regards; however, the effects he observed have since been seen to be transitory (Wagner 1984; see also Appendix Table 1).

The primary reason for Freeman's low estimates that received such popular attention,[3] however, was not on the benefits side at all; it was on the more sensitive cost side. Freeman overstated average college costs by charging to students not only the costs related to instruction, but those for research and public service as well. Generally, analysts have excluded noninstructional costs because these functions are not part of what students perceive they are purchasing when making the college investment decision. Freeman's expenditure overstatement was roughly 14.5 percent, and his 1975 IRR estimate of 9.6 percent would be raised to 10.6 percent by this correction alone (Witmer, 1980).

Freeman's work and subsequent critiques and reanalyses raise two important policy questions. First, have IRR continued to decline to the present and, second and more importantly, are present rates below benchmark standards?

In retrospect, Freeman's finding that rates declined between 1969 and 1974 was not surprising. He examined a period in which the number of college graduates was increasing and business conditions were worsening. In simple terms, the supply of college graduates was increasing unusually rapidly, and demand for those graduates was declining—classical conditions for lower (labor) prices. That such conditions do reduce wages and salaries paid to college graduates had been demonstrated by several other economists (Miller, 1960; Welch, 1970, 1979; Psacharopoulos, 1973, pp. 9, 95–97) and have since been verified (Bartlett, 1978; Welch, 1979; Ashenfelter and Ham, 1979; Cline, 1982; Mattila, 1982; Rosen and Taubman, 1982). Indeed, these factors had been cited by Freeman as plausible explanations for his results. However, the fact that cohort sizes of college graduates would decline by 1980 suggested that Freeman's downturns for inexperienced graduates would abate. In fact, by 1980, new college graduates were finding jobs at about the same rate as in 1960, and their unemployment rate, though not at historic lows, was only about one-half the rate of 1970 (Wagner, 1984, Table 2). This reversal validates the work of Berger (1983), who demonstrated convincingly that the mid-1970s decline was due to the baby-boom effect, including growth in the number of female graduates, and that this effect would persist through the working lifetime of this atypical age-cohort. Berger, however, also shows that this "does not signal a permanent decline in the value of college."

Labor market analysis lends additional insights into future expectations.

[3]His social benefits results were actually most widely quoted.

Using Department of Labor projections to assess future conditions, Rumberger (1980) pointed out that as older, less educated workers are replaced by younger, more educated workers, average educational attainment of the work force will rise, thus dampening the premium paid for a college education. Further, Rumberger projected that growth in professional and managerial jobs to 1990 will be relatively slight, being estimated at only 28 percent of employment growth in the 1980s, compared to 36 and 45 percent in the 1960s and 1970s, respectively. Wagner (1984) is more skeptical about the accuracy of the Bureau of Labor statistics model and its prediction. He thinks it likely that job *restructuring* will occur in order to take advantage of the skills and knowledge held by college graduates in previously lower level jobs.

> To emphasize the point: The alternative I am describing is not one of simply using a person with college-level skills to do the job of a high school graduate. Rather, I ask might jobs be so restructured that firms can take advantage of the competencies of college graduates and the new technologies in expanding product areas? And, I would suggest that the relative prices and productivities of the labor and material inputs might well move employers in this direction.
>
> Wagner (1984)

To date, Freeman's conclusions have proven to be ill advised; the college degree remains a good investment. Rumberger (1980) has shown that the profitability of a college degree declined only slightly in the 1970s. Others have shown that the decline was temporary (Liberman, 1979; Mattila, 1982). Near the beginning of 1986, the Census Bureau (O'Neill and Sepielli, 1985) was reporting a "sharp increase" in the high-school–college income gap between 1958 and 1983, after a decline in 1979. Although by some standards future conditions for college-educated workers have dimmed, so far the financial value of a college degree has been robust beyond the expectations of most observers. Based purely on direct financial rewards, rates of return to the collegiate experience appear to have returned to historic levels or even higher, and these rates probably exceed common alternatives available to youthful high school graduates. The message for interpretation of the meta-analysis results is that mean IRR estimates may to some degree depend upon time periods sampled; but the return to higher education is likely to persist indefinitely because of the socialization function of schooling, the related screening effect, and several inherent characteristics of postindustrial labor markets (Blaug, 1985).

Economic Return Studies as a Basis for Policymaking

Private internal rates of return often are discussed in the process of setting levels of public support for higher education. Although the role and importance of IRR information in reaching these decisions is unknown, we cannot point to any other quantitative information that is more powerful, in fact or claim.

That level of public support should be influenced by private returns may appear somewhat bizarre, but decision making in political arenas often tends to possess its own form of rationality. While accurate private IRR figures and trends ostensibly, though probably mistakenly, are important to public policymaking, to private decisions the relevance is clear.

Professional analysts tend to discredit earnings differentials and alpha values because these measures ignore costs. The former ignores innate and background differences between students and nonstudents as well. IRR studies consider costs and generally attempt to adjust for these student and nonstudent differences, but results often are inconsistent because opinions about costs differ, as do opinions about appropriate corrections and controls. These differences in IRR studies and results are not trivial. Only the earnings figures, like the earnings differentials, are widely accepted. This is not to say that available earnings profiles are considered satisfactory; they merely are the best estimates available. There exists considerable dissatisfaction that historic cross sections of earnings profiles must be used to project future earnings.

IRR STUDIES AS COST STUDIES

The fact that cost estimation methods differ is important because IRR are particularly sensitive to the cost, as opposed to the benefits, of higher education. One reason for this sensitivity is that cost variations of only a few hundred dollars per year may represent a large portion of total college costs, whereas the same amounts are much less, proportionately, in comparison to postcollege earnings. Another reason is that in IRR calculations costs are compounded forward and earnings are discounted backward; thus, the same few hundred dollars spent in the individual's late teens or early twenties will represent a much larger amount later, while the same amount earned in the future will decrease greatly when reduced to present value.

The first realization from this relative cost–benefit calculus is that IRR do not tell us very much about the value or *benefits* of higher education; principally, they tell us about *costs*. Indeed, it is not stretching the point too far to refer to IRR studies as "cost" studies rather than studies of "return." As noted by Douglass (1977), rates of return estimates during the period 1966–1972 were "somewhat lower results as compared with earlier estimates . . . principally because of the rising private costs of higher education" (p. 366). This finding is contrary to the common perception: We believe that when most policymakers—public or private—weigh IRR information, they assume they are contemplating the changing benefits of college, not the changing costs.

To illustrate, the literature has widely reported that the rate of return to elementary and secondary education is much greater than the return to higher education. Yet, to our knowledge, no one has ever emphasized that the explanation is cost difference, not benefit difference. In 1983, male median money income was $10,308 for those with an eighth-grade education, $17,568 for those with 4 years of high school, and $26,152 for those with 4 years of college (U.S. Bureau of Census, CPS, 1985, Table 47). These figures translate into $1,289, $1,815, and $2,146 money income per year invested, for the respective marginal levels of educational attainment (e.g., $17,568–10,308/4 = $1,815). For females the figures are an even more disparate $585, $671 and $1,281, respectively. Clearly, the *benefits* to years of schooling do not decline by educational level even though private rates of return do decline. The reason for the IRR decline by level is that college students absorb a large portion of higher education costs while elementary and secondary students do not. Further, students at the lower levels forego relatively little in the way of earnings. Indeed, IRR for elementary school often exceed 100 percent and may approach infinity (Weisbrod, 1962, 1964) because direct costs are essentially zero, and child labor laws have reduced the economic value of an elementary school child's time to almost nothing. The large social expenditure implies that society believes there are great social values to elementary and secondary education; however, the private monetary benefits (*not* rates of return) are relatively small.

The major point of this discussion, however, is that private IRRs are an inappropriate base for determining public support levels for higher education, not only because these rates pertain to private circumstances, but because what they reflect is primarily how generous society has been, not how valuable the higher education enterprise may be. If society judges private returns to higher education to be low, society can remedy the situation easily. It can increase its share of the costs. The common recommendation in the literature, to increase public subsidies to lower education because rates of return are high there, is easily seen to be misguided advice when it is known that varying return rates reflect primarily how generous society has already been. Elementary and secondary schools probably deserve more financial support, but high rates of return are hardly the reason.

In illustration of the importance of variations on the cost side and of public subsidies, Wachtel (1975, pp. 158–162) estimates that the rate of return to G.I. Bill recipients after World War II was almost twice that to nonrecipients. Siegfried (1972–1973) shows that the rate of return to fellowship holders in economics ranges from 11.4 to 23.6 percent in comparison to 13 percent for those relying completely upon private funds, and Rogers (1969) shows that returns on a "second college degree" increase from the 1–2 percent to the 8–10 percent range if a realistic 50 percent graduate student subsidy is assumed. It might be noted that graduate study subsidies are targeted heavily on higher ability students.

ACCURACY IN COST ESTIMATES

Returning again to our theme of reality and practicality, we are aware that published IRR estimates have and will continue to be used in setting finance policy. What then are the realities of the most important side of the cost–benefit equation? In other words, recognizing that IRR estimates are largely sensitive to costs, what can be said about the accuracy of cost estimates used in IRR analysis?

Private costs may be subdivided into direct, out-of-pocket costs and indirect costs, that is, foregone earnings. For the direct costs,[4] those who conduct IRR analyses almost invariably employ national averages of student expenditures, often, at present, from college estimates such as those submitted annually to the federal government or the College Scholarship Service (CSS). Unfortunately, institutions are provided an incentive to overstate student costs because the amount of aid given to their students, and thus their enrollment levels, are a function of the institution's cost estimate. When researchers employ only tuition data in determining direct costs, errors from this source should not be large; however, when broader cost definitions are used, the errors may be substantial. Leslie (1984) compared student reported expenditures to these hypothetical, institutionally stated costs and found that the average, student-reported expenditure was less for *all* students than was the average institutionally reported figure for the lowest cost student category at the lowest cost institution—the commuting student enrolled at a public, 2-year college. The midpoint of the range of student expenditures reported to CSS by institution was some 58 percent higher than the average expenditure reported by students. Wagner's (1984) work supports these findings. He points out that actual costs have declined since 1970, and his reason is the same given by Leslie (1984): Students simply find ways to reduce costs. During the 1970s, when stated tuitions increased by 2½ times, tuitions actually paid grew by a factor of two. Students met the higher costs by moving out of more expensive independent institutions into lower priced public ones, thus reducing their tuition costs, on average (Wagner, 1984).

Regarding indirect costs, estimates employed in IRR studies also often have been too high. Based upon actual earnings by otherwise equivalent students and nonstudents in the National Longitudinal Study of 1972, Crary and Leslie (1978) found that foregone earnings usually were overestimated (and thus student costs were overstated) by from 16 to 56 percent. Only Becker's (1964) method employed foregone earnings estimates that were approximately correct. Parsons (1974) shows that the principal error made is in underestimating the greater sacrifice of leisure for work by students than nonstudents. Students enjoy less leisure time than nonstudents and work more than is usually assumed (Parsons, 1974, pp. 262–264). One seemingly good estimate is that 18–21-year-old male students earn from 53 to 68 percent as much as comparable nonstudents, and females earn, comparatively, about 32–46 percent as much (Freiden and Leimer, 1981). These conclusions are supported by newer data. Unemployment for recent high school graduates rose from 12 percent in the early 1970s to 16 percent later in the decade and reached 26 percent in the

[4]True direct costs are tuition and fees; books and supplies; those living expenses accruing from college attendance, i.e., that are marginal to nonattendance—all net of subsidies such as student aid. Indirect costs are foregone earnings.

recession of 1982, thereby reducing opportunity costs to college students. Further, part-time enrollments have grown very rapidly, and 92 percent of part-time students are in the labor force; the number of full-time students who work has grown by about 20 percentage points since 1960 but only 10 points since 1980, standing at almost 50 percent in 1985 (U.S. Department of Labor, as reported in *The Chronicle of Higher Education*, January 15, 1986, pp. 29, 32). Both direct and indirect student costs almost certainly are overstated in IRR studies; usually, the error is large.

Beyond accuracy in foregone earnings estimates, the concept of assigning these costs to higher education bears examination. Such an examination is offered by Rogers (1969, pp. 91–92), who points out that foregone earnings are quite different from cash expenditures on education or other kinds of investments. For instance, the individual finds a greater psychological ease in "spending" foregone earnings than in departing with money income; the loss of utility is considerably greater in the latter case. More telling, however, is Rogers's point that if earnings were not foregone, much of the resulting money would not be invested. Since propensities to consume approximate .92 or .93, most earnings would be consumed, not invested. Indeed, one of the great benefits of higher education to the individual and to society is that enrollment is a form of forced savings, thereby building the individual's and the nation's stock of (human) capital. Conceptually, this savings adds greatly to the nation's wealth, just as does any resource savings and capital investment. The "stock" built up, in this case, is human rather than physical capital. In summary, one could argue that the true higher education cost from foregone earnings, at the margin, is the *net* amount invested in the *ceteris paribus* case, that is, the portion of earnings non-college-goers do not spend on consumption. In the absence of such a correction, the private costs of higher education can be argued, again, to be overstated and the private rate of return to be understated.

As a means of testing the importance of quality of cost data, the authors obtained the best cost data believed to be available and calculated IRR for the period Freeman examined—the period seemingly offering the lowest IRR since World War II. The cost data were from the National Longitudinal Study (NLS) of the High School Class of 1972. Actual direct cost data were used, and foregone earnings data were net earnings of high school graduates minus net earnings of otherwise equivalent (SES and ability-controlled) college students. Earnings data were from the Census Bureau. Instead of Freeman's low IRR value of 7.5 percent, the IRR estimate obtained for males from the NLS sample was 11.7 percent, some 56 percent higher, without consideration of any student subsidies. When *average* student aid subsidies are included, the IRR increases by about 1 percentage point.

WHOM DO IRR ESTIMATES "FIT"?

IRR calculation methods employ national average figures. Employment of "averages" is always problematic; in applying private rate of return averages to individual decisions, substantial error is virtually certain. The fact is that no so-called "average" students exist; average cost estimates—those employed in IRR studies—really are a composite formed from the institutionally reported costs of many quite different types of students. Student costs vary tremendously depending upon such factors as type of institution attended and family and government subsidies. Thus, so-called "average" cost is a composite of costs from students who attend private and public universities, liberal arts and state colleges, and community and junior colleges—to name only some of the major institutional types—and who pay full published costs. There is, of course, no such student. As Eckaus (1973) observes, "The use of such averages introduces strong qualifications in the interpretation of the internal rates of return associated with college especially. . . . Although I have no more to apologize for in this respect than other investigators, the procedure is felt to be particularly unsatisfactory" (p. 84). What Eckaus is pointing out is that costs vary so greatly among institutions—for example, between the private and public sector—that average costs will be (relative) overstatements for some students and understatements for others.

Crary and Leslie (1978) show that this problem extends to indirect-cost estimates. They demonstrate that actual amounts foregone for students in 4-year schools are considerably greater than in 2-year and proprietary schools. Further, they show that these costs vary considerably within institutional classifications when students are disaggregated by ability and SES. Surprisingly, high-ability students have the smallest foregone earnings. "Averages," again, do not apply to real persons.

Not only are costs institution specific, the same may be said of earnings, albeit perhaps to a lesser extent. The only known extensive study comparing rates of return across institutional types is a carefully controlled effort by McMahon and Wagner (1982, pp. 161–169). The authors show that community and junior colleges, which offer many technical courses of study, yield high returns, as do private and public research universities and public and private comprehensive colleges. Graduates of liberal arts colleges do not fare as well, except for those who go on to graduate school. Once again, however, the importance of costs arises. Costs at liberal arts colleges are the highest and those (net costs) at private research universities are the lowest. One is well advised to keep the cost sensitivity principle always in mind.

Taking a somewhat different tack, others have examined connections between institutional quality and earnings. Although analysts have spent a good deal of time and effort attempting to define quality, perhaps without satisfying anyone but themselves, a positive relationship always seems to emerge regardless of the measure employed. For instance, Reed and Miller (1970) found a generally linear relationship between college quality and earnings, while Ribich and Murphy (1975) attributed the positive relationship they found primarily to the fact that higher quality institutions require a greater "quantity" of schooling—a conclusion disputed by the research of Johnson and Stafford (1973) and Link and Ratledge (1975). Using the much criticized Gourman ratings (1967), Taubman and Wales (1973) found a strong relationship between quality and income, but only for institutions in the top quintile. This might be expected because of Gourman's apparently highly subjective technique.[5] Informed observers of higher education institutions can identify elite institutions; it is doubtful that they can make accurate subjective discriminations among the mass of institutions below this level, except perhaps to identify those that are thoroughly undistinguished (Taubman and Wale's lower quintile). This conjecture is supported by the work of Solmon (1975, 1985), who has conducted the most thorough analysis of findings and issues surrounding quality and earnings. Solmon has concluded that quality makes a measurable difference only for graduates of the top quartile institutions compared to those of the bottom quartile. Of course, higher quality institutions typically cost more to attend. Overall, Wachtel (1975) concluded that quality, when measured by college cost, adds about 10–15 percent to private returns.

Returns vary also by field of study, and the variations are huge. Eckaus (1973, Chapter 2) estimates the IRR occupational range to be from "negative" to over 20 percent. Returns tend to be highest in the mature professional fields and lowest in the striving professions, such as education and nursing, and in the humanities and fine arts; they are negative for clergymen (McMahon, 1981; McMahon and Wagner, 1981, 1982). Problems in conducting rate of return studies by field, however, are substantial (see Eckaus, 1973, pp. 17–21). Among the problems cited are selecting the appropriate comparison group (to whom among noncollege attendees should the earnings of a physician or history major be compared?), difficulties in separating education from noneducation sources of knowledge and skills, psychic income differences, and worker movement among occupations. Seeborg (1975) points out that the various curricula attract persons of quite different abilities, thus raising additional comparability questions.

Perhaps the greatest variations of all and the most important considerations from the private investment standpoint reflect merely peculiarities in personal and family relationships and circumstances. Beyond the cost overstatements already discussed, very few students personally pay the full cost, whatever it may be. The simplest and least debatable illustration is the student aid recipient whose net cost clearly is less than the list price. Yet only 3 of the 25 studies in the meta-analysis considered this aid in computing IRR. Notwithstanding Freeman's results, the other 2 reported much higher IRR estimates, at 16 and 18 percent, respectively, as would be expected. When one considers the magnitude of student aid—roughly $12 to $14 billion in 1985–1986 subsidies (as opposed to inclusion of full loan amounts)—in comparison to the scale of student self-support, it is obvious that this oversight is serious. For example, in 1980 freshmen met 20.1 percent of expenses through student aid compared

[5]The techniques used by Gourman are largely unknown. Gourman's ratings are not documented and are believed to be highly subjective. (See Webster, 1984).

to 18.8 percent from own sources; shares were only somewhat altered, in the direction of greater student self-support, for upperclassmen (Leslie, 1984). Wagner (1984) has found the same pattern: He reports that direct subsidies to students and their families grew by a factor of four between 1970 and 1982 and that student net costs actually declined.

Additionally, there is the larger and more contentious matter of specifying the decision-making unit for private individuals. If the college investment is viewed as a shared one by student and family, the investment decision is fairly clear where families share in cost payment. This model, however, clearly does not fit the underlying theory of IRR studies. The implicit rationale of the IRR approach, which is a straightforward cost–benefit analysis, excludes such considerations as indirect benefits and "unpaid costs." Subsidies provided by others are not costs to the decision maker. Considering subsidies as costs to the students would lead to incorrect private decisions. Such considerations would be clearly at odds with the rigid cost–benefit bases of IRR studies. The private policy question is how much is the student's cost and how much is his or her benefit? From the student's perspective, only his or her own net investment cost can enter into the IRR analysis unless he or she must share the income gained. Normally, such sharing would apply only to spouses of independent students. Family contributions by others should be considered merely as cost reductions unless the income is shared. Leslie (1984) found that the student's net cost in 1980 ranged from 32 to 40 percent of total private direct cost and, further, that this share had declined by about 10 percentage points over the previous 8 years.

This discussion of "average" students and the cost structures of typical students should include one more important group. These are the persons over 25 years of age, a group composing approximately 38 percent of collegiate enrollments in 1980 (Rumberger, 1984b) and a group that is still growing. Private rates of return for these persons reflect unique circumstances. Many older students work part- or full-time; therefore, their foregone earnings are atypically small or nonexistent. On the other hand, they pay a relatively large share of their own college costs, and spousal contributions presumably are a proper inclusion in their IRR calculations. Further, older students have fewer years to recapture their investment, thus affecting downward their rates of return. Private IRR for older students may be greater or lesser than those of traditional college age, depending upon remaining years of employment and other special circumstances.

Our earlier demonstration of the effects of varying the cost figures was extended to illustrate how personal circumstances may alter IRR. Again using the NLS cost data and mean census earnings data, and by comparison to the 11.7 percent earlier calculated IRR standard for all males, rates for specific groups of individuals can be calculated and considered.

As noted previously, spreading the student aid subsidy across all students raises the IRR by about 1 percentage point. Needless to say, however, students either receive aid or they do not. Among student aid recipients, the IRR rises to more than 15 percent when the amount of aid received is considered. Including average parental subsidies as an additional offset to student costs (also not really justified because students either receive parental aid or they do not) raises the rate to over 17 percent.

Rates also vary depending upon institutional sector. For males enrolled in public institutions, the rates for those who receive aid and, including average parental subsidies, exceed 18 percent. In private institutions the IRR is near 15 percent. Although one may question the assumption that aid recipients receive overall average parental subsidies, the assumption probably is not inaccurate for the students in private colleges. Finally, the authors estimated an IRR for a student whose parents pay all direct costs at a private institution and provide the student with a monthly "allowance" of $250 per month. It is assumed that no student aid is received. For this student the IRR approaches 24 percent.

IRR estimates also were made for various SES and ability groups. Again, only the costs were varied; that is, mean census earnings differentials were employed consistently. The IRR estimates were disaggregated by public and private sector. Subsidies were considered again in two ways: (1) Total subsidies were averaged for all students, and (2) average subsidies were assigned only to those who receive them. For the high-SES, high-ability group, the $250 per month parental subsidy was added on for one of the calculations. It was reasoned that a substantial number of students receive such subsidies.

The highest IRR, at 29.5 and 21.8 percent, were estimated for high-SES, and high-ability students receiving the $250 per month family subsidy at public and private institutions, respectively. The lowest rates tended strongly to be in the middle-SES, middle-ability group where combined parental and direct government subsidies are smallest. Here, IRR range from 12.2 to 14.4 percent. Rates are about equal for low-SES, high-ability and high-SES, high-ability persons because the former receive large government subsidies, whereas the latter receive large parental subsidies. In public institutions, rates for these groups range between 16 and 22 percent and in private institutions the range is from 12 to 20 percent, exclusive of those who receive the extra monthly parental support.

These disaggregated IRR estimates more closely conform to actual student circumstances than do the totally aggregated estimates, although they certainly do not fit anyone precisely. The estimates should provide an IRR of better fit for some students—those who receive student aid, parental subsidies, attend public versus private colleges, have particular abilities and come from particular socioeconomic classes. The greatest shortcoming in these estimates is that mean earnings data are used. Though far from perfect, these IRR are far more useful than aggregated rates for individuals facing the college attendance decision. It should be noted, however, that by employing traditional decision rules all groups reach an affirmative enrollment choice. For most groups the IRR is considerably in excess of benchmark rates.

ACCURACY AND ADEQUACY IN MEASURING BENEFITS

Although the tack taken in this book is primarily to address the hard economic evidence and to evaluate this evidence in its traditional form, note must be taken of the evidence that is not quantifiable, or at least typically is not quantified. It appears indisputable that important private higher education benefits are omitted in the typical private IRR analysis.

The omission is seen simply in Figure 4.2. (The reader should disregard the relative areas of the various costs and benefits.) Conventionally, in calculating private rates of return, the analyst sums all Indirect (I) and Direct (II) costs and, after properly adjusting them to their present value, compares them to the similarly adjusted earnings (or income) of a college graduate in comparison to the earnings/income of high school graduates, the earnings (or income) differentials being the monetay benefits (III) in Figure 4.2. The nonmonetary benefits (IV) are simply ignored. In other words, both costs are included but one of two benefits are excluded. To estimate private returns accurately, both benefits must be considered. As put more elegantly and in reverse fashion by the great Cambridge economist Alfred Marshall,

> The true reward which an occupation offers the labourer has to be calculated by deducting the money value of all its disadvantages from that of its advantages.
> (*Principles of Economics*)

FIGURE 4.2 Cost–Benefit Framework

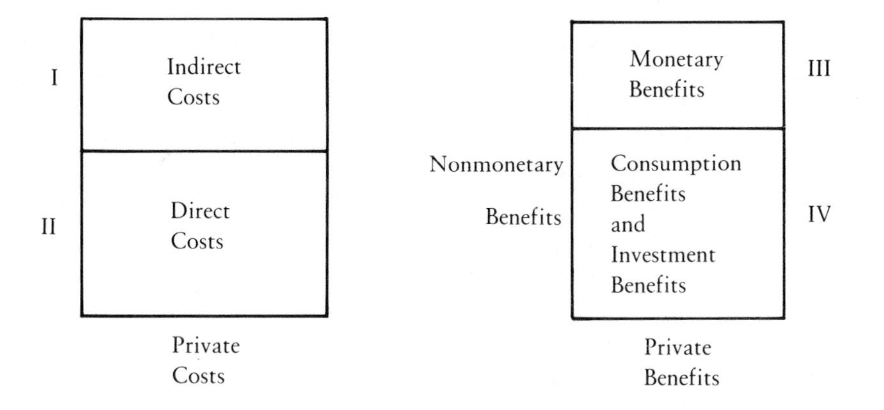

Put similarly, but more broadly by Adam Smith,

> Wages of labour vary with ease or hardship, the cleanliness or dirtiness, the honourableness or dishonourableness. . .
>
> (*Wealth of Nations*)

To ignore such considerations in the calculation of private rates of return surely greatly understates the returns from higher education.

The benefits beyond those represented in conventional rate of return analysis may be categorized as consumption (benefits captured at present) or nonmonetary, investment benefits (captured later). Although these benefits implicitly are substantial and add significantly to the private rates of return stated in this chapter, their full investigation is beyond our purpose. Further, many of these benefits are difficult to separate from social benefits and thus are left to the next chapter, where social returns are discussed.

CONSUMPTION BENEFITS

Many students have more than investment in mind when they decide to attend college. At least part of their cost payment represents a "purchase" of college life, of rap sessions in dormitory rooms or coffee houses, of fraternity and sorority parties and Saturday football games, of pleasures in reading and in rediscovering old truths, and of attendance at concerts and other fine arts events. These activities normally carry over after college, whether at the alma mater or elsewhere (Lazear, 1977). They are manifest in all forms of leisure-time activities, and though difficult to measure in dollar terms, their value clearly is considerable.

Suffice it to say here that the private consumption benefits of higher education must be substantial; otherwise why would so many youth live on campuses when they could save money by commuting? Join organizations such as fraternities and sororities? And attend college full-time when they could greatly reduce costs and thereby increase rates of return by working full-time and studying part-time? Fully 73.5 percent of college freshmen cite "to learn more about things," 61.3 percent cite "to gain a general education," and 32.6 percent cite "to become a more cultured person" as very important reasons for attending college (Astin et al., 1985, p. 47).

NONMONETARY INVESTMENT BENEFITS

Among nonmonetary investment benefits are greater fringe benefits and superior working conditions (Duncan, 1976; Lucas, 1977; Freeman, 1978), a better ability to select appropriate savings instruments (Solmon, 1975), better health and longer life (Grossman, 1976; Feldstein, 1979; Lee, 1982), lower unemployment (Erlich, 1975) and lower disability rates (Lando, 1975), fewer unwanted children (Michael, 1982), and better health for offspring (Grossman, 1982). Psacharopoulos (1975, pp. 134–161) estimates that rates of return rise by about 20 percent when only the value of paid vacations and holidays are considered. College-educated people make more informed purchases (Hettic, 1972; Michael, 1972; Schultz, 1975) and engage in child-rearing practices that enhance formal schooling effects (Hill and Stafford, 1974, 1980; Leibowitz, 1974, 1975; Schultz, 1975) and eventually lead to a greater likelihood of college attendance (McMahon, 1976). Although schooling is associated with the selection of a spouse possessing higher earnings potential (Michael, 1982) and the wife's schooling has been found to increase spousal earnings (Welch, 1974), divorce rates increase with the wife's education. With this exception, all these are benefits accruing directly to college graduates.

Indeed, the nonpecuniary benefits of a college education, at least in some occupations, must be large; how else can we explain collegiate enrollments in such fields as teaching, the ministry, nursing, and social work, where rates of return are very low or are even negative? With just a bit of insight it can be seen that to deny these benefits would be to deny one of the most fundamental premises of economic analysis, the concept of Economic Man.

Conclusion

Where does all this leave us? First, the reality is that rate of return research, especially that which is publicized, has been and will continue to be cited in debates over appropriate levels of public subsidies to higher education. The actual influence of such information in forming political opinions and decisions is unknown but probably is significant. Many private individuals clearly are aware of such information, and its relevance to the private attendance decision is more clear.

Private rates of return to higher education historically have been estimated at somewhat, but not greatly more, than the historic return on benchmark alternative investments. These estimated rates rise and decline with changing economic conditions and size of cohort groups. By these estimates, higher education represents a sound, though not extraordinary, investment.

However, methods employed in estimating IRR have consistently and greatly overstated most higher education costs and thus have greatly understated return rates for most students.

Informed private college investment decisions require identifying one's own specific costs and earnings that are likely after attendance at particular institutions and in particular academic programs. Average IRR estimates, even if they are accurate, can lead to serious mistakes if they are used as a basis for private policy because they really do not apply to anyone.

The benefits of higher education also have been understated. In traditional rate of return analyses cognizance must be taken of such factors as the personal value attached to college attendance and the nonpecuniary investment benefits received.

In summary of this chapter, it would seem that private rates of return, even as conventionally measured, justify additional investment for most persons facing the college attendance decision; that these rates justify additional investment for almost everyone, assuming that IRR are calculated using valid data; and that when all the benefits are included, the college attendance decision represents an investment and consumption choice almost without equal. Finally, private IRR are irrelevant to informed public investment decisions, in that they are inappropriate to social investment decisions and could lead to dysfunctional public policies. As Douglass (in Bowen, 1977, p. 376) points out, however, the "reliability [of social rates of return] is even less."

5

Higher Education as Social Investment

In the last chapter it was posited that policymakers and the public at large often form their opinions about appropriate levels of higher education support through informal impressions of the job market for college graduates and anecdotal information about private rates of return. The presumption often made is that if a college education fails to pay off for students, society should decrease its share of college costs. A major point of Chapter 4, however, was that private rates of return are useful primarily in formulating not public, but individual college investment decisions: Public policymaking must extend beyond private considerations. Theodore Schultz (1971) put it this way:

> It is also true that the price that the student pays for educational services is only remotely connected to the real cost of producing them, and therefore private choices by students, however efficient they are privately, are not necessarily efficient socially (p. 171).

In formulating *public* investment decisions, the analyst typically employs the social rate of return, that is, the return to society on its investment in higher education.

Unfortunately, determining which costs and benefits are public and which are private is often contentious. In fact, we doubt that policymakers are aware of what goes into a social rate of return calculation. Indeed, we suspect that the common misperceptions rival those related to how costs explain differences in IRR among grammar school, high school, and college graduates, as discussed in Chapter 4.

In calculating social rates of return (SRR), the convention is to consider social costs to be the sum of private and social costs, and social benefits to be private benefits only (before taxes).[1] The rationale for including private accounts in SRR calculations is that individuals are part of society. The assumption is that all social benefits are captured by college graduates—more specifically, (only) by the salaries paid to college graduates. Of course, all figures are marginal to those for high school graduates. This counting of (marginal) private costs and benefits also as (marginal) social costs and benefits is conceptually troublesome because analysts use comparisons of private and social rates of return to argue for or against various policy decisions, such as assigning cost shares to society and individuals (e.g., Psacharopoulos, 1981; Witmer, 1983). Perhaps this comingling of private and social cost and benefit data is why individuals and policymakers sometimes have referred to private rates of return in gauging social investments. In any case, in conventional SRR calculations public money (i.e., money raised through taxes and special fees) spent is added to private costs to obtain social costs. Similarly, any social "earnings" should be (but rarely are) added to the earnings of individuals to yield total social benefits. Without these additions, SRR measure only the private monetary benefits, plus the taxes paid. Obviously, there are conceptual and practical problems with conventional SRR analyses.

Traditionally, in public policy formulation the goal of rate of return analyses has been to achieve an optimum level of investment in higher education. If the social rate of return is high, the conclusion reached is that the social investment should be greater; if the rate is low, overinvestment is presumed.

> If the rates of return to education and to R&D are high relative to the alternatives, as they are found to be . . . reduced investments in education and in R&D would be expected to contribute to reductions in productivity growth in the future. (McMahon, 1984, p. 300)

Like the private IRR, a benchmark figure of 10 percent generally has been used to evaluate social rates of return.

In recent years a new goal implicitly has been added to guide public policy. The goal is to improve efficiency by maximizing social rates of return. It is reasoned that if individuals can be induced to pay more of the costs of higher education, SRR will rise and the efficiency of the public investment thus will

[1]True private costs are earnings foregone, tuition and fees, books and supplies, and those living expenses accruing from college attendance (i.e., that are marginal to non-attendance)—all net of subsidies such as student aid. True social costs are private costs plus government support of institutions to provide for the student's education.

be improved. (This logic fails to take into account the inclusion of private costs in social cost accounts!) Since private IRR are high, it is reasoned that individuals will be willing to pay a larger share of higher education costs. Further, since private IRR are higher than social rates, it is judged equitable to expect them to do so (Psacharopoulos, 1981; Witmer, 1983).

These two goals of optimization and maximization potentially are in conflict, although no related discussion has been noted in the literature. The traditional goal suggests higher social investment to induce greater enrollments if social rates of return are high. The newer goal suggests lower social investment in the interests of efficiency, regardless of SRR, even though reduced enrollments would occur due to resulting higher private costs. Perhaps those who urge greater parity in public–private returns believe that social returns are near the optimum level or possibly are even somewhat too low. However, because social returns are a direct function of private returns, higher private costs mean lower SRR, too. Both lines of reasoning suggest a paradox.

There are other issues related to social rates of return to be explored, and there are other ways of viewing higher education payoffs to society. These topics also are addressed in this chapter.

Chapter Overview

Social benefits of higher education are assessed in three ways: (1) *Social rates of return* on undergraduate education range between 11.6 and 12.1 percent—slightly less than the private rate of return values. (2) The percentages of *national income growth* deriving from education and higher education, respectively, are estimated to be 15–20 and 4–5 percent, with another 20–40 percent probably deriving from improvements in knowledge and its applications. (3) *Economic impacts* of colleges upon communities include increases in business volume, which amount roughly to \$1.50–\$1.60 per dollar of the college operating budget, and jobs created, which are estimated at 59 jobs per each \$1 million of the college budget.

Social rates of return generally have been quite stable for 5 decades. Like private rates of return, as conventionally calculated, social rates of return estimates tend to be understated. This is because actual benefits are greater and costs are less than conventional calculations reflect. True private and social rates of return may be roughly equal.

Social Rates of Return

Like the private case, evaluation of the social investment in higher education is attempted most often through rate of return analysis. Calculations of social rates of return conventionally involve the same application of interest or discount rates as do calculations of the private IRR. By convention, social benefits almost always are taken as the pretax earnings of individuals, and social costs—although often not clearly stated—in most cases are specified as the Educational and General Expenditures of institutions (an accounting category) plus all or part of the student's foregone earnings.[2] The heavy reliance upon questionable private cost and benefit data previously noted is evident.

META-ANALYSIS RESULTS

The body of literature containing social rate of return analyses essentially is the same as that of the private IRR studies. (See Appendix Table 1.) That literature contains 30 SRR estimates from 15 studies. Summary data for undergraduate education are presented in Figure 5.1, Table 5.1, and Appendix Table 3; again, most studies are for males or white males (see notes, Appendix Table 2), and the four synthesis methods are employed.

For the 30 results of Method 1, which utilizes multiple estimates by some authors, the mean SRR is 12.1 percent, compared to 12.4 percent for the private IRR from Method 1 in Chapter 4. The median is 12.5 percent. The range of the 30 estimates is from 7.5 to 16.7 percent—a narrower range than for the private IRR—resulting in a smaller standard error of .8 and a 95 percent confidence interval of from 11.3 to 12.9 percent.

For Method 2, in which only a single estimate is taken from each research publication, the 15 estimates obtained have a mean of 11.7 percent, a median of 11.2 percent, and a standard error of 1.3 percent. Thus, the 95 percent SRR confidence interval is from 10.4 to 13.0 percent, with probabilities, as always, decreasing as the outer limits of the interval are approached.

Method 3 limits the sample to consistently designed *and* well-designed studies. Because there were only three of these, the estimate is not terribly useful. The mean SRR of the three estimates is 12.1 percent. The studies are numbers 03, 07, and 27 in Appendix Table 1.

Method 4 eliminates only the least compatible studies and then applies Method 2. For the 11 studies of Method 4, the mean SRR is 11.6 percent, the median 11.0 percent, and the standard error 1.4; hence, the 95 percent confidence interval is from 10.2 to 13.0 percent. Studies eliminated in Method 4 are 08, 23, 30, and 32.

Depending upon the method employed, the mean estimate ranges from only 11.6 to 12.1 percent. Given the small standard errors and the narrow range of means, the true SRR, as conventionally measured, is almost certainly

[2]Note that most of student tuition paid, a private cost, will be reflected in the Educational and General Expenditures Category. Marginal living costs and costs of books and supplies will not be included. Further, the Educational and General Expenditures category contains noninstructional spending.

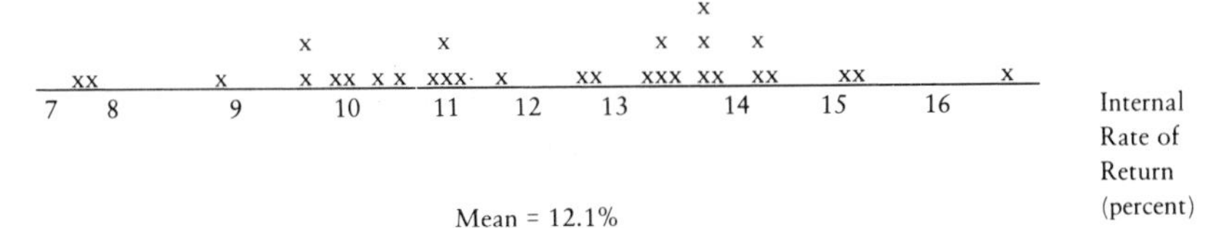

FIGURE 5.1 Social Rate of Return Estimates in the Literature, Method 1

near this range of mean values. The range compares to 11.8 to 12.4 percent for the private IRR.

As in Chapter 4, the SRR also are arranged in temporal order (Table 5.1). The last entries in Table 5.1 show quite stable patterns of 10.6 to 11.7 mean SRR between 1939 and 1973. The mean SRR of 14.5 for 1976 is derived from only three estimates; nevertheless, a temporal increase in SRR is suggested.

How can the .2 to .3 percentage points higher private than social rates of

Table 5.1

SUMMARY OF SOCIAL RATES OF RETURN TO HIGHER EDUCATION—UNDERGRADUATE

		Social RR	(N)*
Method 1	Mean	12.1	(30)
	(S. E.)	(.8)	
	Median	12.5	
Method 2	Mean	11.7	(15)
	(S. E.)	(1.3)	
	Median	11.2	
Method 3	Mean	12.1	(3)
Method 4	Mean	11.6	(11)
	(S. E.)	(1.4)	
	Median	11.0	
By Year	Means		
1939		11.1	(2)
1949		10.6	(2)
1959		11.5	(3)
1969		11.7	(8)
1973		11.6	(5)
1976		14.5	(3)

Source. Appendix Table 1.

*N = Number of estimates represented in the mean estimate.

return be explained? Do private individuals obtain a better "deal"? Do they pay less than their fair share of costs?

The reader will recall that SRR reflect private and social costs and marginal, pretax private benefits. Only because marginal taxes paid by college graduates are small compared to tax support of higher education are social rates of return less than private rates. As noted by Psacharopoulos (1981),

> Contrary to popular belief, the post- versus pre-tax treatment of earnings does *not* make a big difference in a rate of return calculation. It is the addition of *direct cost* of schooling that mainly accounts for the fact that a social rate of return is lower relative to a private rate of return.

Is there a case here for charging private individuals more? Hardly.

Viewing the matrix in Appendix Table 1, it is seen that some of the higher SRR resulted from conservative social cost estimates while others resulted from the special techniques employed for both private and social rate of return calculations. Raymond and Sesnowitz (1975) obtained a high estimate, apparently because they omitted social costs that most others included. From their writings it is clear that Raymond and Sesnowitz were troubled with the conventional social cost and benefit specifications. Liberman (1979) and McMahon and Wagner (1982) calculated SRR at "overtaking" ages—the point in time at which the earnings of college graduates overtake those of high school graduates—and obtained higher SRR values because this method results in larger earnings differentials than if differentials are calculated, as they commonly are, at earlier ages.

In contrast, Hansen (1963), Johnson and Stafford (1973), Carnoy and Marenbach (1975), Freeman (1975), and Wachtel (1975) obtained relatively low estimates by apparently including such institutional expenditures as those for research and public service, even though presumably only instructional expenditures connect directly to the earnings of graduates (the "dependent variable"). The only unusual, evident factor that might explain Taubman and Wales's low estimate is their inclusion of expenditures for the physical plant plus 71 percent of operating budgets rather than instructional expenditures. In contrast with research and public service costs, operating and depreciation costs on the portion of physical plant devoted to instruction should be included in social costs, as should the rental value of the space and the taxes foregone.

Witmer (1980) corrected the cost estimates of Carnoy and Marenbach and others by deleting research and public service expenditures and adding public expenditures for student aid. (It is not clear whether he double-counted some aid by retaining the scholarship and fellowship category present in Educational and General accounts.) In any case, his 13 and 14 percent figures, respectively, approximate the estimates of Liberman and McMahon and Wagner.

In summary, the accuracy of the mean or median meta-analysis estimates is supported by identification of unusual or at least nonnormative methods used in studies obtaining extreme values. If the mean and median meta-analysis results do err, they probably do so on the conservative side, as suggested by Witmer. But even this is only for conventionally performed SRR studies. True rates undoubtedly are much higher, as we shall see.

MAKING SENSE OUT OF THE ESTIMATES

Even with a thorough knowledge of institutional accounting, it is difficult to decide which of the preceding social rate of return estimates is most accurate. Rather than representing differences in accuracy, the varying results appear primarily to reflect differences in values or perspectives. These differences probably are connected to vagaries in the theory undergirding social rate of return analysis. They clearly are related to methodological difficulties.

For reasons already noted, "social" rates of return, theoretically, are supposed to reflect the private costs of and benefits to those who participate in higher education plus the associated costs and benefits paid and received by others (Cohn and Geske, 1986). Private costs were noted in Chapter 4. In practice, they are supposed to include foregone earnings, tuition, books and supplies, and room and board and transportation cost beyond those that would result from nonstudent status—all net of any subsidies such as student aid. Social costs add any public support such as appropriations to institutions and student aid. Again in practice, private benefits are to include private monetary gain (posttax earnings differentials); as per convention, public benefits add the (marginal) taxes paid by these individuals, consistent with the notion that college graduates are part of "society."

The problem with this reasoning is the same one illustrated in Chapter 4, except that the omissions on the benefits side are even more serious. Note that in practice, account is taken of only a small portion of one of the four elements in the cost–benefit equation: Costs to individuals and costs to society are factored in and private benefits are included, but only the taxes paid by college graduates, vis-à-vis high school graduates, compose the (marginal) social benefit. Monetary benefits to others—spillovers—are excluded, as are all nonmonetary benefits. The reason is that these social benefits are not readily observable and quantifiable. Each party, the individual and society, receives nonmonetary benefits, and presumably nongraduates benefit monetarily too (for example, through productivity improvements and upward effects on wage rates, not to mention direct employment in colleges and universities), but such benefits almost uniformly are ignored in rate of return calculations. It is hardly surprising that private, internal rates of return exceed social rates of return in conventional calculations.

Again, social rate of return estimations include only the pretax earnings differentials for college graduates. That benefits to others exist was suggested by the vignette, presented early in this book, related to the formation of Harvard

College and the historical development of higher education thereafter. Suffice it to say here that society continues to subsidize higher education. There is nothing in the purposes and goals of higher education that requires enrichment of private individuals as an end, save equalizing opportunity for the poor. Higher earnings from college attendance hardly can be said to be the exclusive domain of the lower socioeconomic classes. If there are not significant social benefits, why does society continue to subsidize the enterprise? It seems self-evident that social rate of return estimates understate social rates of return by grossly understating the social benefits.

Perhaps this anomaly explains the varying behavior of social rate of return analysts. It may be that some analysts ignore the public expenditures because they cannot identify or specify adequately the related benefits. Perhaps Carnoy and Marenbach, Freeman, and others included costs for research and public service, not out of ignorance as to what constitutes Educational and General Expenditures, but because research and service must yield social benefits, too. From this view, social costs are stated more correctly by the latter group of analysts;[3] however, their estimates presumably are less accurate because of the "missing benefits." If this reasoning is correct, the higher social rate of return estimates contained in the matrix more closely approximate reality than do the lower estimates, although even the former must be too low because of the cost and benefit omission errors noted in the private rate of return analyses of Chapter 4.

NONMONETARY SOCIAL BENEFITS

All this is not to say either that the figures of 11 or 12 percent social rate of return are roughly accurate or that we are more able than others to estimate them. The large unknown is the social benefits. Social benefits are indeed elusive, but they demand some attention here, even though the primary purpose of the book is to examine the traditionally calculated and hard evidence.

Simply put, all or nearly all private and public costs are included on the left-hand side of the equation because they are fairly easy to measure; glaring omissions exist on the right-hand side because the opposite is true. Researchers appear to have been caught up in a bias toward mathematical elegance, without sufficient attention being given to the conceptual and methodological short-comings of their approaches.

Consumption Benefits

Consumption benefits are those benefits captured immediately. They include the college student's private benefits, which were discussed in Chapter 4, plus

[3]The major omission usually is the value of foregone institution rents, depreciation, and capital outlays on collegiate property. (See Brinkman and Leslie, 1983.)

those captured by others. Nonstudents reap many of the same benefits as do students: They attend athletic events, musical and dramatic presentations, and many community service activities. They watch educational television programming sponsored and administered by colleges and universities, and they use college libraries and bookstores, to name only a few of the social consumption benefits of higher education.

NONMONETARY INVESTMENT BENEFITS

The social nonmonetary investment benefits not directly measurable are only somewhat more easily quantified. Consistent with normative definitions, these include the nonmonetary private benefits captured later, plus the externalities—those captured by the others. The private nonmonetary benefits captured by former students are described in Chapter 4.

Among the externalities, that is, the nonmonetary social benefits accruing to others, are lower crime rates as educational levels increase (Spiegleman, 1968; Erlich, 1975) and a greater ability to prevent crime (Erlich, 1975). A causal relation between crime and lower educational levels is demonstrated when crimes of profit are separated from profitless crimes and suitable controls are executed (Erlich, 1975). Higher welfare and Medicaid costs correlate negatively with education levels (Garfinkel and Haveman, 1977, p. 53), whereas greater liberality on social issues such as integration and freedom for youth correlate positively (Beaton, 1975). Community agency volunteers and leaders come heavily from the ranks of the highly educated (Weisbrod, 1962), who also contribute more money to charities (Mueller, 1978; Dye, 1980). The greater taxes paid by the highly educated are, of course, reflected in social rate of return calculations; however, the productivity gains resulting from a highly educated work force spill over to society (Ben-Porath, 1970; Rosen, 1977). Education appears to contribute to research and development (Huffman, 1974, 1977; Mansfield, 1982).

The research and development contribution of higher education, in particular, deserves to be singled out for some elaboration. Again, we turn to Alfred Marshall (1920) for elegant guidance:

> It will be profitable as a mere investment, to give the masses of the people much greater opportunities than they can avail themselves of. For by this means many, who would have died unknown, are enabled to get the start needed for bringing out their latent abilities. And the economic value of one great industrial genius is sufficient to cover the expenses of the education of a whole town; for one new idea, such as Bessemer's chief invention, adds as much to England's productive power as the labor of a hundred thousand men. Less direct, but not less in importance, is the aid given to production by medical discoveries such as those of Jenner and Pasteur, which increase our health and working power; . . . All that is spent during many years in opening the means of higher education to the masses would be well paid for if it called out one more Newton or Darwin, Shakespeare or Beethoven. (p. 216)

Clearly, the assumptions of conventional rate of return analysis, as it applies to research, bear closer examination. Recall that such analyses specify benefits as earnings (differentials) paid to individuals. This approach implies that the entire fruits of the research and research training conducted in universities are captured by the higher wages (again, differentials) earned later by graduate-degree recipients. In other words, the only social product of graduate education is higher pay realized by former graduate students (Tomaske, 1974). If this in fact were the reality, the high social subsidy to graduate education could in no way be justified.

Of course, society in general does benefit from university research. There are some dramatic examples among many cases. Weisbrod (1971) estimated the return to the research leading to the polio vaccine was from 11 to 12 percent, in economic terms alone. Griliches (1958) estimated that the social rate of return on hybrid seed corn research was 700 percent, as of the 1950s, and that the return on all agriculture research ranges from 35 to 171 percent, with only half the cost being paid by public sources.

Importance of the Omission

The omission of nonmonetary benefits in rate of return calculations is serious. Theodore Schultz (1971), often considered the founder of the human capital movement, makes constant references to the problem throughout his book, *Investment in Human Capital.* For example, in regard to the consumption value, he notes, "But all these studies omit the consumption value of education, as Solow reminds me. It is a serious omission. In my papers . . . I have stressed the importance of this consumption value" (p. 142). In regard to social returns in general, he concludes: "The social rates of return are not in good repair either theoretically or empirically. There is all too little evidence on the relationship between social and private rates of return" (p. 155). And still later,

> Economists who have taken a hand in estimating the returns to education have made substantial progress. These estimates and those pertaining to cost have reached the stage where they are becoming useful allocative guides. But so far the returns from the nonpecuniary satisfactions that accrue to students have not been reckoned. Nor are the estimates of social returns in good repair (p. 172).

Very little has changed since 1971. Writing more recently, McMahon (1982) observed that the worst errors still are "errors of omission" (p. 3). He goes on to say that some writers merely ignore the existence of nonmonetary benefits, but that their recognition is mandatory if economic efficiency is to be maintained.

Speculating Regarding Magnitude

Efforts to estimate nonmonetary benefits of higher education had not gone very far by 1987. Although scores of attempts had been made to quantify the value of individual nonmonetary benefits, only a few very tentative efforts to bring these values together as guides to public policy had been undertaken. One of the more notable was by Haveman and Wolfe (1984), who first catalogued "nonmarket" effects of schooling and then assigned values based upon "willingness to pay," as cited in the empirical literature. Converting all values to 1975 prices they report "a conservative estimate" that 1 year of schooling adds annually about $4,500–$5,000 in nonmarket earnings. Using Hansen's (1963) earnings differentials corrected for inflation, they find that the monetary and nonmarket values are very similar, leading them to conclude that "standard human capital estimates may capture only about one-half of the total value of an additional year of schooling." Warning that their estimates are highly tentative, if not speculative, they nevertheless close with the observation that "the misallocation of resources implied by claims of 'overeducated Americans' [Freeman, 1976] may instead represent miscalculations by economists."

Both Haveman and Wolfe (1984) and McMahon (1984) focus primarily on the benefits accruing personally to the college educated, and thus their observations fit into Chapter 4 as well as this chapter. McMahon's estimates derive from weights assigned by students who responded to a nationwide survey asking for their personal values of the nonmonetary returns to higher education. Indexing student responses by setting their values of the monetary returns equal to 100, the overall value of the private nonmonetary benefits was 87. "Locating a suitable career" was indexed at 100 and "Earning a good income in this career" was valued at 88. Among the nonmonetary benefits, "guiding your children" was indexed at 88, "meeting interesting people" at 87, and "developing broad-minded attitudes, concern for others" at 96.

McMahon also disaggregated the data to provide estimates by occupation and degree level. These results are most informative and confirm that in excluding nonmonetary returns, private rate of return studies understate the returns for many groups. An extreme case is clergyman, whose pure monetary return was −16.2 percent (McMahon, 1976, p. 20), but who placed an extraordinarily high value on such nonmonetary values as "broad-minded attitudes, helping others," and "providing volunteer civic leadership." Similar, though less extreme, responses were illustrated by school teachers and others in the helping professions. Applying factor analysis weights to time allocations, McMahon calculated an average private, nonmonetary return rate of 7 percent. Nonmonetary rates for those planning self-employment were particularly high, being 19 percent for self-employed proprietors; other rates were 14 percent for managers, and 13 and 12 percent for doctors and lawyers, respectively.

Earlier, Becker (1975, pp. 117–120) had speculated that the total return to higher education might be twice as high as conventional IRR studies indicate. These newer, empirical estimates, perhaps by coincidence, are of the same order. Haveman and Wolfe's (1984) conclusion that the nonmonetary private and social benefits roughly equal the monetary benefits, coupled with McMahon's private nonmonetary mean return rate of 7 percent, provide a rough indication that conventional analyses may ignore half the benefits of higher education.

Surely, traditional social rate of return calculations are a questionable foundation upon which to base public policy.

Contributions of Higher Education to the Economy

One approach to overcoming the benefits omissions of social rate of return studies is through an estimation of the portion of national economic gain attributable to higher education and related activities. Although by no means mutually exclusive of benefits measured in rate of return investigations,[4] these "growth accounting" studies take a more broad-based approach by attempting to partition the sources of growth in national income into educational and other components. In other words, all growth is accounted for. These studies consider net national income growth as the dependent variable and the classic elements of production—land, labor, and capital—as the independent variables. A portion of the labor contribution to growth is identified as resulting from education. The portion of net national income growth that is unexplained (the residual) is usually identified as growth due to improvements in knowledge and miscellaneous factors, and often is assigned all or in part to education because of the presumed connection between education and knowledge improvement. With all income growth accounted for, the social benefits that were ignored in rate of return studies are now presumed to be included, even though they may be very difficult to identify. Of course, the approach rests on the assumption that earnings are a satisfactory proxy for productivity growth (Psacharopoulos, 1981); that is, the economic growth model specifies national income growth as the equivalent of growth in wealth and productivity gains, as measured through rates of return on investments in land, labor, and capital.

The economic contribution studies may be viewed as trading off some estimation precision for an approach that is more inclusive, theoretically. Becker (1964, pp. 119–120) clarifies the relationship between rate of return results and economic growth results by labeling the former as "minimal social rates of return" estimates because they ignore the intangibles, and the latter as "maximum social rates of return" estimates because all contributions of education are said to be accounted for.

Table 5.2 contains 10 estimates or conclusions regarding the percentage contribution of education to economic growth. Estimates generally are in the 15–20 percent range; of this, approximately one-fourth may be assigned to higher education. Also, education, especially higher education, contributes to improvements in the application in knowledge. Estimates of the knowledge

[4]The growth accounting studies usually employ rate of return on investment data to formulate their estimates. In the case of higher education, this is the rate of return on human capital investment.

Table 5.2

ESTIMATES OF THE CONTRIBUTION OF EDUCATION TO NATIONAL INCOME GROWTH*

No.	Author, Year	Data Year(s)	Present Contribution from Education, and Related Notes
1	Chinloy, 1980	———	Less than 14% when education interactions are removed
2	Denison, 1962	1929–1957	23% from education
			20% from improvements in knowledge application and miscellaneous
3	Denison, 1964	1957–1962	15% from education
		1960–1980	19% from education (projected)
4	Denison, 1984	1948–1973	15% from education
			40% from advancement in knowledge application and miscellaneous
		1973–1981	34% from education
5	Jorgenson, 1984	1948–1973	11% from education
6	Kendrick, 1983	1966–1979	Education "highly significant"
7	Psacharopoulos, 1973	Early 1960s	18% from education, 25% of this from higher education
8	Schultz, 1963	1929–1957	16.5% or 20% from education, 17% of this from higher education
9	Selowsky, 1969	———	"Denison et al. underestimate by 38%"
10	Walters & Rubinson, 1983	———	Education "significant, but less than Denison estimated"

*Estimates are that one-quarter of the growth due to improvements in labor quality through education are assignable to higher education. Additionally, a large portion of income growth due to improvements in knowledge result from higher education.

contribution range from about 20 to 40 percent. Overall, education may contribute as much as 50 percent or more of growth in the economy, and higher education may contribute almost half of this. We do not attempt to synthesize a single estimate because the number of cases are small and, as shall be seen, because of some controversy as to methods. Suffice it to say, from Table 5.2, that higher education makes a most significant contribution to economic growth.

DISCUSSION

Growth accounting studies generally are traced to Solow's 1957 paper, although Denison's name is associated most closely with this line of research. Reporting on the period 1929–1957, Denison estimated that 23 percent and 20 percent of national income growth could be ascribed to education and improvements in the application of knowledge, respectively. The increase in education raised the average quality of the labor force at an annual rate just below 1.0 percent. Extending his work to 1962, Denison (1964) concluded that 15 percent of national income growth could be ascribed to education in the 5 years subsequent to 1957. Also, he projected that education would account for 19 percent of total real income growth between 1960 and 1980.

Denison has updated his results routinely. In one of his more recent works (1984) he attempted to account for the economic slowdown of the mid- to late 1970s. Separating his data into the periods of 1948–1973 and 1973–1981, he compared the contributions of various sources of economic growth in the recessionary/slowdown period to growth during 25 postwar years. From these data, one can examine the contribution of education over time and assess whether the economic value of education is declining. Of course, higher education is only one part of the education variable.

For the 1948–1973 period, education accounted for .53 percentage points or about 15 percent of the 3.59 growth rate. The .53 percentage points were 33 percent of all growth attributable to the three classical factors of production: land, labor, and capital. The remaining 1.99 percentage points (the residual) were accounted for chiefly by "advances in knowledge and miscellaneous determinants." Advancement in knowledge, much of which presumably is related to higher education, represented more than 71 percent of this remaining growth and almost 40 percent of growth overall.

For the 1973–1981 period, the role of education in explaining economic growth actually increased by .08 percentage points. This figure for education was 34 percent of the total growth rate during the economic slowdown. Denison observed, "The striking fact is not that differentials have changed but that they have changed very little, an indication that percentage differences between marginal products of persons at different educational levels has not diminished much in response to the increase in education" (p. 21).[5]

Others, such as Schultz and Psacharopoulos, have pursued the Denison line. Schultz's results were consistent with those of Denison—after a fashion. Schultz (1961) first observed that from 1929 to 1957, national outputs increased 3.1 percent per annum while total inputs increased only 1 percent. He asked how the excess growth could be explained. Second, he observed that each 1 percent real per capita income growth was associated with a 3.5 percent increase in resources committed to education. Schultz went on to calculate that the share contribution of labor growth to national income growth was 75 percent, that education explained from 36 to 70 percent of the per capita labor share, and thus that education explained from 29 to 56 percent of the per capita national income growth due to labor and capital. These values were higher than those of Denison. Later, Schultz (1963) found that his basic, estimated data were considerably in error and that the correct figures for the contribution of education to the economy were 16.5 or 20 percent—values which compare closely with Denison's result of 23 percent. Of the educational contribution, approximately 17 percent was from higher education, not including the contribution from the advancement in knowledge. Using Schultz's method, Psacharopoulos (1973) found that during the 1960s, educational outlays accounted for about 18 percent of national income growth and higher education investments represented about one-fourth of the 18 percent share.

Jorgenson (1984) introduced nonmarket activities into labor income measures and found that from 1948 to 1973, labor contributed 1.1 percent of the 3.9 percent per year in output gain made by the American economy. Of labor's share, labor quality accounted for .45 percentage points and education accounted for about 93 percent of the growth in labor quality. In total, education explained approximately 11 percent of growth during this later time period (.93 × .45/3.9).

Kendrick (1983) used an approach simimlar to that of Denison in analyzing causes of economic slowdown. Examining differences in economic growth among 20 industrial groups. Kendrick concluded that average education per worker was "highly significant in the explanation of industry differences in productivity growth over the period as a whole," but was dampened by other factors during the slowdown between 1966 and 1979 (p. 48). Research and development was significant in all periods, "which confirms the notion that

[5]For the advancement of knowledge variable, the results are perplexing, even to Denison. This factor, which along with "miscellaneous factors" is how Denison labels the residual or unexplained variance term, became a negative value during the economic slowdown. Denison states that "advances in knowledge cannot plausibly be charged with most of the [slowdown]" and the cause must center in the "miscellaneous determinants" (p. 22).

research and development is the fountainhead of technological change" (p. 45). Kendrick's central conclusion was that investments are important to economic growth—"particularly research and development (R&D) and education" (p. 1). In earlier work, Kendrick (1981) had found that in seven of nine countries studied, the contribution of education to economic growth was greater in the slowdown period of 1973–1974 than in the period 1960–1973, thus supporting Denison's (1984) conclusion. McMahon (1984) reported that he obtained "somewhat similar" results to those of Denison (1984), Kendrick (1983), and Schultz (1981, Chapter 4) from a sample taken of the United States and 14 nations of the Organization for Economic Co-operation and Development (OECD).

The national growth accounting studies are not without their critics. Sheehan (1973) argues that such studies confuse "association" with "cause." He asks rhetorically whether education is a cause of higher income, "or does high income enable one to afford more education?" (p. 62). Sheehan (pp. 65–66) further argues that the 23 percent of national income growth Denison attributed to "spread of knowledge" (education), and the 20 percent he attributed to "advancement of knowledge," cannot properly be assigned entirely to education because, in part, such activities are carried out by industry as well. Walters and Rubinson's (1983) skepticism encompasses these points and others. Their major argument is a very fundamental one, which we have made implicitly in other forms: How can earnings returns to (college-educated) individuals adequately represent national economic growth? Using their own set of assumptions, Walters and Rubinson test Denison's work and conclude that education does have a significant impact upon economic growth, though less than Denison suggests. Plant and Welch (1984, Chapter 4) make the same general point: that growth accounting studies really do not measure the contribution of education to economic growth. Their resulting estimate of the educational contribution is smaller than those of others.

Chinloy (1980) maintains that when the impact of education is corrected to "net out" the interactions of education with other factors in improving labor quality, the "main effect" of education is less than two-thirds as great as Denison has estimated. That is, a sizable share of the presumed contribution of education to national economic growth can occur only because of concomitant changes (with education) in gender, employment class, age, and occupation within the work force.

Using the same reasoning, Psacharopoulos (1984) comes to the reverse conclusion. We believe his logic to be sound, that the interaction terms should be assigned to education, at least in part. Psacharopoulos argues that these "growth accounting" studies greatly understate the contribution of education because they ignore the necessary *support* of education in introducing technological changes. Referring politely to the works of Denison and others as "first-generation estimates," Psacharopoulos shows that education is a necessary accompaniment of general investments. He calls this the interaction between education and other forces in promoting growth, and he substantiates that education repeatedly has been shown to complement physical capital investments (p. 339). Among others, he cites the work of Marris (1982), demonstrating that general investment has a weak part in economic growth when not supported by education (p. 340). Thurow made much the same argument in 1970 that Psacharopoulos (1984) dwells upon in his paper:

> Factors may be complementary with each other; possession of one factor increases the productivity of another factor. Education and training provide a good example . . . . Similar complementarities can be seen between human and physical capital. Human capital is of little value without physical capital with which to work, physical capital is of little value without the necessary human skills to operate it efficiently." (Thurow, p. 54)

Psacharopoulos (1984) organizes his evidence in the following manner. First, he points out that the growth accounting studies understate the fact that education must maintain the quality of a growing labor force. He cites Selowsky's (1969) estimate that the growth accounting studies understate the contribution of the education component in the United States by 38 percent due to exclusive attention to the increment, rather than the total contribution of education. Next, Psacharopoulos points out that the first-generation studies ignore productivity gains in farming. Although farming gains are known primarily to be a function of education, this contribution to the economic growth is not identified in first-generation studies (pp. 340–342). In sequence he then shows that concentrated use of wage differentials, which oversample wages earned in the public sector, understates the value added by education because education pays a higher premium in the private sector (p. 342); that sole reference to male earnings biases estimates of the role of education downward because education results in relatively higher earnings for women (pp. 342–343); that adjustments for ability, in growth accounting studies, often are too large (pp. 343–344); and that if "education" is expanded to include on-the-job training, the contribution of education is much larger.

Psacharopoulos concludes his argument by observing that national income is only one of the many ways by which contributions to the general welfare may be measured. He cites lower fertility rates among the more highly educated, lower infant and child mortality, a more equal distribution of income, and improved household consumption (pp. 346–348). These, of course, are matters discussed earlier in the "Nonmonetary Social Benefits" section of this chapter.

Although more reserved in his judgments, Dean (1984, p. 5) seems to agree with Psacharopoulos. He observes that education undoubtedly enhanced productivity by contributing to research and development efficiency and to the speed of innovation application, both of which may not be reflected in salaries of associated, educated personnel. He asks, "Is education, as an input into the growth process, highly complementary to other economic processes. . .?" Mincer (1984, p. 206) describes this situation:

> Consequently, estimates of effects of education on economic growth are understated if they confine themselves to effects on the quality of labor [as per convention] and leave out the effects on technological change and if effects on the growth of technology are not captured in private returns of those contributing to it.

Jorgenson (1984, p. 97) confirms these notions in observing that conventional growth accounting studies fail to capture the effect of education on productivity of individuals in future years and the effect on nonmarket activities that contribute to the social welfare, even for those who do not participate in the labor market. Without taking these factors into account, Jorgenson's estimate is that education accounted for 11 percent of economic growth during the period 1948–1973.

Haveman and Wolfe (1984, Chapter 1) develop perspectives similar to those they raised in regard to rate of return studies. In keeping with a central theme of this book, they discuss the contribution of education to many outcomes beyond earnings differentials. Fertility, health, income redistribution, and the diffusion of technology are examples. In that the growth accounting studies derive estimates of the contribution of education only through rates of return, these estimates are biased downward. Haveman and Wolfe estimate that proper inclusions would increase the usual figures by about two-thirds.

In summary of the growth accounting studies, estimates of the contribution of education to economic growth vary by as much as 2 to 1 or even more; yet all agree that the contribution of education is important not only to the nation but to the lives of the individuals directly involved. Higher education is, of course, only one component of "education."

The (Community) Economic Impact Studies

The final type of study to be included under the rubric of higher education as social investment is the economic impact study (EIS). EIS are studies of the financial contributions of colleges to their communities. Whereas the social rate of return studies and the economic contribution studies examine impacts upon society overall, the EIS draw attention to value added by colleges to their communities, whether local or statewide.

EIS can be viewed as studies of externalities, because they measure benefits accruing to community members exclusive of the benefits to students themselves. Indeed, EIS prove that external social benefits to higher education do exist and that nonstudents benefit monetarily from collegiate functions. Conceptually, it is clear that the "community benefits" of EIS should be component parts of the economic contribution study estimates (the previous section) and of social rate of return studies; however, economic contribution estimates already have been seen to rely upon rates of return, which omit such externalities on the benefits side. Possibly, EIS benefits are included in the residual term of economic contribution studies, and if part of the residual is attributed to higher education, EIS values may be so reflected. Another way to view EIS is that they examine short-term benefits, whereas rate of return studies are of the long term (Linthicum, 1978, p. D-40).

Several cautions must be exercised in interpreting results of EIS. The first of these is the problem just noted—the possible double counting of benefits. At the very least the reader should be made aware of such redundancies. For example, in citing the earnings of college employees as benefits to local communities, EIS obviously duplicate the earnings differentials of college-educated employees already counted in private and social rate of return studies. Even so, *from the community perspective,* it may be argued that college-related local employment contributes to local wealth because many employees, most notably faculty and administrators, would work and reside elsewhere if the college did not exist, thereby taking certain community monetary benefits with them.

A second precaution relates to the motives for and thereby the quality of some EIS, which often appear to have been undertaken for public relations reasons. Many have been completed by colleges and universities or by collegiate systems seeking to show how much an institution or a set of institutions contributes to the community economy: to local businesses who sell their products to colleges; to gains in (nonstudent) citizen incomes; and less directly, to increases in local lending ability and to the financial status of community governments. This motive at times raises questions of researcher objectivity—though not always. In our judgment, the roughly 50 percent of EIS conducted or overseen by members of local economics and business departments within the colleges generally have been completed objectively and carefully, whereas those completed by institutional administrators have tended to be less rigorous and more reflective of the public relations motive. Even these, however, usually have sought to apply a standard estimation method (Caffrey and Isaacs, 1971), thereby enhancing the validity of results. Use of this standard method also enhances the integrative reviewer's ability to assess the researchers' findings, particularly the reliability of results.

APPROACHES TO ESTIMATION

Economic impact assessments have been performed in at least three ways, although one method, the economic base approach (the "standard" method of Caffrey and Isaacs), is by far the most common. An alternative, input–output analysis (Leontief, 1936), utilizes information about transactions among local industries. The method yields accurate results but is costly, in part because data requirements are enormous. Traditional econometric modeling is another approach and one that is inexpensive; however, estimates obtained are often biased upward (Linthicum, 1978, p. 94), and causality often is questionable.

Most economic base studies, whose roots can be traced to the 1950s and 1960s (North, 1955; Tiebout, 1962), employ surveys to obtain the needed financial data. Because the surveys are of causal design, direct inference from expenditures of the institution of higher education to the local economy can be claimed. The required surveys, however, are expensive to conduct.

Economic base studies seek to isolate economic gains attributable to the presence of a college. Economic base theory requires separation of market activities representing mere consumption from those that bring resources into the region or market area. The notion is that the latter are true economic gains because they represent "exports" of goods and services in exchange for outside revenues, whereas consumption activities do not add to community wealth at all, but merely transfer resources from one person to another. Economic base studies, then, require the identification and valuing of indigenous products and services that permit production of "exports." The market activities so identified constitute the "regional specialization" that is highly desirable economically. Natural resources are examples of exportable products that return wealth to a region, as is serving as a transportation hub. Potentially, higher education is another such activity because the function may bring to the community external tax support, donor support, and student spending. The theory prescribes that only these externally provided monies should be counted among the "economic impacts" of EIS.

The major analytical task of these studies, then, is separating the expenditures representing actual gains to the community economy from those that merely are recycled community funds. A companion task is determining to what extent local money is spent elsewhere, such as when community taxes are spent by colleges in purchasing goods or services from nonlocal vendors.

Of the many issues surrounding EIS calculations, classifying the spending of students is probably the most troublesome. Local expenditures by students who are nonresidents clearly are gains to the community, and thus the goods and services these students purchase fit the above definition of "exports." Of course, local funds used to educate these students represent net losses that should be subtracted from associated gains, unless these funds remain locally. Expenditures by students who are residents are more difficult to classify, and the task is not as simple as merely determining attendance patterns if there were no local college. The resident who declines to attend any college in the absence of a local institution may spend more or less than otherwise in the local community, probably depending upon local job opportunities; and the nature of this individual's spending will change, too. The accounting rules for the resident who leaves the community to attend elsewhere are quite different: Not only is the potential for associated local spending foregone, this student usually will take along some local wealth in the form of parental and personal earnings and savings, and local scholarship monies. In the absence of a local college the community also will forego some external wealth transfer, such as from the state and federal government in support of the college, while similarly saving some money in local (college) tax expenditures and for associated municipal and public school services. Overall, the absence of a local college represents not only opportunity lost, but a net debit in local wealth accounts.

The EIS in the literature sometimes fail to consider both sides of the accounting ledger. Some ignore the source of revenues and consider only the expenditures. As already seen, local tax revenues spent to support the local college represent a cost to the community whereas state and federal tax revenues may represent a gain, although this is an arguable point. One might legitimately debate the proper treatment of external tax support because (1) a share of that support derives locally, and (2) some of the tax funds will be spent not on the "community" per se, but for higher education consumption. Only when tax funds are expended locally as wages and salaries and to purchase goods or services is a local economic gain realized—and then double counting is an obvious danger.

Tuition is another revenue source treated inconsistently in the literature. Most tuition revenues represent neither a loss nor a gain for a community: Tuition is usually not a wealth gain because it most often derives locally and therefore represents mere local wealth transfer; but to the extent it eventually is spent locally it does not represent a wealth loss, either. Similarly, state and federal student aid money potentially is a gain to the local economy, whereas the former should not be viewed as a gain in the case of a college or university assessed for its economic contribution, statewide.

Clearly, a problem for the integrative review is consistency in defining the community. The "community" for a community or junior college is much different from that of a statewide, regional, or even national university; and expenditures credited to the "community" will vary accordingly. Authors of EIS legitimately may choose to define "community" differently for a given institution; for example, a state or private university may decide to demonstrate its economic impact either upon the city or upon the state within which it is located. This may or may not prove to be a problem for the review.

The accounting rules for private colleges and universities usually will be somewhat different from those for public institutions. Private, or "independent," institutions typically will receive directly far fewer, if any, state or local public resources, whereas the public services provided and federal tax revenues foregone may differ only somewhat from those of public institutions. Student expenditure accounting normally will differ considerably in the case of independent institutions, whose students are far more likely to be from out-of-state and whose in-state students would be more likely than in-state public college enrollees to attend out-of-state if the independent institution did not exist. Thus, independent institutions tend to impact regional specialization or "export" accounts considerably more than do public colleges. Further, independent colleges may save local and state taxpayers considerable sums that would be required to provide public educational facilities and services for the additional enrollments if the independent schools were closed. For example, Olson (1981) estimated that the existence of the independent collegiate sector in Massachusetts saved the state $242 million in 1981 dollars for (otherwise) public sector enrollments.

The subtleties of "regional specialization" accounting obviously are great, and they often are beyond the consideration of local researchers primed to enhance the institutional image. Still, the problems may not be serious; for example, community and junior colleges that are supported by local property taxes may have as their boundaries the local tax area. From the community perspective, any noncommunity funds expended in the tax area, including any from state or federal governments, represent potential financial gains. In the case of statewide universities considered from a state perspective, "community" gains are represented correctly by resources emanating from out-of-state. Additionally, the more "national" the university in students enrolled and nonstate support realized, the greater will be the economic contribution to the community, whether defined locally or by state. What is required is the defining of the community and then the separation of community and noncommunity shares of community revenues and expenditures.

In each of these problem areas, the assignment of expenditures and money sources may be a function of the accounting stance taken by the researcher. The considerable assignment variation among past EIS researchers has created problems of results comparability for integrative reviewing. Because such studies are often conducted at individual institutions by "shade-tree mechanics" of higher education research, the problem of results standardization is substantial.

THE MULTIPLIER

Many of the quantitative values associated with the analytical problems previously discussed are reflected in a construct known as the multiplier. The multiplier is applied to college-related expenditures and is used to reflect the total amount of wealth generated by those expenditures. The value of the multiplier reflects the frequency with which college-related local expenditures "turn over." Specifically, when a college and its personnel make expenditures in the local area, part of those expenditures become wages, salaries, and profits that are again spent locally, while other amounts leave the community. This process is repeated over and over until all of the original expenditures leave the locality. The figure that represents the continued respending and thus the increased value to the local community of each dollar originally spent is called the multiplier. Taylor and Byrden (1973) of the Industrial and Economics Division of the Denver Research Institute, University of Denver, describe the multiplier as follows:

> Each payment to a first line firm sets off a chain of transactions which involves its suppliers and employees. Thus, retail purchases stimulate industrial activity at

> wholesalers, service organizations and manufacturers; [sic] while these organizations and the first line firms cause "induced" effects through payments to employees and shareholders, some of this income being respent within the community. (p. 16)

Multipliers also can be developed to reflect the number of jobs created by the turnover of money.

In order to obtain an estimate of its own economic impact on its community, an institution may calculate its own multipliers or borrow them from another study. If derived locally, the process involves examining the expenditure patterns (local versus nonlocal, "export" versus "import") of each local industry that is the object of college-related expenditures, calculating industry-specific multipliers from these patterns, weighting each of these multipliers in proportion to shares of college-related expenditures received, and then summing these weighted multipliers to arrive at a total community multiplier for each spending category (e.g., student, faculty/staff, college nonsalary expenditures). (See Lange, 1980, Table 1, for an illustration.)

Although single, overall multipliers often are applied in EIS, research has shown that expenditure patterns vary greatly for each of the spending categories (students, etc.) and thus that most-appropriate multipliers actually are several and varied in size. The standard method developed by Caffrey and Isaacs (1971) specifies four different multipliers, all of which are based upon the sum of local expenditures by the college, its faculty and staff, its students, and visitors to the college. The first of the Caffrey and Isaacs multipliers adds to local expenditures by these four groups local purchases made by local businesses in support or service of those sales. The second adds the resulting fruits of step 1: local expenditures resulting from individuals' earnings associated with the sales of step 1. The third is a jobs multiplier, which uses the local expenditures by the four groups to derive the number of jobs induced from those expenditures. The fourth, a personal income multiplier, adds to faculty/staff compensation a share of spending by the four groups to yield the total personal income generated from the college. Most EIS employ a spending multiplier that combines Caffrey and Isaacs's first and second multipliers, and a jobs multiplier. Very few include a personal income multiplier. Multipliers vary with such conditions as the size of the community, its relative market isolation, and its degree of self-containment. (For a discussion of these issues see California State Postsecondary Commission, 1984, pp. 5–6.) Overall multipliers between 1.0 and 1.7 typically are found for small, rural communities; larger multipliers are the rule for larger, urban communities, and multipliers as high as 2.0–3.0 are said to be expected for broad regions such as states (Linthicum, 1978, p. 93). Our 64 cases generally support this range of estimates in the literature.

Of all 41 college-related expenditure multipliers identified in the integrative review, the mean expenditure multiplier was 1.8 (n = 41), and for jobs it was 2.5 (n = 29). An inflation adjustment lowered the mean to 2.4 (see Appendix Table 4). For comparable and relatively valid, local community college EIS, the multipliers were 1.6 (n = 13) and 2.2 (n = 11; corrected value), respectively (Table 5.3). For EIS of 4-year institutions (Table 5.4), the local multipliers were 1.8 and 2.8 (corrected), respectively (n = 9). For states (Table 5.5), the mean reported expenditure multiplier for *all* studies was 1.9 (n = 15), while the mean reported jobs multiplier was 2.1 (n = 8, uncorrected). These results are consistent with theory.

The reader should be aware, however, that many of these multipliers merely were borrowed from other studies. Of the 41 expenditure multipliers, only 13 clearly were calculated from local data; the mean empirically derived expenditure multiplier was 1.6 (compared to the 1.8 value when "borrowed" multipliers were included). Only three calculated, state, expenditure multipliers (1.3, 1.5, 1.7) were found in the studies reviewed. Of the 29 job multipliers, only 7 were derived empirically and the procedures employed were sometimes questionable. The few jobs multipliers developed empirically are varied in size, commonly ranging from about 1.2 for small towns in rural areas to as high as 5.0 for California (Taylor and Byrden, 1973, pp. 16–17).

Considering the 13 empirically derived expenditure multipliers, those of Trenton, New Jersey (1.4); Pennsylvania (1.7); Atlanta, Georgia (1.5); Harrisburg, Pennsylvania (1.5); Lenoir, North Carolina (1.5); and Washington State (1.3) appear in EIS that seem particularly well done. Local multipliers in these studies are either 1.4 or 1.5. The remaining 7 of the 13 studies are unique either in design (econometric, input–output analysis) or location (rural British Columbia), or obtained somewhat high estimates because of relatively high estimates (with accompanying weights) for student expenditures. The variation in the empirically derived state multipliers (1.7 and 1.3) is easily explained by the much more conservative (though seemingly accurate) approach taken in the Washington study by Eade (1977).

Multipliers in the range of about 1.2 to possibly as high as 2.1 generally appear reasonable for individual communities, while values much higher, upon close examination, almost always are suspect. Among the approximately 73 multipliers of all kinds in the integrative review, with few exceptions, multipliers clearly higher than 2.1 were jobs multipliers that resulted from student and occasionally faculty/staff spending claims that appeared to be overstated.

These high multipliers are artifacts growing out of the incorrect application by most EIS authors of the Caffrey and Isaacs (1971) method of calculating induced employment. Caffrey and Isaacs advise multiplying the sum of all college-related local expenditures and college-associated government services by a value ranging from .00007 to .00009, that is, 70 to 90 jobs per million dollars of these expenditures. Hence, when expenditures are overstated, as student expenditures most commonly are, the jobs multiplier is similarly overstated. Further, it is apparent that almost all EIS researchers have failed to adjust spending figures for inflation. Altmann's (1985) estimate for 1984 was that after the inflationary adjustment 36.6 jobs would be created for every 90 created when Caffrey and Isaacs (1971) published their volume.

Another problem in an integrative review of EIS is that multipliers are not defined consistently across studies. Often what are called multipliers appear merely to be propensities to spend locally, rather than the ultimate value of each dollar spent locally. A multiplier should be applied to *local* expenditures only. Both the multipliers *and* the local expenditure proportion to which the multiplier is applied vary with local conditions.

Like the multiplier itself, the proportion of college expenditures to which multipliers should be applied also varies by community type and category of expenditures. College employees in isolated areas are more likely to spend locally, and jobs are more likely to be filled by local applicants. College purchases, however, may be more likely to be made locally when the college is located in an urban center and local suppliers are present (see column 6, Appendix Table 4). A college located in the outer fringe of a city, on the other hand, may be attracted to nearby, noncommunity markets. For example, suburban Bucks County Community College near Philadelphia and Trenton purchased only 10 percent of its products and services from suppliers located in the College tax area (Mahon, 1979). In any event, the anomalies are many. In varying cases, multipliers may be large but the portion of institutional expenditures to which they are applied may be small. The opposite also may be true.

ECONOMIC IMPACTS UPON COMMUNITIES

The EIS reviewed are not from a random sample of the population of such studies, but rather represent all EIS available in the library of the University of Arizona. We know (El-Khawas, 1986) that approximately 50 percent of all collegiate institutions in the United States have completed EIS and that library holdings, including ERIC documents, are likely to contain a biased sample of all such studies. We also suspect, however, that the more valid EIS will be more likely to find their way into library collections.

Tables 5.3 to 5.5 summarize the results from the more complete and complex Appendix Table 4, the content of which is important to the interpretation of results. It should be noted, parenthetically, that the ubiquitous Caffrey and Isaacs method includes six additional economic impacts not included here—production of durable goods, value of property connected to college activities, community credit base, personal income, net effects on governments and taxes, and business lost due to business operations of the college. The reasons for these exclusions are basically four: (1) very few studies report such data; (2) where they do, the elements included in each category tend to be inconsistent; (3) in the aggregate the values tend to be small and thus relatively inconsequential in comparison to business volume; this situation is in part because (4) values in some cases tend to cancel each other out.

Of the three tables, only Table 5.3 offers results that adequately conform to good integrative reviewing. This table summarizes the impacts of public

Table 5.3

SUMMARY OF ECONOMIC IMPACT BY COMMUNITY COLLEGES UPON THEIR LOCAL COMMUNITIES—CRITICAL VALUES

(1) Author	(2) Multipliers (MP): Spending/Jobs	(3) Business Volume (÷) Budget	(4) Jobs (÷) Budget (millions)	(5) Jobs MP, Corrected	(6) Col. 3 Corrected	(7) Col. 4 Corrected**	(8) Validity/ Comparability
Baum (1978)	1.4/1.7	.5	72	1.9	1.0	51	2
Bess (1980)	1.8/3.2	3.0	178	2.4	3.0	84	3
Butler (1980)	1.3/1.3	.4	56	1.6	.7	47	2
Campbell & Linthicum (1982)	1.4/1.4	.4	42	1.7	.7	44	2
Chestnut (1983)	1.6/3.0	1.5	111	2.0	1.5	64	1
Cosgrove (1984)	2.5/-	3.7	—	—	2.0***	—	3
Jeacock (1983)	1.3/2.2	.8	41	2.3	.8	37	2
Kincaid & Tippett (1984)	1.5/2.1	2.5	84	2.4	2.5	97	2
Littlefield (1982)	1.8/2.7	.7	69	2.4	1.4	55	3 (2 corrected)
Lucas (1977)	1.8/3.8	2.2	127	2.4	2.2	63	2
Mahon (1979)	1.4/2.0	.6	70	1.8	.7	43	2
Philadelphia CC (1982)	1.8/4.6	2.8	131	3.5	2.8	78	2
Poris & Eskow (1978)	1.9/-	2.0	—	—	2.0	—	1
Romano & Herbert (1985)	1.9/2.3	1.8	134	2.1	1.8	66	1
Ryan (1983)	2.0/-	4.1	—	1.9	1.8	65	3
Schimmelpfennig (1983)	1.8/-	2.0	—	—	2.0	—	1
Selgas et al. (1973)	1.5/-	1.5	—	—	1.5	—	1
Means*	1.6/2.4	1.5	87	2.2	1.6	59	—

Note. Col. 8: 1 = Most valid/comparable; 2 = Less valid/comparable but generally acceptable; 3 = Invalid or noncomparable.

*Excludes values for studies rated 3.

**Jobs per million dollars of 1985–1986 dollars.

***Spending eliminated for students who would remain if no local college.

community colleges upon their local economies. The two common metrics employed in all three tables are the ratios of business volume and jobs created to the institution's current budget (specifically, Educational and General Expenditures plus Auxiliary Enterprises). Individuals may multiply the values of columns 6 and 7 by their current institutional budgets and obtain an estimate of total business volume produced and jobs created by the average college, although the jobs estimate requires adjustment to constant dollars. To illustrate, a community college budget of $10 million is estimated, on average, to create $16 million ($10 million × 1.6, from last row of Table 5.3, column 6) in local business volume—that is, in local spending by the college, its employees and students, plus the induced effects (multiplier) of that first-round spending. That $10 million also will create an average of 590 jobs (in 1985–1986 dollars) in the college and local community (10 [number of millions of dollars] × 59 [last row, column 7]). The 1.6, or 160 percent, value for business volume compares with Caffrey's rule-of-thumb estimate of "at least 150% [1.5] and perhaps as much as 300% [3.0]. . ." (in Poris and Eskow, 1978, p. iii). The jobs-created value of 59 per million dollars is considerably higher than Caffrey and Isaacs's inflation-adjusted estimate for 1970–1971.

EXAMINING THE VARIATIONS

As is often the case in integrative reviewing, the more important information to be gained is from examining reasons for the variations rather than from the mean value themselves. Note that the range of uncorrected business volume to operating budget values is large, .4 to 4.1, and the corrected ratio is .7 to 3.0 (Table 5.3). Though more acceptable, even the latter range at first glance seems unreasonably large for similar kinds of institutions. By viewing some of the explanations (Appendix Table 4, column 14), we may enhance our understanding of the ratios and further refine the estimates.

Butler's low, uncorrected estimate of .4 is for a community college in Hampton, Virginia. His estimate is relatively conservative, in part, because he omits the expenditures of all students, visitors to the college, and college part-time employees. Although business volume from visitors typically is small for community colleges, student expenditures typically amount to roughly one-half of total business volume at those colleges that have surveyed student spending and utilized the obtained values. The corrected value of .7 for Butler's study represents the ratio obtained after an average student spending value is imputed and business volume is recalculated. (This is the only correction reflected in column 6 of Table 5.3.) Butler's omission of part-time employees also may be serious; considering faculty alone, the share of community college faculty who were part-time, nationwide, was up from 40 percent in 1972–1973 to 56 percent in 1976–1977 and was still rising (Guthrie-Morse, 1979). Butler's estimate is further reduced by the fact that he uses a relatively low multiplier (1.3 compared to the average of 1.6 [Table 5.3]) for all studies and that he identified a very low local expenditures share (.23). Perhaps most significantly, his data do not originate in expenditure surveys but rather are gross estimates from government documents. All in all, there is little reason to consider Butler's results as compatible with most others.

Return to an issue stated earlier is necessary at this juncture. One of the more critical questions in the calculation of economic impacts is found in the handling of student expenditures: Do such expenditures represent a real gain to the community? As always, the principle should be that only *marginal* local expenditures—that is, expenditures that would not be made in the absence of the college—represent real financial gains to the community. The problem is in isolating and identifying such expenditures.

The difficulty is perhaps nowhere more prominent than in the case of community colleges. Some analysts, including Butler, exclude all student spending, save (sometimes) student aid and earnings at the college, on the grounds that community college students heavily are local residents and that their local spending would be at least as great if they were nonstudents. (Most student aid originates in nonlocal jurisdictions.) Such judgments, however, probably rest on the assumption that in the absence of the college nonstudents would be employed and, moreover, that they would be employed locally. Further, they assume that community college students would not attend elsewhere if the college were closed. As dubious as the first assumption may be, the latter is even more questionable. Romano (1985), for example, reported that only 11 percent of Binghamton, New York, community college students stated they would not attend at all in the absence of the college, and that only 15 percent would attend another local college. Fully 74 percent would attend elsewhere. Poris and Eskow (1978) similarly reported that only 25 percent of students at a community college in a suburb of New York City would remain locally. In a study of all 14 Oregon community colleges, Stevenson (1982) found that 32 percent of full-time students would not attend anywhere and that the remaining 68 percent would transfer (albeit, presumably, some locally). Figures for part-time students were precisely the opposite: 68 percent would not attend anywhere, while 32 percent would transfer.

Although a certain amount of skepticism is nearly always called for in assessing self-reports under hypothetical circumstances, there are other reasons for questioning the deletion of student expenditures. The most important of these is the realization that students leaving the community probably will take with them personal and parental wealth. Poris and Eskow (1978, pp. 30–32) and Romano (1985, p. 38) demonstrate convincingly that these amounts in New York would be much greater than amounts presently spent by students for local higher education. Further, this result does not include "tuition chargebacks" paid in New York, as well as in many other states, when students enroll in nonlocal community colleges. Poris and Eskow (p. 31) maintain also that locally remaining college employees and students would usually replace other employees who would join unemployment ranks or move elsewhere. (This raises subsequent questions, such as geographic sources of welfare dollars.) On balance, Poris and Eskow (1978, p. 32) calculated that loss of their college would represent a net wealth deficit of $35.2 million in comparison to an estimated gain from the college of $26.8 million in business volume alone.

Those few researchers who have worked the calculations all the way through, implicitly or explicitly, reach the conclusion that all community college student expenditures should be counted in EIS. Even this may result in conservative estimates of community impacts, as Romano and Poris and Eskow have shown.

Thus, Butler's treatment of student expenditures may be far too conservative, although he defends his decision by noting "the many postsecondary opportunities afforded peninsula residents" (p. 6). Clearly, local conditions will vary and the generalization made to standardize results for the integrative review may not be completely inappropriate in some cases.

At the opposite end of the range from Butler's results is Cosgrove's budget to business volume ratio estimate of 4.2. A preliminary correction in his budget figure reduced the ratio to 3.7. Further, Cosgrove's high business volume ratio reflects employment of a high multiplier (2.5) and the use of published "student budgets" rather than expenditure surveys completed by students. Further, the documentation of this study is so poor that one cannot be sure what is being measured. Leslie (1984) has shown that student budgets, which are computed by colleges for student aid purposes, tend to be seriously inflated when compared to student-reported figures. When Cosgrove's ratio is corrected by imputing the average student spending values, his business volume to budget ratio drops to 2.0. Use of the mean multiplier value would decrease the ratio further to 1.5, which is very close to the mean ratio of 1.6. Although raising other questions, these calculations do illustrate why the range of ratios is large.

Considering other extreme values, Campbell and Linthicum's (1982) uncorrected business volume ratio of .4 reflects the same omissions made by Butler and, again, use of gross government values due to the lack of any expenditure survey data. Baum's (1978) ratio of .5, too, excluded (most) student expenditures as well as spending by visitors; and he too used government documents rather than surveys to estimate college-related spending empirically. Littlefield's (1982) ratio of .7 excluded most student expenditures and part-time employees; further, his method of calculation was not compatible with other studies. The corrected value for Littlefield is a more normative 1.4.

Among other high values, Ryan's (1983) ratio of 4.1 results from the same sort of high "student budget" data used by Cosgrove and may include all spending in the state, not just the community. The corrected ratio of 1.8 appears plausible, but study documentation is too poor to place much confidence in this estimate. Bess's (1980) data yield a high business volume value of 3.0, but the reasons are not clear because of poor documentation, especially in definitions used. This study probably should be ignored. The Philadelphia Community

College Study (1982) ratio of 2.8 is inexplicably high due to poor documentation. It should be noted that the *state* business volume ratio was only 2.0 for the larger study (Pennsylvania Economy League, 1981) of which this was a part. In other words, the local data are suspect. Finally, the Kincaid and Tippett (1984) study (business volume ratio = 2.5) also is poorly documented.

It is interesting to note that for the studies evaluated as valid and comparable (assigned the value of 1 in column 8, Table 5.3), the range was only 1.5–2.0. This tends to support the mean estimates of 1.5–1.6 and suggests that the extreme values below 1.0 and above about 2.5 roughly balance out.

It should be emphasized, however, that the true economic impact of a community college, in the limited sense it is assessed in EIS, remains open to question. The assumptions favored herein are those that make the most sense to us and are offered simply in an effort to achieve some standardization and an aggregate estimate. Nevertheless, most important values, such as multipliers and assumptions about student spending, do vary across communities, and thus researchers should make their own judgments accordingly. For this reason we have not changed or standardized values unless obvious errors in calculations were made or business volume and job components were omitted. The reader favoring more conservative assumptions, for example, may decide to choose ratios near the lower end of the range of estimates. Our own judgments on these matters, after total immersion in the EIS literature for more than 6 months, are reflected herein.

Regarding the jobs ratios in Table 5.3, many of the same standardization issues pertain. The jobs created by an institution are the sum of persons directly employed, ideally expressed in full-time equivalencies, those induced by the college business volume of the first ratio, and those induced in local government and schools (see Caffrey and Isaacs, 1971). Once again, the treatment of student expenditures is especially important to consistent results; probably second-most important is the jobs multiplier selected.

Whereas in the case of the business volume multiplier, in which the uncorrected ratios were useful in examining results under varying (unstandardized) assumptions, the uncorrected jobs ratios of the EIS are often simply in error. This is principally because the uncorrected jobs ratios often were calculated by EIS authors using a Caffrey and Isaacs formula without correcting for inflation. The corrected jobs ratio (column 7 of Table 5.3) reflects the inflationary adjustment plus the adjustment in jobs resulting from imputation of a student expenditures (column 6) value, where none was indicated. The jobs multipliers also may differ from those reported in the original works because, where necessary and possible, FTE (full-time equivalent) of part-time employment was added (based upon relative earnings, 8 PT = 1 FTE employee [Posey, 1983, p. 6]). Where the number of jobs was not reported, this number was calculated using Caffrey and Isaacs' inflation-adjusted, midpoint estimate of 80 jobs per million dollars (prior to inflation adjustment). Where no multiplier was reported, one was calculated from total community employment and direct college employment figures, if provided. The mean estimate of 13 community colleges was that each million dollars of expenditure creates, directly and indirectly, 59 jobs in the local economy.

The local economic impact ratios for 4-year institutions (Table 5.4) are more problematic for two reasons: There are fewer 4-year school EIS in the sample and the institutions are more diverse. The range of business volume to the budget is from .9 to 2.9, although the estimates cluster in the 2.5–2.9 region. For the nine studies the mean value is 2.2, and range for the jobs ratio is 38–96, with a mean of 67. Again, the more deviant results largely can be explained by reference to column 14 of Appendix Table 4.

The heterogeneity among institutions is especially important in examining 4-year schools. Within the public sector, the differences in funding sources for research universities and state colleges affect the calculus of EIS, or at least should. Not only are the tax revenues of the former less likely to be of local origins, tuition revenues are less likely to emanate from local sources, too. For independent institutions, the same distinctions can be made, but the differences are even more varied and extreme. Private research universities bring vast non-local research monies to the community, and their students are very likely to be from outside the local area. Brown University, for example, attracted 89 percent of its students from out of state (McEnany, 1979). The same pattern applies to prestigious private liberal arts colleges.

The most problematic EIS case is that in which the community is defined as the state (Table 5.5). Authors of most such studies assume that the higher education funds would not be spent otherwise and that the origin of the resources is irrelevant. Such assumptions violate economic base theory. The problems vary in severity depending upon the degree to which the institution or institutional sector being examined is funded with state and local as opposed to out-of-state funds. For EIS of state community college systems, the heavy community college reliance upon state and local funds suggests little impact that can be considered an addition to state wealth. The State University of New York, Office of Community Colleges (1982) concludes that such problems make the statewide impact "impossible to measure" (p. 3).

This issue reminds us that few local, community college EIS reduce local expenditures by the amount of local tax dollars employed. A notable exception to this oversight is the study conducted by Selgas, Saussy, and Blocker (1979), who subtracted out the local tax support of the college, even remembering to subtract the tax multiplier effect in order to take account of the full value of local tax dollars opportunity costs. Fortunately, the size of the error is relatively small for community colleges. For 4-year institutions, the problem is significant both theoretically and in practical magnitude.

Most of the studies in Table 5.5 are of public institutions, and only three make a judicious effort to limit the analysis to nonstate funds. Of these, only two offer estimates that will bear careful theoretical assessment. These are the Olson (1981) study of independent higher education in Massachusetts (business

Table 5.4

SUMMARY OF ECONOMIC IMPACT BY 4-YEAR INSTITUTIONS UPON THEIR COMMUNITIES—CRITICAL VALUES

(1) Author	(2) Multipliers (MP): Spending/Jobs	(3) Business Volume (÷) Budget	(4) Jobs (÷) Budget (millions)	(5) Jobs MP, Corrected	(6) Col. 3 Corrected	(7) Col. 4 Corrected*	(8) Validity/ Comparability
Altmann (1985)	1.8/2.8	2.5	86	2.9	—	80	1
Breslin (1979)	1.9/2.2	.9	105	1.8	.9	39	1
Lange (1980)	2.1/4.0	2.3	97	2.7	—	65	2
McEnany (1979)	1.9/2.1	.9	61	1.8	.9	38	1
Posey (1983)	1.6/2.4	2.5	87	3.1	—	78	2
Rosen (1985)	2.2/1.8	2.8	69	3.5	—	64	2
Salley (1976)	1.5/2.6	2.9	176	3.5	—	96	2
Salley (1979)	1.5/3.1	2.6	137	3.2	—	91	2
Taylor & Byrden (1973)	1.9/2.6	2.4	128	2.4	—	56	1
Mean*	1.8/2.6	2.2	105	2.8	—	67	—

Note. Col. 8: 1 = Most valid/comparable; 2 = Less valid/comparable but generally acceptable.

*Jobs per million dollars of 1985–1986 dollars.

Table 5.5

SUMMARY OF ECONOMIC IMPACT BY INSTITUTIONS UPON THEIR STATES, CRITICAL VALUES

(1) Author	(2) Multipliers (MP): Spending/Jobs	(3) Business Volume (÷) Budget	(4) Jobs (÷) Budget (millions)	(5) Jobs MP, Corrected	(6) Col. 3 Corrected	(7) Col. 4 Corrected**	(8) Validity/ Comparability†
CPEC (1984), State U	2.4/-	—	—	—	—	—	3
U. CA	2.8/-	2.1	75	—	—	—	3
CC	2.5/-	3.8	107	—	—	—	3
Pvt.	2.5/-	1.4	—	—	—	—	3
Eade (1977)	1.3/-	—	—	—	—	—	1
Engler, et al. (1980)	1.7/2.1	—	95	—	—	63	?
Gay & Weintraub (1978)	2.0/2.0	3.5	120	—	2.4	69	3
Hargrave & Buford (1973)	1.5/-	—	—	—	—	—	?
Hogan & McPheters (1979)	1.9/1.9	3.9	162	—	—	99	3
Jackson, et al. (1978)	—	1.5	168	—	—	92	3
Linthicum (1978)	2.0/1.5	1.2	64	—	—	37	2
McEnany (1979)	1.9/2.1	1.5	61	—	1.5	38	2
Olson (1981)	1.4?/2.4?	1.6	80	—	—	63	1
Pennsylvania (1981)	1.7/1.7	2.0	93	—	—	67	1
Stevenson (1982)	1.8/-	—	—	—	—	—	3
Wellsfry (1976)	1.2/3.0	1.7/.7***	191/128***	—	—	89/60***	2
Mean*	1.6/2.1	1.6	98	—	—	59	—

*Excludes values for studies rated 3.
**Jobs per million dollars of 1985–1986 dollars.
***Spending eliminated for students who would remain if no local college.
†1 = Most valid/comparable; 2 = Less valid/comparable but generally acceptable; 3 = Considers only dollars from other states.

volume ratio 1.6; jobs 63) and the Pennsylvania Economy League Study of all institutions in Pennsylvania (business volume ratio 2.0; jobs 67). Not surprisingly, both of these studies include or are solely of independent institutions, whose marginal contribution to the state is considerably more clear. (For a discussion see Olson, 1981.) A third study, by Eade (1977), estimates that the yield from the investment in higher education is 30 percent greater than if related public funds were retained in the private sector.

SUMMARY

Colleges and universities make many direct and indirect contributions to their communities, only some of which are readily identifiable in economic terms. The identifiable economic contributions include additions to business volume, jobs, personal income, the production of durable goods, property values, and the community credit base. According to convention (Caffrey and Isaacs, 1971), business volume should be adjusted to reflect the business lost due to sales of the college. Finally, there is the effect of the college and its personnel upon government. Colleges both consume local government resources and bring new tax resources to the community. Only the business volume and jobs contributions are estimated herein, although it is known from examination of the EIS that the net effects of the remainder are relatively small.

Theory demands that the economic contributions of a college to its community be limited to the "export" of goods and services. A college does not contribute economically, in EIS terms, unless it brings wealth into the community—or, arguably, keeps it from leaving. In keeping with this principle, it is relatively easy to identify and estimate some of the economic contributions of a college and most difficult to identify and estimate others. Almost invariably researcher judgments will differ; and for this reason, the results of EIS often depend upon the accounting stance taken by the researcher.

Unfortunately, the motive of some who have conducted EIS appears to be to endear the college to its local community. Such studies too often have yielded results that are difficult to defend on objective grounds. Nevertheless, there seem to be sufficient numbers of valid EIS so that if they are assessed with care, a sense of the economic contributions of colleges to localities can be quantified. This statement is most apropos for community colleges, the kind of institution most frequently considered in EIS.

A good estimate of the dollar value of the business volume ascribable to an "average" community college is obtained by multiplying the Educational and General Expenditures plus Auxiliary Enterprises of the college by 1.6. Similarly, an estimate of the number of local jobs created may be obtained by multiplying these Expenditure or Budget amounts, expressed in millions of 1985–1986 dollars by 59. Each of these ratios is only a mean effect. Numerous values necessary to composing valid ratios are a function of local conditions.

Most important of these values are the extent to which the college, its employees, and its students spend locally and the degree to which these expenditures in turn are used to purchase local goods and services, thus adding to the employment and incomes of local individuals.

Our estimates of community economic impacts of 4-year schools are more uncertain, primarily because of the fewer valid estimates in our sample. Due to differences in revenue sources, it does seem relatively clear that state colleges contribute more to their local communities per budget dollar than do community colleges, but less than research universities, especially private ones, which are most likely to bring to the community external wealth, both in the form of net tax monies and student spending. We estimate that the business volume ratio for 4-year schools is approximately 2.2 and that the jobs ratio is 67 per million of 1985–1986 dollars.

EIS that seek to quantify the contributions to state economies are the most problematic of all, due to the fact that most higher education resources originate within the state and thus must be considered as transfer payments rather than additions to wealth. The two good estimates available suggest that ratios may be of the order of from 1.6 to 2.0 for business volume and 63–67 for jobs; however, researchers interested in this level would be well advised to follow the nonnormative methods outlined by Eade (1977).

PART III

The Economic Value of Higher Education: The Emergent Social Goals

IN CHAPTER 3, a distinction was drawn between traditional or historic expectations of higher education by society and newer expectations that have emerged in full force since about the time of Lyndon Johnson's Great Society. These newer expectations, ergo higher education goals, are usually labeled "improving educational opportunity" or something very similar; however, the ultimate social goal is achieving a more equal distribution of wealth.

In this section we take a closer look at this important, emergent social goal. We do so for several reasons: Obviously, a matter of major public concern deserves critical examination. Further, pursuit of this goal has been supported with large public expenditures, and examination of higher education financing policy is the purpose of this book. Finally, there now exists adequate research to permit systematic review of this topic even though the form of that research is at times too disparate to allow for a complete meta-analysis.

Three bodies of research bearing directly upon this topic have been identified in the literature: the wealth redistribution studies, the student demand studies, and studies of student aid.

The logical connection among these three areas of research is as follows: First, by definition, any resources collected through a reasonably progressive tax system and reallocated to low-income students will contribute to wealth equitability (the wealth redistribution studies). Second, public subsidies to higher education students potentially can impact equitability, assuming that student enrollments are affected by prices charged (the student demand studies). Third, if subsidies increase the likelihood of college enrollment and graduation for low-income students, additional wealth equitability should result because, all other factors equal, the college-educated earn more than high school graduates. In marginal terms, the major "new" form of the student subsidies is student aid (the student aid studies).

The former of these three groups of studies and Chapter 6 examine the extent to which taxation and public subsidy allocations to higher education serve wealth redistribution, given enrollment patterns by income level. The second group of studies and Chapter 7 appraise student responses to price changes. For Chapter 8 and the student aid studies, the first test simply is whether the aid is directed to low-income persons, because the aid itself represents wealth transfer. To serve its major policy purposes, however, student aid must also allow low-income individuals to attend college, permit attendance at a more expensive college (higher earnings presumably are related to college quality, which presumably is related to prices charged), and contribute to college graduation (the final goal short of measuring income redistribution itself).

6

Equitability in Traditional Financial Support Systems

The first test of the extent to which the "more equal distribution of wealth" goal is achieved through higher education is simply a calculation of who pays the taxes that support higher education and who enrolls. More explicitly, how much of the taxes that support higher education are paid by the various income groups and how much does each receive in indirect tax subsidy through college enrollment? Of course, this measure fails to take into account direct expenses met by the enrolled student and it ignores postschooling benefits.

Unlike the studies reviewed in Chapters 4 and 5, here we do not enjoy the comfort of complete unanimity in the direction of study findings. Whereas rates of returns to higher education are essentially universally positive and are so reported in the literature, the results reported by the wealth redistribution studies vary modestly, and conclusions as stated by the separate researchers are somewhat more mixed. Fortunately, the integrative review largely erases these apparent differences and shows that when rendered comparable, results actually are quite consistent after all.

Before turning to the wealth redistribution studies themselves, a word should be offered regarding methodological problems. For some reason, in these studies methodological brevity is the rule in the published accounts. Thus, often, one cannot be at all sure how the researchers have proceeded. The reason for this lack of study design information is probably explained by the fact that the wealth redistribution studies are conceptually flawed: They remove for examination a single slice of the total cost–benefit, higher education pie, apparently without consideration of the critical importance of the omissions. (For elaboration see the discussion, in the next section of this chapter, of Pechman's [1970] work.) Hence, for example, on the cost side, the studies do not say much about just which taxes are considered in the support of higher education. Student direct and indirect (opportunity) costs, though very real, are ignored altogether. On the benefits side, not only is the specification of benefits solely as tax subsidy received by enrollees fraught with difficulties, there is the further problem of isolating the appropriate expenditures. Presumably, only instruction is the intended object of the wealth redistribution studies; however, there seems to have been little if any attempt to separate out the research and service expenditures, which together often exceed expenditures for instruction. Beyond this, doubtless, no one has considered that within the Instruction accounting category, there is the implicit expenditure for departmental research, which may account for as much as 50 percent of "Instruction" expenditures in research universities (James, 1978).

The organization of this chapter is somewhat different from that of Chapters 4 and 5. Because of the considerable controversy and apparent lack of agreement in the literature, presented first is a brief overview of each study, with conclusions as reported by or attributed to the study author. We save most of our observations and comments for the integrative treatment that follows. This organization permits the demonstration that the primary reason for differences of opinion as to what the research has shown is little more than inconsistency in how researchers have reached their conclusions.

The Wealth Redistribution Studies

The wealth redistribution studies originated in 1969, when Lee Hansen and Burton Weisbrod published their controversial paper, "The Distribution of Costs and Direct Benefits of Higher Education: The Case of California." Hansen and Weisbrod purported to show that the poor subsidize the higher education of the rich and, therefore, that higher education has a regressive effect upon wealth distribution. What followed soon became known as the Hansen–Weisbrod Debate.

Hansen and Weisbrod based their conclusion on the following evidence. (1) Taxes paid in support of California higher education were somewhat regressive: The lowest two income categories paid the highest of certain effective local and state tax rates, whereas tax rates for the seven highest income categories were essentially the same. (2) The subsidies from these taxes were highest at the University of California, were next highest in the California state colleges, and were lowest at the community colleges, whereas attendance rates by family income were in reverse order. (3) When the averages for tax and enrollment patterns were brought together, families with offspring at the University realized a $790 net subsidy; those with children at the State Colleges gained an average of $630; and those with offspring in the community colleges gained $40. Those without children in college experienced a net subsidy of −$650. Hansen and Weisbrod concluded that California higher education was adding to inequality rather than reducing it. The reader should note for future reference, however, that all groups benefited, save those without children enrolled; thus, wealth transfer could not be said to be from rich to poor, but from families without children enrolled to those with children enrolled—particularly to those whose children were enrolled in more expensive institutions. Whereas the impression one gains from Hansen and Weisbrod is that students from wealthier families were benefiting most, this does not mean that the poor were necessarily the benefactors. If regressivity is defined literally to mean money transfer from rich to poor or richer to poorer, then the Hansen–Weisbrod case at least from this evidence was not proven.

In the next year, Joseph Pechman (1970) took strong exception to the Hansen and Weisbrod methods, conclusions, and research perspective. Reanalyzing the Hansen–Weisbrod data, Pechman reached the reverse conclusion, that in general higher education acts progressively in California. Pechman's explanation for his opposing findings was that Hansen and Weisbrod were incomplete in their selection of state and local taxes and used data averages that are insensitive to important tax and enrollment differences. In his analysis, Pechman added progressive corporate income and estate and gift taxes, which he judged to be used in the support of California higher education. Further, Pechman pointed out that only a small share of the taxes considered by Hansen and Weisbrod were used to finance higher education. When actual taxes used for higher education were compared to the benefits received through higher education enrollments, the lowest-income group demonstrated net gains even at the University of California, where low-income enrollments were least. Additionally, Pechman demonstrated that Hansen and Weisbrod's method of employing *average* taxes paid and benefits received yields results that are the opposite of those obtained when those costs and benefits are distributed by income levels. Pechman showed dollar gains for income groups below $12,000 and net losses for those above $12,000. By far the largest net losers were those from families earning more than $25,000. In his implications section, Pechman questioned why Hansen and Weisbrod would take such a narrow view of income redistribution. He argued that costs and benefits can be ascertained only over a lifetime—if even then, because taxes are paid by one generation and benefits received by another. Philosophically, Pechman was highly critical of Hansen and Weisbrod, arguing that any public service essentially favors one group or another (highways and welfare being two examples) and that the issue is not whether a particular group benefits from a particular service but whether the tax system is progressive. Employing the literal definition of progressivity, Pechman showed dollar transfer from richer to poorer through higher education in California.

In his follow-up critique, Robert Hartman (1970) suggested that both Hansen and Weisbrod and Pechman missed the point, which he argued was equalization of opportunity and the provision of below-cost higher education to assure correct enrollment investment decisions. Hartman concluded that both Hansen and Weisbrod and Pechman were correct regarding progressivity–regressivity, based upon the definitions each employed. His illustration of the forms of the evidence presented, however, seemed to support the Pechman perspective.

Following quickly was a study by Windham (1970), who reported that even using the Pechman method, higher education acted to redistribute wealth regressively in Florida. Windham's results almost certainly are the clearest demonstration of regressivity in any state. Employing Pechman's suggestions that costs and benefits be distributed by income level rather than by Hansen and Weisbrod's averaging method and that broad tax measures be considered, Windham showed a transfer of tax dollars from families earning less than $10,000 to those earning more than $10,000. Probably the major reason for his results was the regressivity of state and local taxes in Florida. Under the state constitution there were no personal or corporate income taxes; most tax revenues emanated from consumption taxes. Another major reason, however, was Windham's disinclination to separate out families without enrolled children. This issue, by implication, later became a matter of some controversy, as we shall see. There were other legitimate questions about Windham's methods. One was his apparent inclusion of all federal revenues for higher education, including money for research. Such revenues presumably do not bear *directly* upon the education of students. A second had to do with the fact that some 21 percent of all Florida revenues collected come from tourists. This fact impacted the validity of Windham's cost–benefit calculus. Nevertheless, Windham's conclusion of regressivity in Florida (as of 1970) appears to be a valid one.

At about the same time, and employing the method he developed with Weisbrod, Hansen (1970) published a paper showing that the Wisconsin system was "more egalitarian" than the California system. Hansen reported that families without children in Wisconsin public higher education earned an average of $6,500 and received an average net subsidy of –$240; those with children enrolled at the Wisconsin state universities averaged $6,500 in earnings and $740 in subsidies, respectively; and those with children enrolled at the University of Wisconsin averaged $9,700 in family earnings and $470 in subsidies. Hence the net subsidy as a percentage of family income was –3.7 percent, 11.4 percent, and 4.8 percent, respectively, for the three groups. In California, the subsidy rates for the University and the State Colleges had been about equal. Hansen focused his discussion on the relative progressivity–regressivity for the two states; he did not claim that the Wisconsin system was regressive. The Wisconsin data in fact suggest progressivity if those without children in college are excluded. The basis of the progressivity conclusion, however, is weak because it is based solely on the fact that average family incomes were higher and subsidies were lower at the University of Wisconsin and that incomes were lower and subsidies higher at the Wisconsin state universities.

The same year, Judy (1970) examined the income redistribution question in Canada. Like the United States, Canadian higher education is heavily the domain of the middle and upper classes; indeed, one might anticipate greater inequality in Canada because the many private colleges in the United States drain away many of the children of the wealthy, whereas the private system in Canada is very small. Another difference, of course, was the tax structure; Judy considered federal, provincial, and municipal tax payments. He then compared percentages of university funds coming from each income class with the percentages of university students originating in the same income class. Judy concluded "That no appreciable over-all redistribution of wealth among income classes takes place through the medium of . . . higher educational institutions in Canada." His data, however, showed progressivity when cost shares were compared to benefit shares by income group, with percentage transfers being positive in the lower two income groups and negative in the upper three groups.

Machlis (1973) followed the procedures of Pechman and Windham in judging wealth distribution effects in New York City. Using 1968 data, he disaggregated families with dependent children of ages 18–24 into income categories and calculated what percentage each income group was of the total. Then he compared these percentages to enrollment percentages for identical income categories. Enrollments in the City University of New York (CUNY) were considerably more egalitarian than in the United States as a whole. For example, in the $4,000–5,999 income group, the ratio of New York City individuals in the age group to individuals enrolled was 1.00, whereas the same ratio for the United States was .78. In the highest-income category the ratios were .69 and 1.30, respectively. Community colleges were more egalitarian than 4-year institutions both in New York City and in the United States. Next, Machlis presented tax data by income group, showing the percentage of taxes paid by each category. At the time, New York City taxes were somewhat regressive due primarily to heavy reliance on the property tax, while state taxes were progressive. For the CUNY system, subsidies were positive for all income groups except the highest, with the average net subsidy per family being greatest at the center of the income distribution. The 4-year schools of CUNY followed the system pattern, whereas wealth redistribution was greatest in the community colleges. Machlis finished by adjusting the Hansen–Weisbrod, California data to overcome the "averaging" problem first discussed by Pechman, and then he compared the results to his CUNY data. Machlis showed once again that California redistributed income "from higher to lower" and that the system was only somewhat less progressive than that of New York City.

Few others have reached conclusions supportive of those of Hansen and Weisbrod, and in studies in which this result has occurred the evidence has not been strong. In a more limited but carefully conceived study, Zimmerman (1973) detected a slight "unequalizing effect" by comparing relative subsidies of the highest- to the lowest-income groups at the St. Louis Community College District. The subsidy to the highest-income group was $25 or $15 greater, depending upon the subsidy schedule considered; the largest subsidies, albeit also small ones, were found for the middle-income categories. Like Hansen and Weisbrod, Zimmerman did not show a redistribution from poor to rich, but rather that the upper-income group merely benefited more. In fact, all student groups again gained considerably. Among the important characteristics of this study was consideration of student aid subsidies. Also, Zimmerman cautioned several times about the questionable quality of his data.

Hartman (1972) has been cited as having reached a similar regressivity conclusion, although his evidence was even more fragmentary than Hansen and Weisbrod's. Hartman observed simply that between 57 and 66 percent of the costs of higher education were borne by "nonusers" and that "users" were more likely to come from the upper half of the income distribution. Hartman's work was excluded from the integrative review and meta-analysis matrix due to the very limited nature of his evidence.

Hight and Pollock's (1973) results were mixed. Hight and Pollock employed "the Pechman–Windham approach with a modification" to reexamine the California and Florida data plus data for their own state of Hawaii. Rejecting Hansen and Weisbrod's method of subtracting average tax payment from average instructional expenditure to yield a plus or minus dollar value for each income class, Hight and Pollock subtracted for each group the percent of state–local tax payments from the percentage of students enrolled. They concluded that the California system was progressive because gains were concentrated in income classes ($4,000–8,999) below the mean and because dollar losses were much larger in the highest- than in the lowest-income classes. They noted that the pattern did not change when enrollments were considered by institutional level. In their Hawaii analysis, wealth redistributions were less because of large enrollments of students among the upper classes. Hight and Pollock did not reach a clear conclusion in Hawaii, nor in Florida—although they did observe gains being concentrated in the middle two income categories in the latter case. Hight and Pollock's major conclusion was that varying degrees of tax progressivity and regressivity, combined with varying enrollment propensities by income class, prohibit the making of generalizations from a single state.

Finally, among these earlier investigations, Machovec (1972) evaluated 1970 tax and public higher education enrollment data for Colorado. He included all Colorado General Fund tax revenues and enrollment patterns for Colorado residents at the state universities, the 4-year colleges, and the state-operated junior colleges (6 of the state's 12). Although Machovec found that the lower-income group received a small share of the dividends (enrollment shares and state subsidies), he noted that they also paid a small portion of the pertinent state taxes, resulting in cost–benefit ratios of approximately 1:1. For the middle-income group the same ratio was 1:1.5, and for the high-income group it was 1.3:1. Machovec concluded that "clearly . . . the wealthy were not benefiting at the expense of the poor." He added that if student aid were considered, progressivity would have increased significantly.

Conclusions from what might be labeled second-generation investigations have been more uniformly positive. Probably the most important methodological refinement in these later studies employs what is called the "life-cycle" approach. This correction, which was implicitly recognized by Hansen and Weisbrod and now is widely accepted, reflects the fact that younger and older taxpayers are unlikely to have children eligible for enrollment in college and that their inclusion in these cost–benefit analyses obfuscates the actual transfer of wealth: Their time will come later or has already passed. Because the young and the old are quite unlikely to be enrolled in college and are more likely to be poor, their inclusion lends to the regressivity finding, where that occurs. Pechman (1970), Crean (1975), McGuire (1976), McDonald (1980), and Moore (1982) have written in support of this approach. To our knowledge, no one has written in direct opposition. It seems correct to accept this method as superior because higher education can scarcely be said to contribute to wealth redistribution one way or the other for those who are either too young or have already completed their education, although both the young and the old may pay taxes. More recent wealth studies have limited their analyses to roughly the 35–60 age group, and most have concluded that the financing of higher education and the mix of enrollments therein leads to a redistribution of wealth from the rich to the poor or middle class. Although Crean's (1975) data were drawn from a Canadian sample, they illustrate the life-cycle principle quite well. By focusing on the 35–54 age group and using the Hight–Pollock method of comparing percentage enrollment shares to tax payment shares by income group, Crean found that among five income classes benefits exceeded costs for the bottom two groups, costs exceeded benefits for the top two groups, and patterns were mixed for the middle group. The germaneness of the life-cycle approach was clearly demonstrated by quite different results for families whose heads were younger than 35 or older than 54.

When McGuire (1976) added student aid expenditures and applied the age group limitation to later data (1971–1972) for California, where it all began, he found drastically different results from those of Hansen and Weisbrod. He concluded that the California system was much more egalitarian than they had reported. For the lowest two income categories, percentages of students enrolled in *each* of the three California systems exceeded the percentage of all such (lowest two income categories) California families (Table 6.1). Dollar margins

Table 6.1

WEALTH REDISTRIBUTION SUMMARY TABLE*

Income Class†		Redistributions Dollar Base**					Redistributions Percentage Base***							
		California	California	New York City	St. Louis	Florida	California	Canada	Canada	Colorado	Hawaii	New York	Florida	Wisconsin
		(1)	(2)	(3)	(4)	(5)	(6)	(7)	(8)	(9)	(10)	(11)	(12)	(14)
	(1)	$ −10	$ −10	$ 8	$ 8/499	$ −56/−30	−1.9%	3.1%	9.0%	−.5%	−2.3%	6.3%	−7.5%	
Low	(2)	44	45	43	6/497	−52/−35	5.9	4.5	7.0		−1.1	6.9	1.3	
	(3)	41	41	65	10/509	−7/−14	10.9	−2.7	−1.7		6.1		4.3	
Middle	(4)	14	14	83	16/547			−1.2	−4.9	14.9		8.7		
	(5)	20	20	5	16/536		−1.3				4.0		4.3	
	(6)	$ −156	$ −149	$ −199	$ 7/536	$ 34/32		−2.8%	−9.3%	−14.4%		4.6		
High	(7)						−3.1				.1		2.6	
	(8)						−10.7%				−6.9%	−26.4%	−5.2%	
Conclusion††	(9)	P	P	P	P/N	R	P	P	P	P	P	P	R	
		(13)												
Others	(10)	P												P

*Values are not strictly comparable by table rows because income categories vary. Groupings reflect same or similar categories, taking inflation into account. Calculations by original authors except as noted. (See notes below.)

**Dollar base redistributions reflect average dollar benefits received through enrollment (and related subsidies received) minus average dollar taxes paid by the income group. Base is families with dependent children aged 18–24 except as noted. (See notes below.)

***Percentage base redistributions reflect percentage enrollment share minus percentage tax share, by income group. (See notes below.)

†*Column (1)*. 1964 California data from Hansen-Weisbrod (1969), as calculated by Machlis (1973). Income categories: Row 1 = < $4,000, 2 = 4–5,999; 3 = 6–7,999; 4 = 8–9,999; 5 = 10–13,999; 6 = ≥ 14,000. *Column (2)*. 1964 California data from Hansen-Weisbrod (1969), as calculated by Pechman (1970), with same (estimated) data pooling by book authors. *Column (3)*. 1968 CUNY data from Machlis (1973). Deviations from income categories in Column (1): Row 5 = $10–14,999; Row 6 = ≥ 15,000. *Column (4)*. 1969 St. Louis Community College District data from Zimmerman (1973), corrected to reflect subsidy per *total* households in St. Louis County (1st estimate; 2nd is subsidy per student by Zimmerman). Deviations from income categories in Column (1): Row 1 = < $3,000; 2 = 3–4,999; 3 = 5–6,999; 4 = 7–8,999; 5 = 9–11,999; 6 = ≥ 12,000 (pooled estimate by book authors). *Column (5)*. 1960–1961 and 1967–1968 Florida data from Windham (1970). Double estimate reflects Windham's two tax estimation sources. Subsidies are per *total* households in Florida. Deviations from income categories in Column (1): Row 1 = < $3,000; 2 = 3–4,999; 3 = 5–9,999; 6 = ≥ 10,000. *Column (6), (10) & (12)*. 1968 and earlier California, Hawaii, and Florida data from Hansen-Weisbrod (1969), Hight and Pollock (1973), and Windham (1970), as calculated by Hight and Pollock (1973). Deviations from income categories in Column (1): Row 3 = $6–8,999; 5 = 9–14,999; 7 = 15–19,999; 8 = ≥ 20,000. *Column (7) & (8)*. 1961 Canada data from Judy (1970) and Crean (1975), respectively. Deviations from income categories in Column (1): Row 1 = < $3,000; 2 = 3–4,999; 3 = 5–6,999; 4 = 7–9,999; 5 = ≥ 10,000. *Column (9)*. 1970 Colorado data from Machovec (1972). Deviations from income categories in Column (1): Row 4 = $4–10,000; 6 = > 10,000. *Column (11)*. 1974 New York (SUNY) data from Moore (1982). Deviations from income categories in Column (1): Row 2 = $4–7,999; 4 = 8–11,999; 6 = 12–19,999; 8 = ≥ 20,000. *Column (13)*. 1964 California data (inflated to 1971) from Hansen-Weisbrod (1969), as calculated by McGuire (1976). Only benefits distribution reported. *Column (14)*. 1964–65 Wisconsin data from Hansen (1970). Only average subsidies in University of Wisconsin and Wisconsin State Universities reported.

††P = Progressive; R = Regressive; N = Neutral

favored the lower-income groups both on the average and in the aggregate, with the margin being essentially linear across all three California higher education systems. The largest subsidies went to students from families below $6,000 income. McGuire's inclusion of graduate students refined the results for the University of California. However, McGuire did not consider cost (tax) distributions across the income cohorts; therefore, wealth transfer cannot be shown from his results.

Without considering the life-cycle adjustment but using the Pechman method and adding tuition grant data, Moore (1978) had concluded that in the State University of New York the highest-income group gave up large amounts of resources to the low- and especially the middle-income group. In 1982, Moore (1982) made the life-cycle adjustment and corrected an important error detected in Crean's (1975) life-cycle analysis. (Crean implicitly had assumed that taxes were structured very regressively.) Based upon crude adjustments in his earlier data to impute values to the mid-age group, Moore found that the lower two income classes became even larger net beneficiaries and that the cost was shared by the highest two income classes.

The Integrative Review

From the preceding discussion, even though one obtains a general impression that higher education adds to progressivity, reaching a definite conclusion is not easy. We turn now to the integrative method, which will clarify matters considerably.

After some standardization and organization of the empirical results, the seeming anomalies of the wealth redistribution studies largely disappear. With one exception, Florida, all samples demonstrate improved equality and progressivity through higher education. The Florida exception results from the unusually regressive form of state taxation that existed there in the 1970s.

Table 6.1 presents the integrative review. Studies have been nominally standardized, which makes possible a reasonably good comparison of study findings. The available results lend themselves to comparisons on two separate bases. The five estimates on the left side of the table have been standardized on a dollar basis. This has been done by subtracting average taxes paid by income group from average income group benefits received through enrollments. The seven estimates on the right side of the table have been standardized on a percentage basis; that is, percentage tax shares have been subtracted from percentage enrollment shares by income group. Although these two data forms vary somewhat, they are similar both conceptually and in pattern of results, thus adding considerably to the likely validity of overall conclusions from the integrative review.

Nevertheless, the data in each row and column of Table 6.1 are not strictly compatible because income categories in the studies are not always precisely the same. In order to increase compatibility, a few rough data transformations were made. The size of possible error is believed to be insufficiently large to affect the overall pattern of results.

To gain a good sense of this pattern across studies, dollar income categories utilized in the various studies were arranged in relative, rather than absolute, dollar income groupings, from low- to high-income (see notes to Table 6.1). Often, categories classified in the same row of Table 6.1 varied by $1,000 (e.g., $0–2999 versus $0–3999). Usually researchers have employed differing categories because the income classifications used in data sources vary over time: As inflation increases, categories are changed by data-gathering agencies. The result is that the amount of data incompatibility is less than is suggested by the absolute dollar variations in income categories. There is much more that could be said about this standardization, but in general we believe that category compatibility is quite good and is extremely unlikely to affect the validity of conclusions.

In order to reach overall conclusions from Table 6.1, some decision rules are required. In order to reach a conclusion of regressivity or increased inequality, resources must be redistributed from poor to rich or poorer to richer groups; that is, the flow of resources must be greater toward richer individuals than from them. Usually, comparison of *net* benefits for lowest- to highest-income groups is a satisfactory test to reach a clear conclusion. Comparisons of lower- to higher-income groups supplement the analysis of group comparisons at the extremes.

Columns 1 (Machlis, 1973) and 2 (Pechman, 1970) are formulations of the Hansen–Weisbrod (1969) data in a form that permits an answer to the progressivity–regressivity question. (The Hansen–Weisbrod paper itself does not afford this answer.) It is seen that both the highest- and the lowest-income categories give up resources to the second-lowest- and middle-income groups, but that the average surrender per household is much greater for the highest- than for the lowest-income category. Further, the largest gains are for the second- and third-lowest-income groups. In short, there is more wealth redistribution down the income ladder than up. Column 6 (Hight and Pollock, 1973) is a different way of viewing the California data, and the results are consistent. Employing the enrollment share minus tax share method, it is seen that again the largest "loser" is the highest-income group, and that only the second- and third-lowest-income categories are net "gainers." Hence, row 9 shows a P (progressivity) in each of columns 1, 2, and 6.

One other study bears upon the income redistribution issue in California. McGuire (1976) (row 10, column 13) made several improvements in the Hansen–Weisbrod data by including graduate students and student aid subsidies; he also made the life-cycle correction. The data demonstrate approximately equal dollar benefits per student across the various income groups for the entire California system, even without consideration of cost distributions. Because we know from other studies that the higher-income groups pay more taxes than do lower-income groups in California, we can safely conclude that McGuire's progressivity finding is accurate. This study is excluded from the main part of the table, however, because of the cost data omission. Hansen and Weisbrod's original California study was not included in Table 6.1 because their results were not in a compatible form. Hansen and Weisbrod's conclusion that California higher education contributed to inequality was based upon incomplete and less than fully relevant evidence. The later four studies have since shown the Hansen–Weisbrod conclusion to be ill founded.

New York public higher education systems contribute in an even more progressive manner than does the California system. Machlis's (1973) study of CUNY (column 3) reveals very large transfers from the highest-income group to all other groups. Gains are largest in the middle of the income distribution. Results of Moore's (1982) study of SUNY are essentially the same (column 11): The highest-income group gives up all the resources. One difference is that the lowest-income groups appear to do better in the SUNY than in the CUNY system. This is because city taxes were less progressive than state taxes at the time of these studies.

The remaining studies on the left side of Table 6.1 are Zimmerman's (1973) study of the St. Louis Community College District and Windham's (1970) study of Florida. The Zimmerman study shows slightly smaller net gains to lower-income groups than to wealthier groups; however, all groups gained. This means either that Zimmerman erred or that undefined third parties contributed the unexplained amounts, because gains cannot exceed losses. From evidence provided it is not possible to determine the economic status of third parties; however, as all pertinent state and local taxes presumably are accounted for, the most likely unidentified benefactors are federal taxpayers and donor groups, each of whom are relatively affluent, thereby suggesting some progressivity or, at worst, neutrality in the St. Louis community colleges. Thus row 9 shows a P/N for the St. Louis study.

Windham's (1970) study in Florida is the only one showing clearly regressive redistribution effects, whether viewed in dollar terms (column 5) or percentage terms (column 12; Hight and Pollock, 1973). In Windham's original work (column 5), only the highest-income group (≥ $10,000) received positive dollar transfers. Hight and Pollock's transformations resulted in negative transfers for both the lowest- (< $4,000) and highest- (≥ $20,000) income groups, with the largest negative value (−7.5 percent) for the lowest group.

Hight and Pollock's (1973) results for Hawaii (column 10) also show negative transfers for the lower-income groups, but the negative transfer for the highest-income group was larger. The conclusion is that wealth redistribution through higher education was slightly progressive in Hawaii.

In Colorado (column 9; Machovec, 1972) the pattern is the same, but the magnitudes are quite different. The modest .5 percentage points transfer for the lowest-income group is offset easily by the −14.4 percent transfer for the high-income group, resulting in a clear progressivity conclusion.

Hansen's (1970) study in Wisconsin (column 14, at bottom) is excluded from the main part of Table 6.1 because the results do not really answer the income redistribution question. We conclude that higher education probably acts progressively in Wisconsin because subsidies are higher where mean family earnings are lower and mean earnings are higher where subsidies are less.

The remaining two studies of Table 6.1 (columns 7 and 8) are of Canadian university samples. Although obviously lacking in direct relevance to higher education in the United States, the studies used methods consistent with others tabled, and Canadian enrollment patterns and tax systems in support of higher education are similar to those in many American states. The pattern of results in the two studies are also similar to each other, although magnitudes vary. Positive transfers exist for low-income groups in both studies, and there are negative transfers for all others. As measured by magnitudes, progressivity is considerably greater in the Crean (1975) study (column 8) than in the Judy (1970, column 7) one, because Crean employed the life-cycle correction.

DISCUSSION

The power of integrative reviewing over standard reviewing is demonstrated convincingly in the case of the wealth redistribution studies. Our preliminary perusal of the empirical literature suggested the perennial "six of one and half-a-dozen of the other" conclusion. However, upon closer examination and some standardization of results, a clear pattern and several important principles emerged. First, higher education in most cases does contribute to progressivity. Second, with the exception of Florida, the progressivity conclusion is supported wherever a literal testing of the definition of progressivity is possible: net redistribution of resources down the income ladder versus up. Third, when the analytical methods employed are the most advanced, progressivity is found without exception.

One of the most common problems of standard reviews is that authors of individual studies often use inconsistent decision rules in judging their results. Of 16 wealth redistribution studies originally identified, the study authors concluded, or have been cited as concluding, that higher education led to progressive wealth redistribution in only 9 cases. Five purportedly reached the opposite conclusion and 2 have been cited as reaching neutral or mixed results. The integrative review, however, showed essentially consistent results in all cases except Florida after rough standardization was conducted. Perhaps more than in any other area examined, values of individual authors have played a role in forming conclusions.

As to who benefits from higher education, on the limited criterion of enrollment patterns versus tax incidences, the largest winner would appear to be the middle class, although the evidence is mixed. In all three California studies in Table 6.1, all transfers, though small, are negative for the lower- and higher-income groups but are positive for the middle group. Indeed, one could say that in California the poor do subsidize modestly the higher education of the middle class, and that on this basis the system is slightly regressive. This also is true in Hawaii and Colorado, but is not so in New York, Canada, and probably St. Louis County (community college data only). In the latter three cases, transfers are positive for the lowest-income groups. In New York the gain generally is larger among middle-income families, whereas in Canada transfers to the middle income are negative, but in neither case is the gain at the expense of the poor. In short, higher education appears clearly to be progressive in redistributing wealth from higher- to middle-income families, but such achievements are modest at best in regard to low-income groups, who may, in fact, contribute small amounts to the middle-income group as well.

One of the more important insights from the research literature is gained by a closer look at the meta-analysis matrix (Appendix Table 5), specifically the column headed "Population." States vary in tax progressivity–regressivity, in enrollment rates among low-income students, in student aid funds available, and in mix of public and private colleges; therefore, a conclusion of regressivity legitimately may be reached in one state while the same methodology may yield a correct, reverse conclusion in another. It is not surprising that both studies completed in New York show progressivity, because taxes in New York are toward the high end of the progressivity continuum. The two studies completed in Canada, where tax structures also are progressive, demonstrate progressivity, too. At the other end of the spectrum, Florida, a less progressive tax state, shows regressivity in each of two empirical works. Of five California income redistribution studies, only Hansen and Weisbrod concluded that the system was regressive; further, the other four studies appear to have employed superior methods. Using the questionable method, Hansen (1970) concluded there to be less regressivity in Wisconsin than in California; Wisconsin is known generally to possess fairly progressive tax structures. Colorado, a state probably somewhere near the middle in progressivity–regressivity showed no wealth transfer to the poor, but very little wealth loss also; the middle class did benefit in Colorado, and the wealthy gave up the resources.

Another important consideration is the public sector participation rate among the various income groups. New York, with high public enrollment rates for low-income groups, shows progressivity. The CUNY results in particular are as predicted. Also, the wealthier residents of New York are relatively likely to send their children to private institutions, thus considerably enhancing progressivity in the public sector, which is supported by progressive taxes. Results are somewhat less clearly progressive in California, which has a high participation rate among low-income persons, but a relatively small private sector to drain off wealthier students. Florida, on the other hand, does not have an atypically large private sector to offset its relatively regressive tax system, nor a high participation rate by low-income persons. (Note that most data sources are quite dated, and, thus, that tax progressivity likely has changed, especially when need-based student aid programs are included.)

One of the controversial issues in integrative reviewing is how the reviewer is to treat studies of lesser quality. To this point in this book, major problems with research methods have not arisen in sufficient numbers to affect results. In the wealth redistribution studies, the "life-cycle" adjustment creates more extreme results, but does not change results direction. Nevertheless, it is worth observing that although we have not found arguments against the adjustment in the literature, one certainly could argue that family heads younger than 35 and older than 55 or 60 are taxpayers, too, and that exclusion of these persons from the analyses, though probably methodologically correct, is still a matter of judgment.

Finally, a number of years after the Hansen–Weisbrod–Pechman debate began, John Conlisk (1977) tested one of Pechman's fundamental theses: that the Hansen–Weisbrod approach was based upon faulty logic because of the intergenerational transfer problem. Pechman (1972, p. S256) had argued that the traditional way of viewing costs and benefits in which benefits are distributed to students according to the income class of parents "Sweep(s) the problem created by intergenerational transfer . . . under the rug." Pechman had held that a more useful way of viewing the problem was to recognize that costs are paid by one generation and benefits are received by another and that there is no way of merging the benefits and costs in one generation to evaluate the equity problem. The reader will remember that basically the same point was made in Chapter 4, where we wrote of invalid cost specifications in traditional IRR calculations.

Conlisk (1977) proceeded to check the Pechman proposition by constructing an intergenerational transfer model. Acknowledging that the "true debate" concerns equity in a real-life situation far more complex than his simple model, Conlisk reasoned that "if the logical connection between equity and net benefits does not hold up in a simple economy [his model], it seems improbable that it will hold up in a complicated one" (p. 148).

In building his model, Conlisk broke up the population into income classes and then tested to see whether each class reaped more benefits than it paid out in taxes for schooling. From examining "counterexamples," that is, cases in which the Hansen–Weisbrod finding was not supported, he decided that not only was the Hansen–Weisbrod thesis disproven, but the fact that counterexamples abounded showed their thesis to be highly unreliable. Conlisk concluded by observing that the debate "favors Pechman's side."

In a published "comment" on Conlisk's paper, Johnson (1978) agreed that Conlisk demonstrated many plausible examples whereby "inequality will fall" over generations even when subsidies in the first generation appear regressive. However, Johnson believed Conlisk's conclusions to be in error. Johnson reasoned that one should properly question any policy that leads to (some) regressive cases and that if education fails to increase income, as in one of Conlisk's counterexamples, public subsidies should be removed.

Conclusion

Our general conclusions from the income redistribution studies are comprised of several parts. First, it seems extremely unlikely that, overall, higher education is a generally regressive force, as was originally posited by Hansen and Weisbrod. As measured by the wealth redistribution studies, if anything it is most likely that the system contributes moderately to progressivity in most states and in the nation as a whole. Further, if student aid is considered, the total contribution of progressivity probably is consistent and the effect substantial. If student aid is not considered (aid was relatively small when the early wealth redistribution data were collected), the overall margin likely is not large, so that in states with regressive tax systems, low participation rates among poorer youth, and a small private higher education sector, higher education may have a modest-to-perhaps-moderate regressive effect. In such cases, however, the regressivity most likely will be from low- to middle-income families, rather than to the wealthy ones, as some observers suggest. In general, however, we question the conceptual bases of the wealth redistribution studies.

It may be more correct to view progressivity or regressivity as a personal rather than a social phenomenon. As Robert Hartman (1970) states:

1. Poor people pay taxes and very few of them use public higher education. Those who do, gain thereby; those who don't, don't.
2. Middle income people are heavy users of the system. Their taxes don't cover the costs.
3. A few rich people use the system and gain handsomely thereby. The rest of the rich pay substantial taxes and get no direct return. (p. 521)

The present system of financing higher education, with heavy reliance upon federal and substantial reliance upon state need-based student aid, almost certainly contributes to enhancement of the wealth equitability goal that was assigned directly to higher education as early as the 1960s. The probability that the system contributes directly in a negative way seems very small indeed, although exceptions may be found in a few states having highly regressive tax structures, particularly if less precise research methods are used or if researcher bias leads to questionable decision rules in reaching conclusions. Indeed, the inconsistencies in methods and decision rules largely explain why different researchers have reached varying conclusions.

7

Money as a Potential Instrument of Public Policy

The wealth redistribution studies of Chapter 6 examined the effects of higher education financial support structures in redistributing money from rich to poor. These structures, it should be observed, were not designed for the purpose of improving equity; therefore, to some extent success in this regard largely would have been accidental. In Chapter 8, we examine the more purposeful attempts to enhance educational opportunities for low-income students and ultimately to redistribute wealth more fairly. This chapter concentrates upon what are known as the student demand studies—how students react to higher education price changes. The major impact of this chapter is that in demonstrating how students react to college costs, the potential of financial interventions in effecting public policies is revealed.

Historically, higher education opportunity has been addressed through no- or low-tuition policies. This has been true in both the private (independent) and public sectors. Indeed, prior to World War II, public college tuitions were zero or only about $100, and private tuitions were only perhaps 2 or 3 times as great. Public tuitions were kept small primarily through state support of

An earlier version of this chapter appeared in *The Journal of Higher Education,* Vol. 58, No. 2 (Mar/April 1987).

institutions, whereas private colleges were heavily subsidized through voluntary support, especially from various interest groups such as churches.

When public expenditures for colleges and universities grew dramatically after the war, financing systems began to draw more attention. The higher expenditures had resulted in large part from enormous enrollment increases. The rising costs, coupled with an increasing awareness of the social importance of providing higher education opportunity to low-income persons caused policymakers to reexamine the old ways of doing things. Higher education pricing policies drew immediate attention, for of all possible public intervention strategies, financial subsidies were, and continue to be, politically the most acceptable.

The assumption is that cost is an obstacle to opportunity. The question is, to what degree? That is, how effective are financial subsidies in promoting opportunity? Does the low public tuition that is possible only through very large public subsidies of institutions enhance opportunity? To what degree and for whom? Further, what happens when tuition prices are raised and the resulting savings expended on student aid for low-income youth? It is worth observing that directly or indirectly the wealth redistribution studies were motivated by these same questions. Was the existing system of low public tuition and high public institutional support effective and efficient in serving low-income individuals?

The Student Demand Studies

Economists, and a few educators, turned to demand theory for a framework to guide exploration of these questions. Demand theory suggests that the quantity of a good or service demanded (e.g., higher education) is a function of the money income of the buyer, the price of the good or service, prices of alternatives, and buyer tastes or preferences. Thus, demand for higher education, that is, enrollment, should be related to tuition and other prices charged. If this is so, price subsidies should be effective. Further, if low-income persons were shown to be more price responsive than higher-income individuals, subsidies (student aid) awarded on the basis of need should be more effective than low tuition, which benefits everyone.

META-ANALYSIS RESULTS

Twenty-five student demand studies were subjected to meta-analysis. Results were standardized to a student price response coefficient (SPRC) per $100 of price change. Specifically, the SPRC values reflect the change in the enrollment rate of 18–24-year-old potential first-time students facing a $100 increase in the average 1982–1983 tuition and room and board price of $3,420.

The results of all studies were in the expected direction; that is, enrollments declined when prices increased and increased when prices were reduced. The average SPRC for the 25 studies was about −.7; that is, for every $100 increase in tuition price, one would expect, under 1982–1983 price conditions, a drop of .7 percentage points in the first-time enrollment rate among 18–24-year-olds. Because the enrollment rate for this age group was about .33 in 1982, the $100 price increase would represent an enrollment decline of about 2.1 percent, all other factors equal. However, the initial impact on overall enrollment would not be as great because the .7 figure was derived primarily from studies of first-time students. Upperclassmen are less responsive to price changes because their investment has already begun and because they will not have to pay the higher price for as many years. Of course, a 2.1 percent decline in first-year enrollments presumably would translate into comparable enrollment declines after 4 or more years.

The range of results from the meta-analysis is substantial, as would be expected from very disparate study populations (see Appendix Table 6). The standard error for the 25 estimates is .09; however, almost 40 percent of the variance is a result of one study. When this study is removed, the standard error drops to .07, meaning that we may be 95 percent certain that the "true" SPRC lies between −.5 and −.8.

ONCE AGAIN, THE QUESTION OF "FIT"

As we have already seen, however, meta-analysis results may be valid average estimates while fitting no particular case. The circumstances are very similar to those of the private rate of return studies, in which the average cost figure for a U.S. college student was a blend of public and private, 2-year and 4-year, and other cost components. Just as there is no such composite student in the IRR studies, there is no such student facing $100 cost increases in a composite public/private and 2-year/4-year institution. Further, just as IRR vary with the institution attended, so does student response to price. A student who selects a low-cost community college is unlikely to respond to a $100 price increase in the same way as would an otherwise identical student attending an expensive private college. This is not to say that results from studies of differing populations need necessarily vary, because price responses of particular mixes of students within numerous mixes of institutional settings may to some extent balance out.

In any case, for national or even state policy purposes, a mean or average estimate from very disparate studies may serve a useful purpose as an indication of overall enrollment reactions to price manipulations, although such utility would be better served by estimates gained from studies of the entire higher education system rather than from averages of limited and biased samples (in the external validity sense). States, too, may be guided most appropriately by results from broad-based studies, except where their interests are more parochial, for example, are limited to the public sector. For individual institutions or institutional systems, similar care should be used in selecting SPRCs for policy application. With this backdrop, we may now look more closely at the meta-analysis results and receive some guidance for policy. In the process of viewing study and results differences we can learn a good deal about how price response varies by study conditions.

NATIONAL AND REPRESENTATIVE ESTIMATES FROM STATE STUDIES

Several studies are useful to national higher education financing policy and, with proper caution, to policy in many states. Seven of the student demand studies were of the U.S. population of public and private institutions, and another five, though limited to particular states, also included both sectors. A good SPRC estimate for these institutions would be between −.5 and −.8 if a standard research method were employed. For the studies employing national samples, those by Hopkins (1974) (SPRC = −.6), Corazzini, Dugan, and Grabowski (1972) (SPRC = −.5), and Tannen (1978) (SPRC = −.8), appear to have the greatest generalizability. The Hopkins and Tannen studies are perhaps most useful to present policymaking because both consider student aid, which today is a major force in financing policy. Inclusion of student aid should give more accurate estimates of price increase impacts because aid reduces the net effect of price increases. These two studies do differ, however, in how they specified price (the dependent variable). Whereas Hopkins employed a net tuition specification (tuition net of aid), Tannen used a broader definition: net tuition plus foregone income and room and board. Because deductions for student aid are proportionately larger in the case of tuition than for broader prices, we might have expected a higher SPRC for the Hopkins study, but this was not the case. Reconciliation of estimates may lie in the fact that Tannen limited his sample to males, who would be expected to be more price sensitive than a sample that included females, because the former pay a substantially larger share of their own costs (Leslie, 1984). That is, one would be less sensitive to a price if someone else paid a large share of it. The lower SPRC found by Corazzini et al. probably can be explained by their failure to net out tuition increases for student aid offsets, leaving us to favor the Hopkins SPRC estimates of −.6, but not yet willing to dismiss Tannen's figure of −.8. Again, these figures are from national samples and reflect price response in public and private institutions as combined and weighted in the population.

The remaining four national studies are each sufficiently unique or faulted to preclude easy reconciliation of results. Bishop's (1977) relatively low estimate (−.4) probably is due to his limiting the potential alternative for students to the lowest cost nearby college. Hight's (1975) higher result (−1.1) from data for 1927–1963 is widely attributed in the literature to a failure to separate effects from changes in the supply of higher education, over time, from effects due to changes in prices. The low estimate (−.2) from Jackson (1978) is for student aid, rather than tuition or other prices. As will be seen in Chapter 8, students perhaps react more strongly to direct price changes than to student aid subsidies. Finally, we are not at all clear as to what to make of Hoenack and Feldman's (1969) estimate of −1.0. We believe this high estimate is a result of their unique formulation of the student's attendance decision. Our suspicion that their result is upwardly biased is reinforced by the results (−.5) of Corazzini et al. (1972) from the same data source, Project Talent, and the closer conformance of Corazzini's findings with those of others.

The pattern of estimates from the five other broad studies of all institutional types supports this conclusion. With one exception, these studies of state rather than national samples achieved results in the range of from −.6 to −.8. Barnes's (1975) study in North Carolina obtained a −.6 SPRC and included student aid. Kohn, Manski, and Mundel (1976) arrived at the same figure from Illinois and North Carolina data even though they ignored student aid. The aid effect probably should have been relatively modest in the Kohn et al. study in any case because their price specification was very broad. Lehr and Newton (1978) found a comparable SPRC of −.7 in Oregon when aid was included, and Wilson (1977) obtained an only slightly higher estimate (−.8) from responses to commuting costs in Minnesota. Only Radner and Miller's (1970) results are at notable variance (SPRC = −.3), and again the literature is helpful in evaluating this result. Critics have consistently identified the source of Radner and Miller's downward bias as resulting from inadequate price variations in their sample.

Putting the results of these 12 studies of combined public and private samples together, the SPRC estimate of from −.6 to −.8 emerges as very plausible, indeed likely. One could, with some caution, go even farther and extend the appropriateness of this range to states not greatly different from the national institutional mix, in other words, to those with a significant but not overwhelmingly large independent sector and with price structures near the national median.

SPRCs IN SPECIFIC CASES

As we move away gradually from broad national and state studies of all kinds of institutions, we would expect only modestly different results, and this is what is found. Public enrollments compose more than 80 percent of national higher education (headcount) enrollments, and results from studies limited to the public sector vary little from combined sector results. Clotfelter's (1976) national sample of public institutions yielded an SPRC of −.5. This estimate, which is near the low end of our range of from −.6 to −.8, is plausible, in part, because it did not reflect expenditures for student aid. Ghali et al. (1977) obtained a slightly higher figure, −.6, by including student aid. Their estimate was from Hawaiian public higher education, which has few nearby private competitors. Orvis's (1975) results from a Minnesota study of response to commuting costs, however, are notably higher (−1.1). Orvis (1975), Wilson (1977), and Hoenack and Weiler (1975) all employed a similar price specification and obtained similarly high results. This may be due, in part, to a relatively high sensitivity to commuting costs, but it seems more likely that the SPRCs calculated are incompatible with other estimates. It appears that the commuting elasticities (percentage changes in enrollment per percentage point change in commuting costs) reported are own-price elasticities, which do not take into account enrollments lost to other institutions as prices rise, and thus indicate greater price sensitivity than actually exists overall.

On the other hand, SPRCs should be higher in the public sector because students, on average, are less wealthy, and $100 cost increases are proportionately larger than in the private sector. We would have expected SPRCs of −.7 or −.8 for these studies of the public sector; comparable estimates were a bit smaller.

Moving on to other institutional classifications, the aforementioned study by Hoenack and Weiler (1975) was of a 4-year public sample in Minnesota. Hoenack's (1968) estimate for another public 4-year school, the University of California, was −.6. Although this estimate may seem a little low for a public institution, the University of California is permitted to admit primarily high-ability students, who would be expected to be less price responsive. Campbell and Siegel's (1967) study, which was the first student demand study completed, also yielded an SPRC of −.6, even though controls were lacking. Campbell and Siegel examined only 4-year institutions, but they considered both public and independent ones. Their result, too, seems plausible. If estimates of from −.6 to −.8 appear accurate for institutions overall, and estimates from −.7 to −.8 seem plausible for the public sector mix of 2-year and 4-year institutions, SPRCs of from perhaps −.6 to −.7 appear likely for public 4-year schools overall. Results of this magnitude are not disputed by Hoenack's and Campbell and Siegel's findings.

The remaining studies are of institutional types in which more extreme results would be expected. For reasons already mentioned, reasons having to do with the relative wealth of enrollees and of institutional costs, we would expect higher price response at community colleges and lower response at private institutions. We would also expect the open-door policies of the former and the generally greater selectivity at the latter to contribute to this pattern. Generally, this is what was found.

The SPRCs for four community colleges were +1.3, −1.0, +.5, and −2.4, respectively. The first of these values (AASCU, 1977) reflected an experimental price reduction in 2-year public colleges in Wisconsin. This explains the positive sign. The second value, −1.0, was obtained when prices subsequently were raised again in the same institutions (AASCU, 1977, No. 2). It may be instructive that the price response was greater when prices were reduced than when they were raised. The third SPRC, +.5, probably should be discounted because the study (Berne, 1980) included only persons who applied to a particular New York community college, and the relevant independent variable was tuition net of student aid. This study has no counterpart among other studies in the meta-analysis. The final, high SPRC of −2.4 was reported by Sulock (1982) from a national study of community colleges. The extraordinarily high value is, of course, suspect, although adjustments for student aid would explain some of the deviation from other community college SPRCs, particularly because community colleges enroll a disproportionate share of low-income and minority persons. We calculated our own community college SPRC from national data for 1967–1972 in order to check the Sulock data and obtained a 1982 equivalent value of −.9 after controlling for unemployment, race, family income, student aid, community college market share, urban–rural residence, and previous higher education experience. Our value is more consistent with results of other studies and intuitively appears to be more plausible in relation to results in other kinds of institutions.

SPRCs at independent colleges, as expected, are low. Funk (1972) reported a value of −.2 for Creighton University over the time span 1959–1970. Tauchar (1969) obtained a value of −.3 from a California sample of Catholic high school students who were queried about possible attendance at Roman Catholic colleges. The highest estimate, though toward the low end of the overall SPRC distribution, was obtained from a national sample of midselective private colleges (Knudsen and Servelle, 1978). This relatively high SPRC of −.6 might be explained by the uniqueness of the sample, but part of the explanation probably was the correction for student aid.

METHODOLOGICAL ISSUES

The necessary standardization process for the student demand studies is complex arithmetically if not conceptually. The process involves (1) transforming results to a common measure of student response to price change; (2) correcting all values to reflect consistent price levels; and (3) converting data from various age-group populations to a common age base. The standardization techniques employed for this study were based upon those developed in a landmark study by Jackson and Weathersby (1975), who calculated an SPRC for a hypothetical first-time student from a family earning $12,000 in 1974 and facing a college cost of $2,000 per year.

Each of the three adjustments listed bears elaboration. Consistent with Jackson and Weathersby, the SPRC employed for this book was the change in participation rates among 18–24-year-olds as a result of a $100 higher education price increase. For most studies, at least some conversion is necessary.

Often, researchers report (statistically controlled) percentage enrollment variations as prices change for a single institution over time. For comparability to other studies, such institutional enrollment changes must be converted to enrollment *rate* changes. When enrollment changes are reported as an SPRC/ $100, the institutional enrollment percentage can be calculated by multiplying by .33, the enrollment rate for eligible 18–24-year-olds in the common base year of the study (1982). However, many studies report student response to price change in another form, the price elasticity of demand, Σ. This elasticity is defined in the following: Σ = E/P, where E is the percentage change in enrollment and P is the percentage change in price. Because the SPRC = E/ $100 price change, the SPRC = Σ after the $100 is converted to a percentage figure, provided that both values are expressed in or are converted to enrollment rates. (For example, suppose Σ = .5 for a $500 price change on a base price of $5,000. Then, by substitution, E = Σ × $500/5000 = .5 × .1 = .05 and the SPRC = .05 × $100/500 = .01; that is, SPRC = 1 percent.)

Conversions of elasticities to SPRCs may be straightforward; however, there are important exceptions as shown by Chisholm and Cohen (1982, pp. 18–19), who identify errors made by Jackson and Weathersby (1975). Chisholm and Cohen show that the mathematical properties of elasticities are such as to render comparisons across studies hazardous, particularly time-series studies. Employing the arithmetic procedures above, Jackson and Weathersby utilized tuition elasticities to estimate enrollment effects at a $2,000 total cost basis. Their use of elasticities would not produce errors in the case of time-series studies if the rate of tuition change were the same as the rate of total cost change, but such has not been the case, and the problem is especially serious in converting data from old time-series studies. Using Campbell and Siegel's (1967) landmark study as an illustration, we observe that the tuition increase was 148 percent of total direct cost increase between 1927 and 1963. Because Campbell and Siegel indexed their data (1927 values = 100), their tuition elasticity of −.44 equates to a total cost elasticity of −.65. The result, *ceteris paribus*, is almost a 50 percent understatement of the Campbell and Siegel SPRC by Jackson–Weathersby—from this error alone. When only elasticities are provided, errors can only be avoided by returning to the original cost information and calculating SPRCs from those data. The standardization procedure used for this chapter was to convert tuition elasticities to total cost elasticities (actually, tuition plus room and board elasticities) where necessary.

Standardizing price levels is the second necessary task. For this chapter, all such values were converted to academic year 1982–1983 constant dollars. Directly related to this point, Jackson and Weathersby made an additional error that materially affected their results. After using the average 1974 total cost value of $2,000 to convert elasticities to SPRCs, they then deflated again by the 1974 CPI (Consumer Price Index) value.

Further, it is believed that a superior deflation mechanism exists. In this study, student costs are deflated by a national student cost index created from actual tuition and room and board costs over time. The argument is that in making the enrollment decision students respond to changes in the actual prices they face—tuition, room and board, and so forth—not to the market basket prices of the CPI. An investment framework would argue more for the CPI deflator because under this framework students are presumed to weigh costs and benefits of alternative investments.

The third and final major correction that may be required is in converting all participation rates to the 18–24-year-old base. Many studies report results in terms of later college participation rates among high school sophomore or juniors (Project-Talent-based studies) and high school seniors (SCOPE [School to College: Opportunities for Postsecondary Education]-based studies, among others). These rates are as much as twice as high as the 18–24-year-old participation rate, and adjustments to achieve comparability to the 18–24 age cohort are mandatory. Again, Jackson and Weathersby, whose work is considered seminal in this area, neglected to make this adjustment. At one point in their analysis, Jackson and Weathersby (1975, p. 643) speak of the "eligible" population, but the participation rate employed differs from the rate for 18–24-year-old high school graduates, the group typically considered as "eligible" in the literature, or from the rate for 18–24-year-old high school graduates who have not completed 4 years of college. It is worth noting before leaving this discussion that Jackson and Weathersby's errors often cancel out.

Although these are the major comparability issues, there is no doubt that some problems remain. One of the potentially more troublesome of these issues to the reader concerns comparability of SPRCs between micro and macro studies where own-price and cross-price (prices charged by competitors) elasticities may be confused or interpretations may be contentious. Specifically, the issue arises in studies of single institutions versus studies of the entire higher education environment; enrollment effects upon individual institutions may be confused with effects upon the entire system. From a macro perspective, our primary interest is in the discouragement effect of tuition increases; that is, how many students do not participate in higher education because of price increases? From the micro (institutional) perspective, interest primarily is not in discouragement from *overall* participation but only from enrollment in the institution itself: Some of the students who leave an institution when tuition is raised will attend elsewhere. In deriving their estimates from tuition and enrollment data for a number of institutions, cross-sectional study results reflect explicitly the impact of whatever prices are charged in the sample. Time-series studies, on the other hand, include such forces in a somewhat different way: They implicitly factor in price changes of other institutions as they occur over time, without specifying what those price changes are. Because the time-series and cross-sectional results reported in the matrix do not seem to vary much, this difference apparently is not important.

DISCUSSION

What then do the student demand studies tell us? First, they clearly tell us that students respond to price and that the effect is not trivial. For the nation as a whole, a change in the 18–24-year-old enrollment rate per $100 price increase probably would be in the range of from .6 to .8 percentage points downward. Because this enrollment rate is .33, enrollments would probably decline from 1.8 to 2.4 percent for every $100 price increase. This percentage translates into lost higher education opportunity for approximately 50,000 first-time students and for smaller numbers of upperclassmen who already have an investment stake. A rough estimate is that within 4 years, roughly 200,000–250,000 fewer enrollments would result annually from the $100 increase, all other factors equal.

The studies tell us also that we probably should expect greater enrollment effects in community colleges and lesser effects in private colleges. These differing effects might be due to differences in institutional costs and selectivity and in family income levels of students attracted. Further, as one goes up the cost, selectivity, and student/family income scales within these institution classifications, SPRCs should decline. Although numbers of studies here are small and thus conclusions must be tentative, approximately .9 *eventual* (within 2 years?) percentage points declines in the enrollment rate for community colleges (about 2.7 percent enrollment declines) and a range of from about −.2 to −.5 percentage points in the rate (eventually, from −.6 to −1.5 percent in enrollments) for independent colleges would be suggested. These estimated declines for overall enrollments are based upon the assumption that effects upon first-time students will accumulate for each of 4 years of enrollment and that some effect, albeit a reduced one, will be noted upon upperclassmen in the first year of the increase and thereafter, so that the *net* effect in 4 years will roughly approximate the effect upon first-time enrollments in the first year of the increase.

For public institutions, SPRC estimates of −.7 or −.8 appear sound when 2-year schools are included, and values of perhaps −.6 or −.7 seem appropriate when they are excluded. Sensitivities near the low end of these narrow ranges may be expected for more selective and prestigious universities, and sensitivities near the high end may be anticipated for less selective and prestigious state colleges.

RESPONSES TO VARIOUS PRICES

These sensitivity values would seem to fit tuition price increases best. Sensitivities for price increases in room and board or combined totals probably are not as great, especially when incidental costs and foregone earnings are added. From limited information it appears also that students may be less sensitive to student aid.

These conclusions, however, are by no means certain, in part because evidence is scant and sometimes inconsistent. A few studies in the meta-analysis compared sensitivities; these usually support our conclusion. For example, Bishop (1977) found tuition price sensitivities to be about 5 times greater than those for opportunity costs and about 60 percent greater than for those for room and board and commuting, although he acknowledges that the true effects "probably are much less." The tuition sensitivities reported by Kohn et al. (1976) also are about 5 times greater than commuting sensitivities and are twice as great as room and board sensitivities. Chapman's (1979) results comparing tuition and commuting costs are consistent. Jackson's (1978) results for student aid would seem to follow the pattern; not only is his student aid SPRC (−.2) low, he reports that students appear to react strongly to receiving aid but not to the amount.

On the other hand, Hoenack, who has specialized in use of commuting elasticities, believes that student sensitivity to commuting costs are little different from other costs when the value of the student's time is added to transportation expenses. Further, Manski and Wise (1983) obtained roughly equal student sensitivity values for several kinds of prices. This result is especially puzzling because the model employed was the same one used by Kohn et al. (1976), who obtained very different results. Differing samples may explain the inconsistency; however, the more likely explanation is in Manski and Wise's averaging of their unusual cost specification, which was schooling costs expressed in dollars per month divided by family income. It is likely that SPRCs vary by income level, as reported by Kohn et al., but balance out in the averaging of cost to income ratios employed by Manski and Wise.[1]

A CLOSING NOTE

The student demand studies demonstrate convincingly that monetary subsidies possess the potential for achieving or at least advancing the equal opportunity goal. Although a detailed, empirical examination of the relative effectiveness of student aid versus low tuition in meeting that goal would be interesting, such an analysis is extraneous to our purpose, which is to examine this "marginal" higher education goal in terms of the corresponding marginal financing mechanism—student aid. Low tuition is a historical financing device that we can only assume was created in response to historic goals, such as

[1]These and other matters contained in this chapter are elaborated in our paper "Student Price Response in Higher Education: The Student Demand Studies." *The Journal of Higher Education,* 58 (March/April 1987).

"preparation of trained men and women," "education of an informed electorate," and so on.

There may remain, in the minds of some readers, one other matter that bears exploration. For the skeptic who has observed very little apparent enrollment impact from increasing higher education prices in recent years, we offer the following. First, higher education list prices until quite recently have not risen significantly in real terms. Second, students often have avoided price increases by moving to lower cost institutions, with the result that overall enrollment rates remain unaffected. Third, since 1972, need-based student aid programs have grown astronomically. For those probably most sensitive to price, such aid ameliorates the effects of tuition increases. In effect, students have succeeded in passing increased costs on to others. For example, from national data bases, Leslie (1984) found that between 1973 and 1980 the students' share of total costs declined from 28 to 18 percent, while parents and government made up the difference.

There are other reasons that are beyond, or only indirectly involve, price considerations. Demand is known to be affected not only by price but by the money income of the buyer, by tastes and preferences, and by the value of the good from a consumption or an investment perspective. For example, as Campbell and Siegel (1967) show, the influence over time of tuition on participation rates becomes apparent only after one controls for changes in income. The growing interest in higher education on the part of women illustrates the effects of a change in preferences. Their increased participation rate has offset a decline in the rate for males and in the process probably obscured the effects of tuition increases as well. The value of a college education, as measured by the rate of return on investment, has apparently remained high in comparison to alternative opportunities, although the precise figures have been the subject of some debate. Finally, many colleges and universities have acted to enhance the real or perceived value of what they offer. The introduction of new programs, more aggressive marketing, and the like serve to counteract higher tuition. Other actions, such as lowering admission standards, may also have had a confounding effect on the relationship between tuition and enrollment. Demographic changes, of course, are another important influence on enrollment. It may be instructive to note that despite a clear conceptual connection, the relationship between higher education enrollments and key demographic changes is not straightforward. That relationship too is masked by countervailing forces. How else are we to understand the fact that the recent decline in the number of high school graduates has yet to be accompanied by a decline in overall higher education enrollments?

8

The Effects of Student Financial Aid

The explicit goal of need-based student financial aid is to ensure that, given a minimal level of academic competence, all students have an equal opportunity to participate in higher education. Specifically, the intent of such aid is to remove financial barriers that could prevent individuals from enrolling in college, unduly restrict their choice of institution, or bring about their premature departure from college. The questions for policymakers, taxpayers, and those who work in higher education are whether student financial aid is effective in achieving these goals and, if so, to what extent.

Government-sponsored student financial aid as we now know it began in the mid-1960s. By the mid-1980s, the Federal effort alone had leveled off at around $10 billion annually, including about $1 billion in veterans benefits. Federal subsidies of Guaranteed Student Loans (GSL) are part of that $10 billion. Although the amount borrowed through the GSL and other government loan programs is included in some analyses under the rubric of student aid, in fact only the government subsidy constitutes aid, with the remainder representing a student rather than a government expenditure. The states contribute approximately another $1 billion, and the institutions at least another $3 billion (differences among reporting procedures across the nation make the latter figure difficult to determine precisely), making the total package about $14 billion.

These billions of dollars affect student demand for higher education by lowering the net price students must pay. Whereas in the previous chapter we examined the effects of increases in the cost of college, here, by implication, we examine the effects of cost decreases that come about through the student aid mechanism. Theoretically, there is little mystery about the effects of student aid. Aid recipients should enroll in larger numbers, attend higher-cost institutions more often, and complete their education with greater frequency than comparable nonrecipients because their net, or true, costs are lower.

In practice, however, determining the actual effects of student aid is a formidable task, due to a variety of methodological problems ranging from mundane data issues to the subtleties of econometric modeling. The data problems are substantial. As of the mid-1980s, a comprehensive, national student aid data base did not exist, making it impossible to determine, for example, how much total aid a given individual received or the magnitude of the net price faced by the student after aid has been awarded.

Other methodological problems stem from the sheer complexity of human behavior. Researchers have had difficulty in isolating the effects of student aid from a myriad of other influences. In all likelihood, the aid effects are relatively weak compared to factors known to be important, such as parents' education. It would be surprising, would it not, if nothing more than a reduction in the net price of attendance could overcome years of relative deprivation of many kinds experienced by typical low-income families? Furthermore, there is evidence to suggest that the college attendance decision routinely occurs early in the high school years, well before at least the specifics of the student aid picture could be expected to have much effect (Hearn, 1980).

Student aid itself is complicated. It can take the form of an outright grant, a job, a loan with varying degrees of interest subsidy, or, quite often, some combination thereof. Conceivably, the effectiveness of student aid could be related to its form as well as its amount.

The supply side of the equation is not without its problems, too. Student aid researchers usually assume that the number of enrollment places expands indefinitely to meet any level of demand. Serious conceptual and statistical problems may arise if the assumption does not hold. However, in reality, phenomena such as enrollment caps at major public universities and even the deliberate downsizing of a few such universities have occurred during the last decade, and many of the elite private institutions have traditionally maintained enrollment ceilings. Institutional budget cuts, which were common during the late 1970s and early 1980s, reduced the outreach efforts and the availability of services that are vital in stimulating and maintaining the enrollment of low-income students. Strictly speaking, then, the assumption of unlimited supply of enrollment places is probably invalid. The quantitative relationships are murky, however, and it is conceivable that supply limitations, although real, have little material effect.

In what follows we first discuss briefly the various approaches that have been used to analyze the effects of student aid. Then we review what has been learned about the effectiveness of student aid with respect to each of its three purposes: improving access, providing choice, and contributing to persistence. Each goal is examined individually because that is how researchers typically deal with them, but interaction effects are also noted.

Analytical Approaches

Three distinct approaches have been used to measure the impact of student aid: econometric analyses of enrollment behavior, surveys of student opinions on the impact of student aid, and calculations of higher education participation rates. Findings based on all of the approaches will be examined in this chapter. None of the three is without its weaknesses, but taken together they do provide a reasonably sound basis for evaluating the effects of student aid.

In the econometric approach, researchers typically use multivariate statistical techniques. As is generally true of statistical modeling of complex phenomena, this method is subject to various threats to the accuracy and reliability of the estimated effects. These threats include biased parameter estimates resulting from omission of a variable that belongs in the model, misleading measures of statistical significance resulting from collinearity among the independent variables, misinterpretations of estimated effects because of a failure to "identify" the model properly, and so on. Still, all things considered, this is the preferred method for determining the effects of student aid because the econometric approach affords the researcher the best opportunity to control systematically the influence of intervening variables (i.e., events or characteristics that mask the true relationship between student aid and enrollment).

A second approach to assessing the impact of student aid is to ask students how they perceive that impact on their own attendance decisions. Unfortunately, there is a good chance that these impressions of the effect of student aid will be biased upward. Students have an obvious interest in keeping their cost of attendance as low as possible, and they are likely to be prone to exaggerating the effects of financial factors on their decision to enroll or remain in college.

The participation rate studies are similar to the econometric analyses in that they examine actual behavior, but they resemble the impressionistic studies in the simplicity of their methodology. They address the following question: Do changes in higher education participation rates for target populations move in the same direction as changes in the overall amount of student aid? Often, this approach is the form of practical political test used to assess public policy initiatives. If participation rates and student aid amounts move in the same direction, then one has *prima facie* evidence that the student aid initiative is working, whereas a lack of such correlation may be viewed as a policy failure.

Although popular and seemingly straightforward, this approach is the most seriously flawed because, in effect, it fails to recognize the complexity of the phenomena being investigated. Although one can readily observe participation rates over time along with changes in the amount of student aid, one cannot readily ascertain the extent to which other socioeconomic dynamics (including the composition or type of aid) may have caused whatever rate behaviors are observed. Typically the studies include no formal control over the influence of these other factors, apart from an occasional adjustment of the income categories to reflect the movement of prices in the economy.

Not only the methodology, but the underlying assumption of this approach can be challenged. Carlson (1976) reasons as follows:

> Equality of opportunity in higher education does not imply equality of demand. That is, there is no reason to expect or even desire that all types of individuals should enroll in colleges and universities in equal proportions. Because of varied preferences across segments of the population, the usefulness of enrollment rates as measures of access and choice is very limited and without any solid foundation. (p. 10)

Of course, this reasoning is not beyond question either, as it assumes that in these matters one safely can ignore the reasons for varied preferences. It is not within the scope of this book, however, to pursue issues of social and political philosophy. Our task is to assemble the evidence that will indicate whether student aid does what it purports to do. Many individuals consider participation rates to be an important part of that evidence, so it is appropriate to discuss them in this chapter.

In reviewing the findings of the studies that comprise each of these approaches, two questions will be addressed: Does student aid have any effect? If it does, what is the magnitude of that effect? As might be imagined, the first of the two questions is by far the easier to answer. Indeed, for the second question we shall have to be content with "ballpark" figures in most instances. To the extent that such figures can be firmly established, however, we will have accomplished something of value, given the current scarcity of even rough estimates.

The emphasis throughout this discussion will be on the impact of aid on low-income students, the primary target population of most need-based student aid. Low-income students are either independent students with low incomes or, more often, dependent students from families with low incomes. The effects of student aid on middle-income and high-income students will occasionally be discussed as well. The former have at times been the target of aid policies, and the latter often serve as a benchmark for gauging the effects of student aid programs on lower-income groups.

Integrative Review Results

In examining the effects of student aid, varying degrees of integration will be achievable. We are, after all, examining three issues—access, choice, and persistence—from the perspective of three methodological approaches. In some instances, the studies to be reviewed generate results that, when standardized, can be the basis for meaningful measures of central tendency, such as mean or modal values. In other instances, the review will be able to go no further than assembling results in a manner that makes it possible for patterns to be observed.

ACCESS

Student aid either lowers the cost of attendance through grants or makes additional funds available to students through loans or work opportunities. Either way, student aid makes it easier financially to attend college. But does student aid do more than that? Is it at least partly responsible for the fact that some students attend at all? What proportion of students now attending college are doing so partly because of student aid? What proportion would not have entered college in the absence of student aid, or some portion thereof? These are the questions addressed in the studies reviewed in this section.

The review will be organized around the three methodologies described above. Findings from econometric analyses will be examined first, followed by those from student opinion surveys and participation rate calculations. This way of proceeding is desirable because the nature of the evidence varies so greatly among the three approaches. In a concluding section, and occasionally before then, the summary findings are compared across methodologies.

Econometric Analyses

Nine econometric studies were found. Data on the seven studies used for the integrative review are shown in Table 8.1 (additional details can be found in Appendix Table 7). The data show the percentage of full-time low-income enrollment that is dependent on student aid—that is, the percentage of students who would not be enrolled without aid. As expected, the effect on students from low-income families is by far the strongest. Without aid, mostly in the form of nonrepayable grants, the enrollment of low-income students would be reduced by about 20–40 percent, depending on the estimate. The estimated effect on middle-income students is much smaller: The range across five studies is 7.4–19.5 percent. Other results of the econometric studies are that the magnitude of the impact of student aid varies by type of aid, sex, race, and level of academic achievement. The seven studies differ in important respects: the manner in which income categories are delineated, the type of aid whose effects are examined, and the assumptions about the rules governing the awarding of aid (e.g., whether an award can be treated as a substitute for other aid). These differences limit the comparability of the results shown.

Four of the studies (Carroll, Mori, Relles, and Weinschrott, 1977; Jackson, 1978; Manski and Wise, 1983; Blakemore and Low, 1985) are based on data

Table 8.1

THE IMPACT OF STUDENT AID ON ACCESS: ECONOMETRIC STUDIES. ESTIMATED PERCENTAGE OF FULL-TIME ENROLLMENT DEPENDENT ON GRANT AID (BY LEVEL OF FAMILY INCOME)

	Family Income		
	Low	Middle	High
Range of Effects as Estimated in Various Studies	41.5	19.5	3.5
	37.3	14.1	3.0
	37.0	12.4	2.4
	34.4	11.1	
	32.1	7.4	
	30.8		
	20.6		
	19.5		
Mean	31.7	12.9	3.0

from the National Longitudinal Study (NLS) of 1972, which surveyed approximately 22,000 high school seniors across the nation. All four studies use complex statistical techniques and a great deal of control over factors that might be expected to influence the decision to enroll, factors such as characteristics of the students themselves, their families, or the high schools they attended, and the costs and other features of the colleges they plan to attend. It is important to note that the Basic Educational Opportunity Grant (BEOG) program was not yet funded in 1972. (BEOGs were renamed Pell Grants in 1980; the original name will be used in this chapter for studies that examine effects of this aid program in the 1970s, while the current name will be used for studies involving grant aid from 1980 onward.) The federal programs operated by the Office of Education in 1972 consisted of loans, College Work Study, and Supplemental Educational Opportunity Grants (SEOG). Veterans assistance, the largest program at that time, was not a factor in the NLS because this survey was administered to students before they had the opportunity to be in military service. In contrast, another large grant program, Social Security benefits for 18–22-year-olds with deceased or disabled parents, was a factor even though it was not need-based. Grants were also available from the institutions, of course, as they had been from the early years of higher education in this country, but the focus of this type of aid has traditionally included merit as well as need. The same is true for Merit Scholarships, which came into existence long before the 1970s.

Blakemore and Low (1985) found that financial aid offers in the form of grants have a significantly different impact on students of varying ethnic background, level of academic achievement, and family income. They estimated that a 30 percent drop in total grant aid per capita would result in the following percentage enrollment declines: white males, 5.2; white females, 7.1; black males, 8.5; and black females, 4.7. Among students with a 2.75 grade point average (GPA) and a family income of $11,000 or less (1982 dollars), the percentage declines were as follows: white males, 8.3; white females, 12.0; black males, 6.3; and black females, 3.5. The percentage declines were estimated to be much greater for students with lower (2.25) GPAs, but much smaller for students with higher (3.5) GPAs. For example, enrollment among low-income, low-GPA white males would decline 13.6 percent, compared to only 3.5 percent for low-income, high-GPA black males. Blakemore and Low did not provide aggregate data. To derive the composite figures shown in Table 8.1, we used their estimated rates for students with average GPAs along with weighted averages reflecting the relative number of enrolled students by sex and race, and we assumed that the effects of totally eliminating grant aid would be a linear extension of the effects of eliminating 30 percent of such aid. Race and gender differences in response to grant aid are explored in greater detail in an earlier study by Blakemore and Low (1983), with results similar to those reported here.

Manski and Wise (1983) used data from the NLS to build a simulation model that predicted the impact of the federal BEOG program on 1979–1980 freshmen enrollment in postsecondary education institutions. They derived alternative estimates based on whether BEOGs would replace or be complementary to other aid awards. Under the assumption that BEOGs would be substituted for other aid, their model estimates that low-income enrollment would decline by 37.3 percent in the absence of the BEOG awards. Enrollment of middle- and upper-income students, who together received 40 percent of all BEOG money in 1979–1980, would decrease by 11 percent and 2 percent, respectively, without the BEOG awards. The estimated effects of BEOGs on enrollment are of course more positive assuming that they complement other aid.

Manski and Wise concluded that the BEOG program is indeed effective in increasing access, but that a significant fraction of BEOG funds is spent as a pure subsidy. They calculated that in 1979–1980 only about 25 percent of BEOG awards went to students who would not otherwise have enrolled, compared to 39 percent in 1977–1978, when the BEOG program had less liberal income-eligibility requirements (i.e., it was limited more to low-income students). Since then, those requirements have been tightened again.

Carroll et al. (1977) also used data from the NLS to simulate the enrollment effects of BEOGs, but their approach differed from that of Manski and Wise in several important respects, including statistical techniques and objectives. The purpose of the Carroll et al. analysis was to investigate how various ways of implementing the BEOG program would affect the number of students induced to attend college. Among the policy alternatives examined were award ceilings, the percentage of cost covered by the grant, the percentage of need covered by the grant, and so on. The estimated enrollment effect of 20.6 percent, which is shown in Table 8.1, is the mean value for ten different simulations based on variations in these award rules.[1]

Carroll et al. found that none of the BEOG policies they considered had much effect on the enrollment behavior of nonwhite males. Nonwhite and white females were about equally responsive to aid. White males were more responsive to aid than were nonwhite males, but less responsive than were the females of either ethnic group. The results reported by Carroll et al. differ most from those of Blakemore and Low with respect to nonwhite males. Taken together, the results of the two studies suggest that the ethnic background and gender of students make a difference in the impact of student aid, but that more research needs to be done to sort out what is apparently a complex set of relationships and interactions among ethnicity, gender, and economic status.

Carroll and colleagues' findings are more congruent with Blakemore and Low's with respect to the differential impact of aid on students of differing academic abilities. The latter investigators found that low-income students of low ability were nearly four times as sensitive to aid offers in deciding whether to attend college than were low-income students of higher ability. For students of all income levels, Carroll et al. estimated that students in the lowest ability quartile were about twice as responsive to BEOG awards as students in the highest quartile. As these authors point out, high-ability students will attend college in relatively large numbers regardless of aid, but the same is not true for low-ability students. Many of the latter apparently require a cost reduction in order to achieve a favorable cost–benefit ratio for attending college.

One of the ways in which Jackson's (1978) study differs from the other three NLS-based studies is that he compared the impact of the awarding of aid with the impact of the amount of aid awarded. He found that the offer of aid has a much greater impact on access than does the amount of the award. This result is not totally surprising. The amount of aid, given some level of family income, is largely a function of the cost of attending a particular institution. Thus, for many students the amount of aid may have more effect on the choice of institution than on the basic decision to attend college.

In contrast to Jackson, Carlson (1975) reported that the amount of aid did have a statistically significant effect on enrollment. Carlson also estimated that loans and work study were only about half as effective as grants in stimulating enrollment of low-income students. Interestingly, loans were more effective than grants with respect to the enrollment of middle-income students.

[1]The percentages shown in Table 8.1 reflect the estimated percentage of students who would leave higher education without grant aid. The data in Carroll et al. (1977) is presented in the form of additional enrollment. For example, the mean effect for the 10 policy alternatives is a 26 percent increase in enrollment over the amount that would be present without the aid. That translates into a 20.6 percent drop in enrollment if the aid were to disappear. Given that aid is a fact of life, the latter mode of presenting the results seems more appropriate.

One other econometric study, Berne's (1980) analysis of factors affecting enrollment at community colleges, examined the effect of the award amount. In this case, one would expect the amount to influence access because at this type of institution, typically the lowest-cost alternative, many students are likely to be deciding between higher education enrollment and some other option. As expected, Berne found that the greater the amount of grant aid, the greater the positive effect on enrollment.

Crawford (1966) calculated that the presence of student aid led to an increase of 14.8 percent in the enrollment of financially needy National Merit Scholars of 1958–1959. The students involved, both those awarded as well as those denied aid, were highly talented (for example, both groups had average combined Scholastic Aptitude Test [SAT] scores of about 1250). Inasmuch as the work of Blakemore and Low and of Carroll et al. shows that the impact of grant aid on high-ability students is much less than on those with low or medium ability, and given the known correlation between academic performance and family income plus the greater response to aid by low-income youth, it is reasonable to assume that Crawford's estimate understates substantially the effect of aid on students overall, and especially on low-income students. If one adjusts Crawford's finding to reflect the impact of ability, by using the mean of the relationships estimated in the Carroll et al. and Blakemore and Low studies, the result is a low-income enrollment effect of about 37 percent.

The eighth econometric study did not contain sufficient data to present findings in the form required for inclusion in Table 8.1, but, in general, the results support those of the other studies. In this study, Weinschrott (1978) simulated the effects of grants and loans on the enrollment of students at several income levels, using data from the NLS. He found that grant aid induced additional enrollment of low-income students, while loans increased the enrollment of middle-income students. The average effects for loans, expressed as elasticities, were about 88 percent as large as the average effects for grants.

Finally, in simulating various effects of the Tuition Assistance Program (TAP) in New York, Mullen (1982) estimated that for every additional $100 in the average grant award (1982 dollars), low-income enrollment in New York higher education would increase by about 1.2 percent. Mullen suggests that the enrollment gain would have been larger had it not been for the presence of substantial amounts of aid available prior to the inception of the TAP.

Several studies presented usable data on the relative impact on enrollment of a decrease in tuition versus an increase of the same amount in grant aid. Theoretically, one would expect there to be little difference except that tuition tends to be known further in advance and is more definite. Despite the attention given to student aid in the media and, presumably, by high school counselors and college admissions recruiters, knowledge about student aid is anything but universal within the target population. For example, Olson and Rosenfeld (1984) report that 52 percent of surveyed parents of high school seniors in 1980 knew nothing about BEOG/Pell Grants. Given a lack of knowledge about the availability of aid, tuition should have a slightly greater impact than a comparable amount of grant aid (Hyde, 1978).

The empirical evidence in the access studies is inconclusive. Manski and Wise (1983) found that the estimated parameters for tuition, dormitory costs, and discretionary grant aid (not including BEOGs) were roughly similar for 4-year colleges and vocational-technical schools, but grant aid was nearly four times as potent as tuition at 2-year colleges—a relationship that the authors could not explain in terms of their model. In Blakemore and Low's (1985) model, a change in tuition was, on average, about three times as effective as a comparable change in grant aid. The difference in impact was smaller for males and greater for females, favoring tuition in both instances. Carlson (1975) estimated that a $100 increase in grant aid was just slightly less effective (.86, to be precise) than a $100 decrease in tuition as a way of increasing enrollment. In a study that will be discussed in more detail in the section on choice, Schwartz (1985) estimated that grant aid had more than twice the impact of a comparable amount of tuition at 4-year institutions, but warned of estimation problems. Only Carlson's finding and some of the estimates in Manski and Wise would seem to be plausible, but no more than that can be said on the basis of the available studies. Clearly, more research is warranted on this important question.

Surveys of Student Opinions

A second approach to assessing the impact of student aid on access is to ask students how they perceive that impact on their own attendance decisions. Table 8.2 shows the results of asking aid recipients whether they would attend college without a particular form of grant aid. All aid was need-based except in the Springer (1976) study of the Social Security program. Typically about one-fourth to one-half of those asked indicated that they would not attend either full-time or part-time without the aid. The 22 data points range from 22.5 percent to 67.1, with a mean value of 42.6 percent. As expected, the reported effects are greater for students from low-income families: The mean values were 45.4 percent for the lowest-income group and 35.1 percent for the middle-income group.

The results obtained by Fenske, Boyd, and Maxey (1979) for the Illinois state student aid program show an increasing effect of the program over the decade in which surveys were conducted. (The results of the first survey, in 1967, were exceptionally low; they are not included in Table 8.2 but can be found in Appendix Table 7.) The reason for this growth in the perceived impact of the Illinois aid programs is not apparent, nor do the authors of the study venture an opinion on the matter. They also found a larger effect for those awarded grants as opposed to merit-based scholarships. This was to be expected, they indicated, because the latter individuals presumably have greater motivation to attend and more options for financing their college education without

Table 8.2

THE IMPACT OF STUDENT AID ON ACCESS: STUDENT OPINION SURVEYS. ESTIMATED PERCENTAGE OF FULL-TIME ENROLLMENT DEPENDENT ON GRANT AID, BASED ON SURVEYS OF STUDENT AID RECIPIENTS (BY LEVEL OF FAMILY INCOME)

	Family Income		
	Low	Middle	Others
Range of Effects as Estimated in Various Studies	67.1	44.9	36.0*
	65.3	43.7	
	53.8	37.1	
	50.9	27.5	
	50.5	22.5	
	50.4		
	50.3		
	46.5		
	45.8		
	44.6		
	43.4		
	37.5		
	36.5		
	32.8		
	26.9		
	23.7		
Mean	45.4	35.1	36.0
Overall mean = 42.6			

*Social Security beneficiaries (Springer, 1976).

state student aid. However, mixed results were obtained by Fife and Leslie (1976) in their analysis of the grant and scholarship programs in New Jersey, perhaps because of differences in regulations governing the two types of aid.

In commenting on the differences among the states in their study, Fife and Leslie attributed the relatively small effects in California, 36.5 percent for low-income and 22.5 for middle-income recipients, to the availability of an inexpensive alternative should aid not be forthcoming. At that time, the state's community college system had no tuition.

The studies shown in Table 8.2 reflect the views of student aid recipients only. There are several student surveys that assess more broadly the effect of student aid on access. In a survey of high school seniors, Leslie et al. (1977) found that among those planning to attend college, 43.5 percent of low-income students, 27.7 percent of middle-income students, and 15.0 percent of high-income students said they could not attend without student aid. In a survey of Kentucky high school seniors who were eligible for need-based state aid but were denied assistance because of a shortage of funds in the aid program, Foreman, Lunceford, and Elton (1984) found that 44.8 percent of those who subsequently did not attend college attributed their failure to attend to insufficient student aid. During the 1950s and early 1960s, there was concern about the loss of talent represented by very able, low-income high school graduates who did not go on to college. A series of studies was done to estimate the portion of that loss that could be attributed to a lack of financial resources. Crawford (1966) reviewed five of those studies: The mean of the effects he reported was 47 percent. That is, an average of 47 percent of nonenrolled, highly talented recent high school graduates indicated that lack of money was the primary reason for their decision not to enroll in college.

How do the results of the student opinion studies in Table 8.2 compare with the results from the econometric studies? Because the aid-recipient surveys address the effect of state grant programs only, as opposed to that of all grant aid in the econometric studies, a straightforward comparison is not fully appropriate. Nonetheless, the results from the two sets of studies appear to be reasonably similar. For example, if we assume that two-thirds of low-income students receive grant aid, then according to the aid-recipient surveys the amount of enrollment dependent on grant aid would be .67 × .454 (from Table 8.2), or 30.4 percent. This figure is at the midpoint of the 20–40 percent range obtained from the econometric studies. If 33 percent of middle-income students are awarded grant aid, then .33 × .351, or 11.6 percent, of middle-income enrollment would be lost if grant aid were eliminated. The comparable range in the econometric studies was 7.4–19.5 percent.[2]

[2]The number of students who are in a particular income category and who receive aid can only be estimated. The .67 figure for low-income students is probably conservative. The number of Pell Grants awarded annually, around 2.5 to 2.9 million, is about the same as the number of full-time low-income students (see the summary at the conclusion of the access section). In 1981–1982, 67 percent of Pell Grants went to students with individual or family incomes of $15,000 or less (Gillespie and Carlson, 1983, p. 17). Although a Pell Grant is the cornerstone for most need-based aid, it is fair to assume that some low-income students who do not receive Pell Grants receive some other form of grant aid. Thus, .67 is a conservative estimate of the proportion of low-income students receiving grant aid. The .33 figure for middle-income students is less certain. In 1981–1982, about 860,000 Pell Grants went to students from families with incomes over $15,000. Based on an estimated 3.2 million full-time middle-income students, that translates into 26 percent receiving the most basic form of grant aid. Presumably there are middle-income students who receive grant aid, but not in the form of a Pell Grant. According to an analysis of the High School and Beyond survey (Carroll, 1984), the percent of middle-income students in 1981–1982 receiving grant aid in some form averaged 38 percent (unweighted) across four institutional types. Presumably, some of these students received merit rather than need-based grants, so the figure needed for the calculation in question is probably somewhat less than 38 percent but more than 26 percent. The 33 percent figure used to calculate the middle-income enrollment effect is simply a "ballpark" estimate. In any case, any figure within 10 percentage points of 33 percent would still result in estimated enrollment effects within the 7.4–19.5 range established in the econometric studies.

Participation Rate Calculations

It is not possible to integrate the results of the participation rate studies in the manner accomplished in previous sections and chapters. Income categories, which are needed to isolate the target populations, vary widely among the studies. On some occasions the focus is on the very poor, while in other studies the focus is on families with less than the median income. The studies also differ with respect to the age category for which participation rates are calculated, such as 18–21-year-olds versus 18–24-year-olds. In addition, the studies examine different intervals of time within a 22-year period (1961 to 1983).

Table 8.3 presents data from those studies. Two general observations are in order. First, because many different populations are represented in the table, the comparability of rows of data is limited. Second, the studies provide data either for consecutive years or for years separated by long intervals of time. The sometimes substantial year-to-year variability in participation rates documented in the former studies would seem to put at risk any conclusions one might draw from the latter studies. For example, one of the more recent studies (Lee and Associates, 1984) comparing rates for college-eligible 18–24-year-olds uses 1969 as a starting point and 1974 as an intermediate point. Leslie's data for that age group (though not limited to the college-eligible population) shows that the rates in 1969 were substantially higher than in the years immediately preceding or following it. The opposite was true for rates in 1974. Thus, while the decline from 1969 to 1974 recorded in the Lee study did take place, the data are somewhat misleading with respect to overall trends in participation rates—if one can speak meaningfully of overall trends.

Probably the best known of the participation rate studies was done by Hansen (1983), who looked at the average of participation rates for the fall of 1971 and 1972 compared to the average of rates for the fall of 1978 and 1979, for 18–24-year-old dependent students from families with incomes above versus below the median. Despite the massive increase in student aid during this period, the participation rate for low-income students actually decreased. As shown in Table 8.3, the average for the early period was 16.0 percent compared to 15.7 percent for the later period. Meanwhile, the rate for students from families with above-median incomes increased slightly, from 34.4 percent to 34.6 percent. Thus the ratio of below- to above-median income participation rates deteriorated. In other words, individuals from families with incomes below the median lost ground absolutely as well as relative to individuals from more affluent families.

Hansen's study received a good deal of criticism. In essence, the critics argued that participation rate data can be generated in a variety of ways and that Hansen had made some inappropriate choices. The data in Table 8.3 show that other studies examined nearly the same period as Hansen but came to different conclusions based on different age groups, income categories, and student classifications. However, the results from these other studies are not one-sided with respect to Hansen's findings.

Table 8.3

THE IMPACT OF STUDENT AID ON ACCESS: PARTICIPATION RATE CALCULATIONS

Author Year of publication	Population: 1982 income/age group	Percentage of Individuals Enrolled or Planning to Enroll in Higher Education																		
		1961	1966	1967	1968	1969	1970	1971	1972	1973	1974	1975	1976	1977	1978	1979	1980	1981	1982	1983
Leslie 1977	< $9100			13.9	17.0	18.2	15.8	16.7	16.7	15.0	14.6	17.2								
	$9100–$18200			27.1	28.3	29.2	27.2	27.0	26.5	23.7	23.2	26.7								
	Families with full-time 18–24 dependents																			
Suter 1977	< $9,500																			
	White						19.9						20.0							
	Black						15.2						20.2							
	18–24 dependents																			
Peng 1979	< $14300																			
	Men			22.1	23.1	25.9	20.7	22.0	21.5	19.9	19.5	20.2	18.9							
	Women			17.5	21.9	23.5	20.8	23.7	23.9	20.3	21.4	27.4	26.4							
	> $42900																			
	Men			71.0	66.7	70.5	63.7	61.9	57.3	56.8	56.0	56.5	54.5							
	Women			65.2	58.3	58.6	59.3	61.6	56.4	56.4	59.5	63.6	63.1							
	18–24 dependents																			
Frances 1980	< $14300			20.0	22.5	24.8	20.8	22.8	22.6	20.1	20.3	23.5	22.4	22.6						
	$14300–$28600			37.9	38.5	38.8	36.6	35.4	34.2	31.2	31.7	35.1	36.3	34.4						
	> $42900			68.3	63.0	65.2	61.7	61.8	56.8	56.6	57.5	59.6	58.2	59.8						
	18–24 dependents																			
Longanecker 1980	< $9100				35.0						33.0				34.0					
	$9100–$18200				47.0						35.0				35.0					
	> $48500				76.0						63.0				60.0					
	17–22 dependents with h.s. diploma																			

Davis & Johns 1982	Lowest quartile**		12.4		22.4				17.2			20.6			
	Below median**		34.7		45.6				44.5			45.2			
	Full-time freshman														
Frances 1982	< $6100							9.5				14.3			
	$6100–$12100							19.1				18.0			
	> $30300							50.8				50.4			
	Families with full-time 18–24 dependents														
Tierney 1982a	Lowest quartile						12.1				13.4				
	2nd lowest quartile						12.7				13.3				
	18–34-year-olds														
Hansen 1983	Below median				16.0					15.7					
	18–24 dependents														
Lee & Associates 1984	< $13000														
	18–24 dependents*			39.2				33.0					33.0		
	Men			42.8				34.0					29.7		
	Women			35.6				32.1					36.1		
	18–24 independents*			12.7				15.0					15.9		
Lee, Rotermund, & Bertschman 1985	< $10000														
	Black									32.7				22.7	
	Hispanic									23.5				26.7	
	White									27.6				25.8	
	18–24 dependents*														
Clowes, Hinkle, & Smart 1986	Lowest SES quartile														
	Recent h.s. graduates														
	Men	30.0				32.0								39.0	
	Women	29.0				33.0								42.0	
Lee 1986	< $10900									30.3			28.2		25.7
	$10900–$21800									36.0			34.6		31.3
	> $32600									49.9			52.8		52.4
	18–24 dependents*														

*College eligible: high school graduates, not institutionalized, civilians, without a bachelor's degree.
**Enrollment shares; income levels are for families with head of family between 35 and 64 years of age.

Tierney (1982a), for instance, looked at the participation rate for 18–34-year-olds in the lower-income quartile. Over the period from 1973 to 1979, the participation rate of this group increased from 12.1 to 13.4 percent. The role that student aid played in this advance is debatable, of course, as is true for most participation rate changes. Frances (1982) calculated participation rates for families that had less than $6100 (1982 dollars) in inflation-adjusted income and that had one or more 18–24-year-old dependents enrolled full-time in college. Those rates increased from 9.5 to 14.3 percent between 1974 and 1980. According to Frances, her results are in direct contradiction to Hansen's.

Another study focused on a particularly appropriate target group. Clowes, Hinkle, and Smart (1986) compared participation rates for recent high school graduates over a 21-year period. One of the data disaggregations they made was by socioeconomic status (SES), which in part is a measure of income. As shown in Table 8.3, participation rates for women increased substantially in the lowest SES quartile, going from 29 percent in 1961, to 33 percent in 1972, to 42 percent in 1982. For men, the comparable figures are 30, 32, and 39 percent, respectively. As is true for the results of the Tierney and Frances studies, the upward movement in participation rates for these low-SES students certainly presents a more favorable picture of the presumed effects of student aid than that provided by Hansen's data.

Rates also increased in the other SES categories in the Clowes et al. study. If one takes a ratio of participation rates over the full period, the lowest SES quartile will be seen to gain slightly vis-à-vis the highest SES quartile, but not from 1972 to 1982, when considerable ground was given back by the lower quartile. This result, that the poor did not do well relative to the affluent during the 1970s, a period when student aid increased dramatically, supports Hansen's findings.

Table 8.3 contains additional data suggesting that low-income students have not gained ground on high-income students since the early 1970s. Davis and Johns (1982) calculated the percentage of full-time college freshmen coming from families with less than the median income (for all families with heads of family between ages 35 and 64) for each of 4 years. If there were no barriers to entry and all else were equal, one would expect that 50 percent of the freshmen would fit that criterion. As the data show, in 1966 only 34.7 percent of all freshmen surveyed came from families with below-median incomes. By 1971, the number had jumped to 45.6 percent, but it was to go no further, slipping to 44.5 percent in 1976 and edging up to just 45.2 percent in 1980. Davis and Johns also examined the percentage of freshmen coming from families at or below the first quartile of income for all families. In this case the "no barrier" indicator is, of course, 25 percent. The figures show a very substantial gain from 1966 to 1971, going from 12.4 percent to 22.4 percent. By 1980, however, the figure had slid backward to 20.6 percent.

Hansen (1983) was criticized for excluding independent students from his analysis of participation rates. This criticism applies equally well to most of the participation rate studies. As the "population" column in Table 8.3 shows, most of the studies focus exclusively on dependent students, despite the fact that the proportion of students who are classified as independent is increasing and that a very large proportion of these students receive student aid (especially grants). As indicated in the table, the participation rate of independent students increased from 12.7 percent in 1969, to 15.0 percent in 1974, to 15.9 percent in 1981 (Lee and Associates, 1984). According to St. John and Byce (1982), the proportion of independent students who receive federal grants increased from 27 to 37 percent between 1976 and 1979. About 40 percent of all Pell Grant awards now go to independent students (Hossler, 1984). If independent students were to be included in the calculation of participation rates, the observed changes in rates would probably present a more favorable *prima facie* case for the positive effects of student aid. In any event, as Hansen and Stampen (1986) point out, the shift of student aid resources toward independent students marks a significant change in the functioning of federal student aid, especially because nearly 60 percent of independent aid recipients are 25-years-old or older.

The increasing participation of women in higher education is a well-known phenomenon. How about low-income women? Have they kept pace? The data in Table 8.3 show how sensitive this question is to the population and time interval examined. Measured from 1967 to 1976, low-income, 18–24-year-old dependent women increased their participation almost 9 percentage points (Peng, 1979). For the population of college-eligible 18–24-year-old dependents, the low-income female participation rate hardly changed at all from 1969 to 1981 (Lee and Associates, 1984). Among recent high school graduates, low-income females increased their participation rates substantially between 1972 and 1982 (Clowes et al., 1986). The difference in perspective is even greater for their male counterparts—a dramatic decrease for the 18–24-year-old college-eligible group versus a substantial increase for recent high school graduates (a difference only partially explainable, it would seem, by starting one interval in 1969 and one in 1972). The role played by student aid in these developments is certainly not obvious.

The overall (non-income-specific) participation rate for blacks, when measured in terms of high school graduates, went into a sharp decline after peaking in 1976 and equaling the white participation rate in that year. By 1982 it was lower than in 1967 (Marks, 1985). When measured by the participation rate among college-eligible individuals from families with less than $10,000 income, blacks experienced a substantial 10 percentage point drop in participation between 1978 and 1982 (Lee, Rotermund, and Bertschman, 1985). Hispanics have done somewhat better. In terms of overall participation rates for high school graduates, they, too, experienced a decline: from 35.5 percent in 1975 to 29.9 percent in 1981. However, as shown in Table 8.3, low-income Hispanics increased their participation rate from 23.5 percent in 1978 to 26.7 percent in 1982, compared to the large decline for blacks and a small (1.8 percentage points) drop for whites (Lee et al., 1985). Some observers, such as Marks (1985), attribute the decline in black participation rates in part to the increasing emphasis on loans, as opposed to grants, in federal student aid. If this is correct, other forces must be operating on Hispanics.

Participation rates are the result of a complex network of interrelated socioeconomic factors. A complete discussion of these factors is well beyond the scope of this book. We are compelled, however, to at least mention a few matters that must have played an important, although not fully understood, role during the period analyzed in the participation rate studies.

Many of those studies use the late 1960s or early 1970s as a pivotal point in calculating participation rates and rate changes. This is the time when the nation's military involvement in Vietnam both reached its peak and began a precipitous decline. The war itself, the draft, educational deferments from the draft, the end of the draft (in 1973), and the creation of large numbers of individuals eligible for veterans benefits surely must have affected participation rates. Indeed, as Lee (1986) and others have emphasized, even the basic arithmetic of participation rates was affected, because at least some rate calculations are based on a definition of the college-eligible population that excludes persons living on military bases or overseas. Nearly 2.4 million 18–24-year olds were in the military in 1969, compared to just 1.2 million in 1973.

As important as were Vietnam and related matters, participation rate behavior suggests that the most important long-term influences are basic movements in society. Developments in the 1960s related to civil rights, the women's movement, and egalitarianism in general may have been the driving forces behind the increase in participation rates for lower-income individuals during the late 1960s and through much of the 1970s. These developments interacted in complex ways with the war and the nascent and then full-blown federal student aid programs. For example, one of the forms taken by egalitarianism in many states was an effort to make higher education, often in the form of community colleges, available to virtually everyone. It is likely that this effort to increase the supply in itself led to an increase in the demand for higher education, particularly among low-income students who are the primary targets of federal student aid programs.

Economic factors are important, too. For example, participation rates for all students increased substantially in 1975. That was a year in which funding for BEOGs increased substantially over the prior year; however, it was also a time of economic recession, which meant that enrollment probably increased in part because of the lower opportunity cost of attendance. In addition, 1975 was a year when the average increase in tuition was smaller than the increase in the Consumer Price Index, another reason for an enrollment increase.

From the perspective of the low-income student, the economics of student aid deteriorated from the mid-1970s to the early 1980s. In the first place, the amount of grant aid available on a per-student basis declined in real terms.

The maximum Pell Grant award in 1983–1984 was $1800. To equal the purchasing power of the maximum grant in 1974, the 1983–1984 maximum would had to have been $3000 (Lee et al., 1985).

Second, grant aid per student compared to the cost of attendance declined markedly. By 1982–1983, the dollar value of a Pell Grant had declined to about 30 percent of student costs at public universities, one-third less than in 1978–1979 (Marks, 1985).

Third, the composition of available aid changed, which may have affected the extent to which overall aid was a stimulus to low-income enrollment. From fiscal year 1976 to fiscal year 1981, for example, the proportion of student aid in the form of grants decreased from 77 to 50 percent of all federal and state aid (Gillespie and Carlson, 1983), when all loan monies, rather than just the loan subsidies, are included. If just the loan subsidies are used in the calculation, and assuming that they are worth about one-half of the face value of the loans, the comparable change in the proportion of grants is from about 86 to 65 percent; calculated in the same way and with the same assumption, the proportion of grants continued to decline, reaching a level of just over 50 percent by 1986. These changes were due to growth in the loan programs and to a decrease in grants in the form of veterans benefits. At one point in the mid-1970s, veterans educational benefits totaled more than $4 billion a year. By the early 1980s, this program had shrunk to about $1 billion annually. In 1 year alone, 1976, the number of veterans enrolled declined by 370,000 (Stampen, 1980). The decline in special grant programs continued well into the 1980s, as the educational benefits program within the Social Security system was phased out entirely by the middle of the decade. At its peak, the program distributed grant aid totaling more than $2 billion annually. Cutbacks in these programs must have had a negative effect on absolute low-income enrollment rates, even though the programs were not need-based.

Singular, even accidental, events can be important, too. For example, Stampen notes that clerical errors in 1978 resulted in an inadvertent doubling of BEOG rejections (from 20 to 40 percent of applicants, or 500,000 in all). This development may have been partly the reason why historically black institutions experienced an enrollment decline in 1978 after enjoying enrollment increases in every year from 1970 through 1977.

There do seem to have been circumstances, then, that might explain why the theoretically expected, empirically demonstrated (in the econometric studies at least) positive effects of student aid are not more apparent in the historic participation rates of low-income students. Of course, one can never be fully comfortable with these *ex post facto* explanations, anymore than with the rate data themselves. More than anything else, perhaps, the plausibility of the explanations shows how difficult it is to assess the effect of student aid on the basis of participation rates.

Regardless of how participation rates may have changed, the fact remains that low-income students still attend at considerably lower rates than do high-income students, despite the presence of great amounts of student aid. It is the interpretation of this fact that is problematic. The explanations offered by investigators suggest that perhaps the money barrier comes and goes to some extent and that it may have grown in the early 1980s. However, the relatively low participation rates for low-income students may not be due solely to a money barrier, at least not the barrier that student aid is designed to overcome, that is, the cost of attendance. Borus and Carpenter (1984), using data from the 1979 and 1980 National Longitudinal Surveys of Youth Labor Market Experience, found that when family background variables such as lower parental education were controlled (held constant), the percentages of poor youth going on to college were not statistically different from those who were not poor. When those family characteristics were not statistically controlled (i.e., when they were allowed to have their natural effect), youth from poorer families were less likely to attend college. This finding suggests that further enhancement of the participation rate of low-income students might require an earlier intervention of some kind other than conventional forms of student aid.

Summary for Access

Overall, the results for access are as follows. All of the econometric analyses and student opinion surveys indicate that student aid, at least in the form of grants, does increase the enrollment of low-income individuals. The results of the participation rate studies do not lend themselves to unambiguous interpretation, but most studies indicate that a greater proportion of eligible low-income individuals were participating in higher education in the early 1980s than prior to the advent of the major federal grant program (BEOG/Pell).

The econometric analyses suggest that about 20–40 percent of low-income enrollment is the result of grant aid. How many students do these percentages represent? Rough estimates, pegged to 1982–1983, can be developed as follows. Data on the number of full-time, low-income students in higher education are not readily available. The most recent data available are for 1978–1979 (in Frances, 1982). If $12,000 in 1978 dollars is chosen as the cutoff point for low-income families—median income in calendar year 1978 was $17,640—then 37.4 percent of all full-time students in higher education in 1978–1979 came from low-income families. If the proportion of low-income students remained about the same into the 1980s, and given that higher education enrolled about 7 million full-time students per year during that time, then the full-time, low-income group would have numbered about 2.6 million. Given that number, the econometric results indicate that in 1982–1983 about 500,000 to 1 million low-income students were enrolled in college because of grant aid. If 45.9 percent of all full-time students continued to come from middle-income families (defined as families with incomes from $12,000 to $30,000 in 1978), as they did in 1978, and the enrollment of 13 percent of such students is dependent on grant aid (the mean value from Table 8.1), then grant aid accounted for the enrollment of 415,000 middle-income students. In all, then, the econometric studies suggest that in 1982–1983 about 900,000 to 1.4 million full-time students were enrolled because of student aid in the form of grants. The midpoint of those figures, 1.15 million, is about 45 percent of the annual number of Pell Grants awards and represents roughly 16.4 percent of all full-time students in that year.

Comparable estimates based on the student opinion surveys in Table 8.2 lead to rather similar conclusions. About 51 percent of all full-time students receive some student aid, not counting Guaranteed Student Loans (Anderson, 1984). If we assume that about 10 percent of the recipients received no grant aid in 1982–1983, that would leave about 3 million students receiving grant aid of some kind (an assumption is required because of the lack of recipient information that cuts across types of aid). In any case, 3 million would seem to be a conservative estimate, given that the Pell Grant program alone accounted for 2.5 million recipients. Multiplying 3 million by 42.6 percent (the overall mean value from Table 8.2) yields an estimate of 1.3 million students whose enrollment in 1982–1983 depended on grant aid.

A third estimate can be generated using the results of the student demand studies in Chapter 7. The modal result from those studies was that a $100 decrease in tuition is accompanied by a 1.8 percent increase in enrollment. Let us assume, for the sake of argument, the correctness of Carlson's (1975) estimate that $100 dollars in grant aid is .86 times as effective as $100 in tuition. Then for every $100 in the average grant aid offer, we would expect a 1.55 percent enrollment increase among those offered aid. To obtain a rough estimate of the amount of grant aid available for low- and middle-income students, the target population, let us assume that they received all of Pell, SEOG, veterans benefits, and state grants, plus $1 billion in institutional grants, for a total of $7.3 billion in grant aid (as of 1982–1983). The number of full-time low- and middle-income students is 5.3 million, based on the data from Frances (1982) previously cited. Dividing the total amount of grant aid by the total number of students results in an estimate of $1400 as the average aid offer. The arithmetic, then, is simply $14 \times .0155 \times 5.3$ million, and the result is an estimate that grant aid was responsible for the enrollment of roughly 1.2 million full-time students. In reality, of course, students will be offered aid that is less than or more than the average, or they will not be offered any aid, so the arithmetic is a considerable simplification. The assumption is that these phenomena will have a tendency to cancel one another, so that the simplification can stand as a reasonable estimate. For example, if some students do not receive aid, then the average award to those who do will increase, which in turn will result in a larger portion of the aid recipients enrolling than would have been the case with smaller average awards.

Whether readers will attribute the similarity of these three estimates to the discovery of truth, to chance, or to the ingenuity of the authors of this book will depend, perhaps, on the extent to which they are comfortable with the numerous assumptions and intermediate estimates used. From our perspective, the estimate that best reflects the studies reviewed is that in 1982–1983 the enrollment of about 1–1.3 million full-time students was dependent on grant aid.

CHOICE

By lowering the cost of attendance, student aid helps make it possible for individuals of limited financial means to participate in higher education in some form. The question addressed in this section is whether student aid also helps make it possible for those same individuals to attend the full range of higher education institutions.

Student aid achieves its purpose to the extent that it reduces the number of occasions when income dictates where a student enrolls. The issue is sometimes framed as though it were a matter of ensuring that students can attend their first-choice institution. This is a less satisfactory way of defining the objective. It is highly probable that student and family income play an important role in shaping the initial choice set, that is, the range of institutions initially considered to be viable options. If disproportionately large numbers of low-income students have low cost and less prestigious institutions as their first choices, and there is some evidence for this suggestion (Munday, 1976), then realizing those choices would not achieve the goal of equal opportunity.

With few exceptions, the research studies reviewed in this section focus on the enrollment distribution of students from different income levels. The distributions considered important are those between high cost and low cost institutions, public and private institutions, and institutions that differ by status: 2-year and 4-year colleges, and universities. Because control (public versus private) and status typically are correlated with price, most studies are in effect examining enrollment choices in relation to the price of attendance. Nonetheless, the other distinctions are important in their own right. There is evidence to suggest that an individual's postschooling economic and social position in society is heavily influenced by the type and caliber of college he or she attends (Trusheim and Crouse, 1981). Other interests are at stake as well. Allowing students a wide range of choices has the secondary effect of promoting institutional diversity. Appropriately configured, student aid will reduce the tuition gap between public and private institutions, thereby helping the latter institutions remain competitive, especially among low-income students.

For expository purposes, the studies reviewed are again organized by their general investigatory approach: econometric analyses, student opinion surveys, and compilations of participation rates (in the form of enrollment shares by type of institution). As was true for access, the number of studies concerning the effects of student aid on student choice is modest given the complexity of the issue. Nonetheless, the studies are sufficient to show beyond any reasonable doubt that student aid does help ensure choice. They also provide some idea of the magnitude of that effect.

Econometric Analyses

A total of 23 econometric analyses were found that analyze how student financial aid impacts on student choice. No one analytic approach was used in all of them; instead, three distinct approaches predominated. In the first set of studies to be reviewed, the focus is on choice effects as viewed from an institutional perspective. In the second set of studies, the research centers on the choice effects of federal and state student aid programs. In the third set of studies, student choice patterns are examined without reference to specific institutions or aid programs. Only one of the three approaches leads to results that can be synthesized quantitatively, but each approach leads to findings that are of some interest. A brief outline of several important findings will serve to organize the presentation that follows. Further details on the individual studies can be found in Appendix Table 7.

The econometric studies converge around the following results:

1. Institutions can improve their ability to recruit students by using student aid. In situations in which students are clearly choosing between two or more institutions, student aid that reduces the net price difference by $100 will have a positive enrollment effect of about 1.8 percent on the higher cost institution.
2. The effect of Pell Grants on student choice is unclear. The studies that have examined this issue have come up with conflicting results. The positive choice effects of state student aid programs have been more clearly established.
3. Application and enrollment patterns for a variety of students at least hint that student aid has had a beneficial effect on student choice.

In addition to these findings, some patterns mentioned in the previous section again appear. Students from low-income families are the most sensitive to the price of attendance and to the awarding of student aid. Aid in the form of grants has the largest effect on the enrollment behavior of students from low-income families.

The largest group of studies, 10 in all, examined the choice effects of student aid from the perspective of institutions in direct competition for students. The estimate of the effect of a $100 decrease in the net price difference between competing institutions is based on 4 of those studies (Berne, 1980; Tierney, 1980; Tierney, 1982; Tierney and Davis, 1985). The methodology used in these studies was standard regression or logit analysis of the choice behavior of students who had applied to more than one type of institution. The choices examined were between public and private institutions, different types of public and private institutions, and between community colleges and other types of institutions. In all of the studies, a great deal of control was exercised statistically over student and institutional characteristics. The net price variables consistently performed as one would expect theoretically.

The four studies produced 11 data points. The data initially took the form of changes in enrollment probabilities. These data were standardized to reflect the percentage change in enrollment that would be experienced by the higher cost institution (in the various institutional pairings) if it reduced the price differential with the lower cost institution by $100 (in 1982 dollars). The value of 1.8 percent is both the median and the mean value for the results distribution, although the range is large (.8 percent to 3.6 percent).

By extrapolation from the 1.8 percent figure, the impact of aid that changes the net price difference by $1000 would have a positive low-income enrollment effect on the higher cost, aid-awarding institution of 18 percent. In other words, for every 100 low-income applicants who would have chosen an institution with significantly lower costs, the higher cost institution would enroll 18 additional students, from the 100 applicants, by raising its average aid award by $1000. This figure should be used with caution, however. In two of the studies (Tierney, 1982b; Tierney and Davis, 1985) the authors warn that the certainty of the estimated effects are inversely related to the size of the change in the net-price differential, and, of course, linear extrapolation typically carries some risk. Still, some comfort can be taken in the fact that the estimate does not seem out of line when viewed from the perspective of the results of the studies on access and, more generally, the results of the student demand studies in Chapter 7. In addition, in Tierney's (1980) study in which he examined the choice between attending a public and a private institution, nearly 18 percent of the enrollment choice behavior of students from low-income families was explained by student aid after controlling for a variety of student and institutional characteristics. These two virtually identical percentage figures, while they address the same underlying issue, do so in fundamentally different ways. Thus, the most that one can say of their similarity is that it suggests that these studies may have given us a reasonably good fix on the order of magnitude of the effects in question.

The remaining studies from the institutional perspective offer some additional support for the direction if not the magnitude of the preceding results. In one segment of a study by Astin, Christian, and Henson (1980), the focus was again on students who had applied to, and been accepted by, more than one institution. In these situations, it was found that grants generally were the most influential form of aid. For students choosing between two private institutions, the size of the difference in grant aid offers was highly correlated with subsequent student choice, with students favoring the institution that offered the most aid. For the choice between a public and a private institution, the most important variable was the net cost at the private institution.

In a study by Jackson (1977), using a different methodology, an institution that offered some aid to all its applicants could expect to increase its matriculation rate of accepted freshmen by nearly 17 percent (although increasing the average aid award had only a miniscule effect on enrollment). At a public university, Fields and LeMay (1973) compared matched samples of individuals who had applied and been accepted for admission and who had applied for aid. Some of the students subsequently were awarded aid and some were not. Among those awarded aid, the matriculation rate was 33 percent higher than among those denied aid. A difficulty in interpreting this result is that no control was exercised in the analysis over aid offers that may have come from other institutions. Hoenack and Weiler (1979) found positive choice effects for student aid at a public flagship university. Miller (1981) showed that loans and work study have a negative impact on enrollment when substituted for grants in the aid award packages at an elite private institution.

In a simulation study of college-specific grants and loans, Weinschrott (1978) found significant positive effects and negative cross effects for grants. That is, college-specific grants tended to increase enrollments at the institutions awarding them, and the increases came at the expense of other institutions. Most of the effects occurred for low- or middle-income students. Four-year institutions at various cost levels were able to attract additional students. College-specific loans did not have widespread effects, but there was some evidence that loans from medium to high cost institutions attracted some students away from low cost 2-year and 4-year institutions.

In the section on access, we reviewed strong and fairly consistent evidence that grant aid, often in the form of Pell Grants, induced additional enrollment in higher education. One of the issues addressed in a second set of choice studies is whether Pell Grants, known as BEOGs at the time when most of the studies were conducted, and designed primarily as a means of ensuring access, also have a demonstrable effect on the overall distribution of students by institutional type. To be more specific, has the Pell Grant program resulted in a shift from 2-year to 4-year institutions, or from public to private institutions, or from less costly to more costly institutions? An affirmative answer to one or more of these options could be taken as evidence that Pell Grants do contribute to choice as well as to access. Similar questions can be asked about state student aid programs.

The evidence with respect to BEOG/Pell Grants is conflicting, to say the least. As noted in the discussion of access, Carroll et al. (1977) used a simulation model to examine how the predicted effects of the BEOG program would change depending on the award rules. They found that in almost all cases enrollments at higher cost institutions were enhanced the most, in comparison to enrollments at lower cost institutions, by the presence of BEOGs, regardless of the rules. Carroll et al. examined 10 different policy sets for BEOGs. Measured by the increase in low-income enrollment, the average effect for public institutions was 23.6 percent compared to 40.6 percent for private institutions, an advantage for the latter of 17 percentage points. The differences were even greater for institutional segments within the sectors. For example, public 2-year colleges gained only 14.5 percent compared to a 49.4 percent gain at high tuition public 4-year institutions. Medium and high tuition private institutions gained the most, 135 and 115 percent, respectively. Low tuition private institutions were the one exception to the general trend of these results; their low-income enrollment gain was only 3.2 percent. The relative percentages reflect in part, of course, the original (pregrant) enrollment of low-income students. The small low-income enrollment at higher cost private institutions contributed to the extremely large percentage increases in the simulation exercise.

In Weinschrott's (1978) study, general grants, that is, grants that can be spent at any institution, were found to increase enrollments at several types of institutions. The largest increases were predicted to occur at low cost 2-year colleges and low cost 4-year colleges. Smaller increases were predicted for middle and high cost 4-year colleges. The pattern was nearly identical for loans, except that grants influenced low-income students, while loans had their effect on middle-income students.

Weinschrott's findings are, in a sense, somewhere between those of Carroll et al. and those of Manski and Wise (1983). As indicated, Carroll et al. found very strong choice effects, in that BEOGs dramatically increased low-income enrollments at middle and high cost 4-year institutions. Weinschrott found that public grants and loans led to only modest increases of that kind, while Manski and Wise found almost no increases at all at 4-year institutions in their study of the BEOG program. In the Manski and Wise study, almost all of the enrollment increases occurred at 2-year colleges or vocational-technical schools. The Astin et al. (1980) results seem to support those of Manski and Wise and of Weinschrott: Receiving a BEOG tended to be associated with enrolling in less selective institutions, including less selective private institutions. Astin et al. cautioned against drawing conclusions about causal effects, however, citing the possibility that some institutions may actively encourage students to apply for BEOGs after the students have already applied and been accepted.

Schwartz (1986) found that public grants (including Pell Grants) accounted for about 22 percent of the low-income enrollment, 12 percent of the middle-income enrollment, and 3 percent of the high-income enrollment in 4-year colleges. Schwartz looked for but did not find evidence that either loan subsidies or private grants affected enrollment at these institutions. Confirmation of the direction of these effects for public grants can be found in Carlson (1980). He found that when tuition and the percentage of federal aid in the form of grants were held constant, an increase in federal aid was accompanied by an increase in the enrollment rate for students of all income levels in 4-year public institutions. Both the Schwartz and Carlson data included SEOGs as well as BEOGs. Since SEOGs are used predominantly by higher cost institutions, this could help account for the positive effects of public grants on enrollments at 4-year institutions.

The Schwartz and Carlson findings appear to represent fairly strong support for the beneficial effects of grant aid on choice, given the tendency of low-income students to be underrepresented in 4-year colleges. Schwartz's study is especially important because he used a data sample, the High School and Beyond survey of high school seniors of 1980, that is a better representation of the aid picture in the 1980s than is the NLS, which is used in so many of the other econometric studies. His results, however, as well as Carlson's, do not indicate how the overall pattern of enrollment is being affected by grants. Conceivably, the enrollment gains at public 4-year colleges could have come at the expense of 2-year colleges, which typically would be viewed as a gain for choice, or at the expense of private colleges, which typically would be viewed as a loss for choice, or at the expense of neither, which could be interpreted as a gain for choice and probably access as well. (In a related analysis of the same data, Schwartz [1985] concludes that whereas public grants lead to an increase in wealth neutrality with respect to enrollment in public 4-year colleges, a decrease in tuition would lead to a decrease in wealth neutrality.)

Kehoe (1981) found that state grants had greater power to discriminate between students' institutional choices than did BEOGs. His analysis focused on in-state versus out-of-state institutional choices.

All this adds up to a complex and somewhat confusing picture of the effects of BEOG/Pell Grants, which have come to be the most ubiquitous form of grant aid. Low-income students can qualify for a Pell Grant by attending virtually any type of higher education institution. Because Pell Grants are so widespread, it may be difficult to determine accurately their differential effects on different types of institutions. In many, if not most, instances Pell Grants are the base upon which an aid package is built. Thus, it is not surprising that although Pell Grants *may* tend to be associated with enrollment at less expensive institutions, SEOGs have been associated with enrollment at more expensive institutions (Astin et al., 1980). Pell Grants suffice at the former institutions. Supplemental aid is more often needed at the higher priced institutions where a Pell Grant is not sufficient, even if it is a larger award than would be given at a lower priced school. Financial aid officers commonly employ campus-based aid (SEOGs, NDSLs, and CWS) and then the institution's own funds to "fill out" the student aid package after the Pell Grant amount is known. Perhaps, therefore, it is not surprising that it is easier to assess the relationship of Pell Grants to access than to choice.

Using a very different approach than in any of the previously mentioned studies, Zollinger (1984) constructed hypothetical college choice sets for a sample of Illinois state scholarship recipients. The choice set for each student consisted of institutions that the student might reasonably attend given the student's academic ability. He found that financial aid increased the proportion of students who were able to afford the least costly one-quarter of the institutions in their choice set from 13 percent to 44 percent, a gain of 31 percentage points. Generally, there was little difference in the impact of aid with respect to male versus female students or students of low versus high academic ability. By contrast, although aid increased college choice for minorities, blacks and other minorities were still not able, on average, to attend colleges in their choice sets as frequently as white students. The amount of available aid apparently was not enough to compensate fully for generally lower family income among the minority students, especially blacks. Zollinger concluded that aid is helping to enhance choice, but that college choice remains linked to family income.

The first set of studies in this section examined choice effects from the institutional perspective. The second set investigated the extent to which the Pell Grant program can impact or has impacted on choice, as well as the effects of state grant aid programs. A third set of studies consists of analyses that, while they are less cohesive than the previous two sets with respect to method or central focus, collectively at least hint at the beneficial effects of aid. The common feature among these studies is analysis of student application and enrollment patterns.

In a replication of an earlier study (1973), Spies (1978) found that in 1976 the effects of family income on the enrollment choices of high-ability students were smaller than those he observed in 1971. Taken together, the results of Spies's two studies suggest that the advent of additional student aid in the early 1970s had increased choice. In the 1978 study, controlling for family income, parental education, and academic ability, he also found that students applying for aid were more likely than nonapplicants to apply to high cost institutions and that low-income minority students were more likely than their nonminority counterparts to apply to high cost institutions.

In a broad-based analysis of the effects of student aid on enrollments in the private sector, Leslie (1978) found that about one-half of the change from 1965 to 1975 in the private college enrollment share could be explained by changes in public (federal and state) aid expenditures. Using several estimation methods, he concluded that public student aid had added about 250,000 students to private collegiate enrollments in 1975, or about 11 percent of total private enrollments in that year.

Among SAT takers in 1981, Baird (1984) found that family income had no apparent effect on the percentage of students who were able to attend their first-choice college. Although the percentage attending 4-year colleges generally increased with family income, the lowest-income category was an exception. Students from low-income families had a relatively high rate of attendance at 4-year colleges. Shaut and Rizzo (1980) examined the enrollment behavior of students who received 1973–1974 Tuition Assistance Program (TAP) grants in New York. Differences in family income were not a factor in students choosing high cost versus low cost institutions. Mullen (1982) simulated the effects of the TAP and found that private institutions experienced enrollment gains at the expense of public institutions. Munday (1976) examined a national sample of 1972 freshmen aid applicants and found that they tended to enroll at colleges whose students were, on average, different from them in terms of educational development (ACT scores) and family income. This was not the case for students generally. Munday attributed the difference in behavior to the effects of student aid.

Surveys of Student Opinions

Table 8.4 shows how the students themselves perceive the impact of student aid on choice. The studies shown differ in a number of ways that limit their comparability. Most critical in this regard are differences by level of student income, by type of student aid, and by type of institution. Deriving a measure of central tendency would not be appropriate. Nonetheless, the studies indicate clearly that student aid is enhancing choice in the opinion of a substantial portion of the students surveyed.

As shown in Panel A, in some instances as many as 40 to 50 percent of the students queried felt that financial aid was an important factor in their choice of institution. The perceived effects of particular state student aid programs are, with one exception, somewhat smaller than the effects of all aid. This is to be expected on the assumption that the impact of aid is directly related to the amount of aid. In the Schwartz and Chronister (1978) study, for example, the maximum aid award was only $600 (1982 dollars), hardly enough, one would think, to affect the enrollment choices of large numbers of students attending private institutions. In the one instance in which state aid had a very large impact (Foreman et al., 1984), the authors of the survey concluded that they were measuring the effects of more student aid dollars than just those provided through the state program. The authors of the Illinois studies (Fenske et al., 1979) noted that their results are artificially low because the results reflect the responses of only those students who would not have dropped out of school in the absence of aid; that is, students who were relatively insensitive to financial aid. They also noted that the Illinois aid program benefited private institutions far more than public institutions.

The Astin et al. (1976, 1979, 1982, 1985) data shown in Panel B are taken from the annual fall Cooperative Institutional Research Program (CIRP) surveys. The figures represent the percentages of freshmen students who indicated that the offer of financial assistance was a "very important reason" for attending their present college. The most interesting feature in the data is the growing percentage of students who consider aid to be important in their choice of institution. The percentages increase from one measurement period to the next in 22 out of 24 instances. Similarly, in a study of student aid in South Carolina, Blackwell (1978) reported that students perceived aid as being a more important choice factor in 1977 than in 1972.

Another result of interest in Panel B is that more women than men consider aid to be important in choosing their present college. The margin of difference is small, 3 percentage points in 1985, but it grew steadily from 1976 to 1985. Fully one-third of students at private 4-year colleges considered aid to be im-

Table 8.4

THE IMPACT OF STUDENT AID ON CHOICE: STUDENT OPINION SURVEYS

A. Percentage of Aid Recipients Whose Enrollment Choices Are Affected by Student Aid: By Level of Family Income

Location of Aid Program	Family Income			
	Low/Needy	Middle	High	All
Illinois				
Grants				
1976	10.2			
1973	8.4			
1970	13.0			
1967	11.6			
Scholarships				
1976	23.0			
1973	21.1			
1970	31.3			
1967	33.0			
Kentucky Grants	56.6*			
	39.5**			
Virginia Grants	22.6*	15.4*	4.9*	
Educational Opportunity Grants	24.6			
All Aid				
New York	51.0			
Portions of Pennsylvania & NY	42.2	32.2	21.2	
Six metro areas				45
National				40

*Students at private institutions.
**Students at public institutions.

B. Percentage of Students for Whom the Offer of Financial Aid Was an Important Reason for Their Choice of Institution

Type of Institution, Sex of Aid Recipient	Data Year	Aid Type	Family Income	Percent Affected
	1985	All	All	
All institutions				20.2
Private universities				28.7
Private 4-year				34.0
Predominantly black institutions				48.0

Table 8.4 (Continued)
THE IMPACT OF STUDENT AID ON CHOICE: STUDENT OPINION SURVEYS

Type of Institution, Sex of Aid Recipient	Data Year	Aid Type	Family Income	Percent Affected
Men				18.6
Women				21.7
	1982	All	All	
All institutions				16.7
Private universities				25.4
Private 4-year				30.5
Predominantly black institutions				28.3
Men				15.4
Women				18.0
	1979	All	All	
All institutions				15.9
Private universities				22.9
Private 4-year				26.1
Predominantly black institutions				31.4
Men				15.1
Women				16.7
	1976	All	All	
All institutions				13.6
Private universities				23.0
Private 4-year				25.3
Predominantly black institutions				26.7
Men				13.4
Women				13.9

Source. Compiled from data collected through the annual Cooperative Institutional Research Program (CIRP) surveys and published in Astin et al. (1976, 1979, 1982, 1985).

portant in their choice of institution in 1985, an impressive figure it would seem, given that students at all income levels are represented in the response rates. The percentages are generally higher for students at predominantly black institutions than for students at all institutions, probably because a greater proportion of the students at the black institutions are from low-income families. Low-income students receive more aid and, as we have shown, are more responsive than more affluent students to aid offers.

Only two of the student opinion studies (Leslie et al., 1977; Schwartz and Chronister, 1978) provide results disaggregated by level of family income. Both studies corroborate the familiar pattern in which the impact of aid is much greater among low-income students than among students from middle-income or high-income families.

ENROLLMENT SHARE CALCULATIONS

The few enrollment share studies that focus on choice provide interesting results, although, as is often true for this type of study, the results are difficult to interpret. As the data in Table 8.5 show, some of the enrollment share percentages are strongly negative from the perspective of the choice goal. According to the Leslie (1977) and Astin (1985) compilations, the tendency of low-income students to be disproportionately enrolled in 2-year colleges has not lessened during the student aid era. Indeed, the data indicate that the disproportion has increased. Another negative, underscored by Astin, is that the number of low-income students at the most selective public universities would have to more than double for low-income students to achieve proportionate enrollment levels at those institutions.

The compilation developed by Davis and Johns (1982) is generally more positive. It documents the enrollment behavior of students from families with incomes below the median. As the data in Table 8.5, Panel A, show, these students increased their representation in universities from 1966 to 1980. Nonetheless, it is only in 2-year colleges that these students meet or exceed a 50 percent enrollment share. They come close to the 50 percent mark in public 4-year institutions, 47.9 percent in 1980, but fall far short at other types of 4-year institutions.

The evidence is fairly positive from the standpoint of enrollment of low-income students in private, relatively high cost institutions. Using CIRP data, Leslie (1977) shows that students from families with less than $18,200 income substantially increased their enrollment share at private institutions during the period from 1968 to 1975. He found that median family income for freshmen enrolled in private institutions actually declined during this period. Of course, his data reflect the early period of the student aid era. The Davis and Johns data indicate that 4-year private institutions in particular were enrolling a much higher percentage of below-median-income students in 1980, 37.1 percent, than in 1966, 26.6 percent. Private 2-year colleges and private universities also show gains over that period, but the latter show a sharp decline, 30.3 percent to 25.7 percent, from 1976 to 1980, to a point where below-median-income students are enrolling at about half the rate one might expect if family income were not a factor.

Like the participation rate studies in the section on access, all of these enrollment share results, negative and positive alike, are "uncontrolled," and therefore of somewhat limited value. One cannot simply take the results at face value. For example, if student aid brought about a substantial increase in the number of low-income students participating in higher education, and if the increase in enrollments of more affluent students did not keep pace, the enrollment shares of low-income students would increase at high cost institutions even if the relative distribution of low-income students across institutional types remained the same.

The data in Panel B of Table 8.5, adapted from Fife and Leslie (1976), provide modest support for the premise that student aid enhances choice. The data portray the effects of state student aid programs on enrollments by type of institution. Enrollment norms for all students are compared to the enrollment distribution of aid recipients. From the public versus private perspective, the aid programs in California and New Jersey had the greatest impact. Students had to compete for the aid awards. Those who were successful chose to enroll in private institutions at a higher rate than did students overall. There also were substantial movements among institutions by degree level. In both states, the biggest gainers were universities. It is unclear how much of the enormous increase at public universities in California can be attributed to student aid. That state's public universities are highly selective. Anyone able enough to be accepted probably was able enough to win a state scholarship, and vice versa. Conceivably, the enrollment distribution of the best students in the state would not be much different from that of aid recipients, although the award rules favored the private sector (the maximum award level was much higher for students attending private institutions). Students at public 2-year colleges in California were ineligible for the state aid program. This was not true in New Jersey, but relatively few participants in that state's aid program elected to attend a 2-year college.

The results are less clear in the other two states where the aid awards were need-based rather than competitive, and the regulations were less restrictive. In Pennsylvania, recipients of state aid attended private institutions a bit less frequently than did students generally, but recipient enrollment in universities exceeded state norms. The biggest movement of students was from public 2-year colleges to public universities. The relatively high tuition at public universities in Pennsylvania is probably part of the reason for the results in that state: Many students could not afford to attend universities without aid. The aid program in New York apparently did little to shift enrollment between the public and private sectors. The university segment gained enrollment as a result of the aid program, but the other 4-year institutions lost enrollment.

A lesson to be drawn from the results in Panel B is that state student aid programs can have very significant effects on enrollment patterns. The precise nature of those effects will depend on the structure of higher education in a state, especially selectivity and tuition levels in the public sector, and, of course, on the particulars of the aid programs themselves. The complexity of the situation on a state-by-state basis, including the role of federal student aid, is explored at some length in the study by Astin et al. (1980) mentioned earlier.

Perhaps the most discouraging finding to come out of the enrollment share studies is the continuing failure of minority students to achieve proportionate representation among the various types of institutions. By the early 1980s, according to Astin (1985), blacks, Hispanics, and Native Americans were still overrepresented in public 2-year colleges and underrepresented in public and private universities. Blacks were underenrolled in 56 out of 65 "flagship" public

Table 8.5

THE IMPACT OF STUDENT AID ON CHOICE: PARTICIPATION RATE CALCULATIONS

A. Participation Rates over Time in the Form of Enrollment Shares

Author/Year	Population/ 1982 Income	Institution	Enrollment Percentage 1966	1968	1971	1975	1976	1980	1983
Astin 1985	Freshman	Public 2-year	23.6						22.2
	Lowest income	Public 4-year	28.4						19.7
	quintile	Public university	16.8						12.0
Davis & Johns	Freshmen	Public 2-year	40.0		54.0		56.5	54.3	
1982	Below median	Private 2-year	38.8		45.7		55.7	53.9	
	income*	Public 4-year	46.1		50.5		48.3	47.9	
		Private 4-year	26.6		34.6		32.9	37.1	
		Public university	22.9		28.9		34.6	32.9	
		Private university	21.7		27.2		30.3	25.7	
	Below lowest	Public 2-year	14.8		27.9		24.8	26.2	
	income*	Private 2-year	13.4		23.9		24.4	29.1	
	quartile	Public 4-year	18.1		26.0		21.3	25.2	
		Private 4-year	10.7		17.1		11.8	16.0	
		Public university	10.1		15.6		11.7	12.4	
		Private university	6.6		11.0		11.0	9.6	

Leslie 1977	Freshman				
	< $18,200	2-year	23.4		29.3
		4-year	21.0		22.2
		University	15.4		12.8
		Public		22.1	27.6
		Private		15.5	22.0
	$18,200–27,300	2-year	29.3		28.8
		4-year	26.5		24.5
		University	25.6		21.0
		Public		26.8	22.7
		Private		21.2	18.1
	> $27,300	2-year	47.3		41.9
		4-year	52.5		53.3
		University	59.0		66.2
		Public		51.1	49.7
		Private		63.3	59.9

*Income levels are for families with head of family between 35 and 64 years of age.

(continued)

Table 8.5 (Continued)

THE IMPACT OF STUDENT AID ON CHOICE: PARTICIPATION RATE CALCULATIONS

B. Enrollment Percentages: Aid Recipients* versus All Students

	California		New Jersey		Pennsylvania		New York	
Institutional Level/Control	Scholarship Recipients	State Norm	Scholarship Recipients	State Norm	Scholarship Recipients	State Norm	Scholar Incentive Recipients	State Norm
All levels								
Private	41.7	14.1	43.1	30.4	40.9	44.7	35.5	34.3
Public	58.3	85.9	56.9	69.6	59.1	55.3	64.5	65.7
University								
Private	23.8	3.8	15.5	6.2	10.0	9.5	11.6	13.2
Public	52.8	11.6	18.6	14.4	30.9	21.6	9.8	2.8
Total	76.6	15.4	34.1	20.6	40.9	31.1	21.4	16
4-year								
Private	17.8	10.0	24.8	19.2	29.7	34.1	18.0	19.6
Public	5.5	14.0	31.0	28.0	21.6	19.1	12.8	22.9
Total	23.3	24.0	55.8	47.2	51.3	53.2	30.8	42.5
2-year								
Private	0.1	0.2	0.9	4.4	1.4	3.1	2.8	1.4
Public	0.0	60.3	7.1	27.1	5.1	14.6	47.8	40.0
Total	0.1	60.5	8.0	31.5	6.5	17.7	50.6	41.4

Source. Adapted from Fife and Leslie, 1976, p. 330.

*The California and New Jersey programs were competitive; the Pennsylvania and New York programs were need-based.

universities; Hispanics and Native Americans were only slightly better off, being underenrolled in 48 and 46 of those universities, respectively. Data tabulated by the National Center for Education Statistics (Plisko, 1984) show that overrepresentation in 2-year colleges is greatest for Hispanics. In 1982, their percentage share of enrollment in 2-year institutions was 6.2 percent, compared to just 3.0 percent in 4-year institutions. Blacks are better off in this regard, with a 10.3 percent enrollment share at 2-year colleges, compared to an 8.0 percent share at 4-year institutions. The latter percentage is down, however, from 8.5 percent in 1976.

Summary for Choice

The impact of student aid on student choice is difficult to analyze, perhaps more so than its impact on access. The process of choosing an institution is complex. There are several points in the process when student aid, or the likelihood thereof, could be influential. For instance, general notions about the availability of aid would be important at the time when students and their families initially think about the range of attendance possibilities. The attendance decision itself would more likely be affected by actual offers of aid from specific institutions.

The aid picture also is complex. At least two things happen with the introduction of aid, other things being equal. On the one hand, more institutions become affordable to low-income and, to a lesser extent, middle-income students. At the same time, relative prices, or price differentials, change. One or the other may be the more important development in a given situation. For example, aid can be an enabling device for students who very much want to attend a particular institution. With aid they will enroll at that institution, and the relative prices of other options will make little difference. On other occasions, perhaps when personal preferences are not strong, relative prices become more critical and the best aid offer is likely to influence the attendance decision.

The evidence assembled in this section, at least with respect to the econometric and student opinion results, provides confirmation for what one would expect theoretically. Student aid is an effective way of changing net-price differentials among competing institutions. An institution can increase its enrollment share by increasing the amount of aid it offers, other things staying the same.

There is less agreement in the studies about the effects of the federal government's BEOG/Pell Grant program. Much depends, it would seem, on how the institutions react to such aid. More institutions become affordable because of the aid, presuming that they do not raise prices commensurately in concert with the aid. If they do raise prices, they may end up with the same number of students as before the aid but with more revenue per student. This helps the institutions but does little for choice; that is, it does not lead to a redistribution of students. Although the evidence would be circumstantial at best, we may be seeing something of this situation in the disparity between the results of the opinion studies and most of the econometric studies, on the one hand, and the enrollment share studies on the other. The results from the latter studies are ambiguous at best. The former tell us that aid does work. The resolution may be that aid has worked well enough to maintain the distribution of students, more or less, while helping to strengthen the financial position of the institutions. The enrollment share of private institutions, for example, is essentially unchanged since the early 1970s, when the rapid growth in aid began, after precipitous declines in the 1950s and 1960s.

PERSISTENCE[3]

Studies analyzing the effect of student financial aid on persistence will be handled differently from those dealing with access or choice. Relevant studies of persistence are numerous, and they typically compare, in quasi-experimental fashion, the behavior of individuals in a treatment group to the behavior of individuals in a control group. As a consequence, in dealing with these studies we can proceed more in the manner of a conventional meta-analysis. First, the results of the studies are standardized in the form of abstract effect sizes. Then the effect sizes are averaged and the averages tested for statistical significance. Various subsets of studies are examined in similar fashion. In addition, the average effect sizes are interpreted, albeit somewhat loosely, using terms such as "moderate" or "small," and they are transformed into percentages that reflect the relative likelihood that individuals with certain attributes will persist in college.

Whenever possible, the effect size for a sample was calculated as the sum of the treatment group mean minus the control group mean, divided by the control group standard deviation (Glass, 1976). When means or standard deviations were not provided, various algorithms were used to convert other types of statistical results, such as *t*-scores or chi-squares, to comparable effect sizes. In most studies the treatment group consists of aid recipients and the control group consists of aid nonrecipients. In some situations, for example, in comparing the behavior of males and females, all individuals in the analysis are aid recipients.

The effect of student aid on persistence can be addressed in two ways. One way is to compare the behavior of low-income students who receive aid with the behavior of low-income students who do not receive aid. The econometric studies of access and choice are structured in this fashion, but this is not true for most studies of persistence. The alternative is to compare the behavior of

[3]We are grateful to Tullisse A. Murdock, who permitted us to synthesize this material from her Ph.D. dissertation. See Murdock (1986).

aid recipients with that of nonrecipients, without reference to student (or family) income, and to look for evidence that the effects of income disparities have been neutralized. This is the approach taken in most persistence studies. Because most student aid goes to low-income and, to a lesser extent, middle-income students, the premise is that student aid will have been shown to be successful if the persistence rate of aid recipients is the same as that of nonrecipients.

The initial literature search uncovered 62 persistence studies. A number of them were eliminated from further consideration, including those that dealt with student perceptions rather than actual persistence measures, included graduate, foreign, or athletic scholarship students, had ambiguous measures of persistence or financial aid, or failed to provide adequate descriptive or inferential statistics to permit the calculation of an effect size. In the end, 49 studies containing 85 data points (samples) were used for the meta-analysis.[4]

FINDINGS

The baseline analysis examined 46 samples in which the persistence of aid recipients was compared to that of nonrecipients. These samples differ in several ways, including measures of persistence and types of institutions, students, financial aid, and research methods. Ignoring these differences for the moment, the overall impact of aid on persistence, as measured by the mean effect size for all 46 samples, is a statistically significant +.132. Cohen (1977) suggests that an effect size of this magnitude can be considered "less than small." With respect to persistence in college, a positive difference of .132 between aid recipients and nonrecipients means that, on average, a person receiving financial aid has a persistence likelihood greater than 55 percent of the nonrecipient group.

As Figure 8.1 shows, there is considerable dispersion of effect sizes around the overall mean. Thirteen of the studies show negative results: aid recipients persisting less well than nonrecipients. By contrast, six studies found positive effect sizes ranging from .44 to .52. An effect size of .5 might be called "moderate"; it would mean that the average aid recipient would have a persistence likelihood greater than 69 percent of the nonrecipient group. Only one study (Haggerty, 1985) reported a larger effect size, .91. A possible reason for this exceptional figure is that all of the students in the analysis were at least 24-years-old. Unfortunately, no additional evidence regarding this possibility can be offered, as none of the other studies focused on older students.

[4]With few exceptions, the persistence studies are not mentioned by name in the text. Because the results of the studies included in the analysis could be treated in a common manner, there was no need to include in the text either a selective or exhaustive enumeration of the various studies. The interested reader can find a detailed listing of the individual persistence studies in Appendix Table 7, beginning with study number 58.Many of the studies are discussed in Murdock (1986).

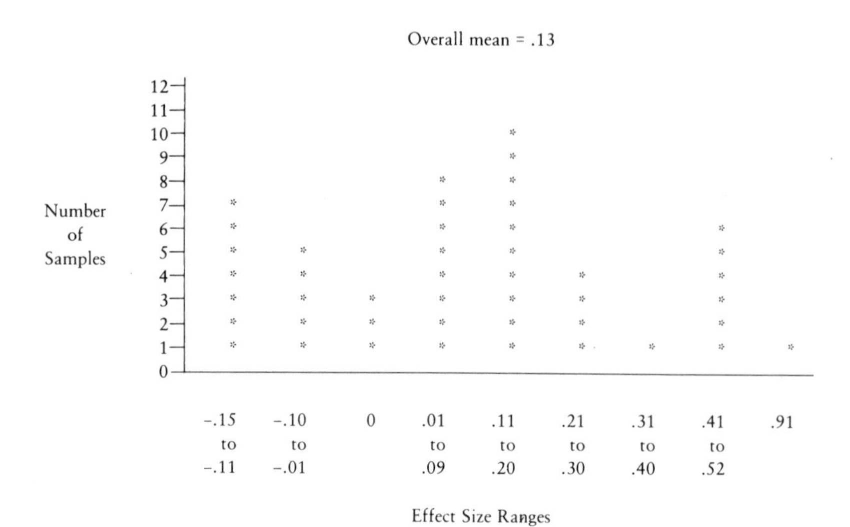

FIGURE 8.1 Impact of Student Aid on Persistence; Dispersion of Effect Sizes for 46 Samples.

The overall average effect size of .132 can be interpreted as indicating that student aid is working. As noted earlier, the persistence studies are structured in such a way that if aid recipients are shown to persist as well as nonrecipients, then, by implication, student aid can be said to have accomplished its goal of equalizing educational opportunities across income categories. Indeed, from this evidence it would appear that aid may even be giving a slight edge to recipients. Further analysis will show, however, that this is probably not true, and that the best supported overall conclusion is that aid works as intended but does no more than that.

Table 8.6 summarizes the meta-analysis results for the impact of student aid on persistence. First, an overview of the table will be helpful. The effect sizes appearing in Panels A through E are averages for various groups of samples. Panel A shows results for samples in which the persistence of aid recipients is compared to that of nonrecipients. Results shown in Panels B through E are from samples in which the persistence of different types of aid recipients are compared. Both weighted and unweighted average effect sizes are shown, in accord with accepted practice. As the data indicate, weighting (by the size of the respective treatment groups) seldom affects the conclusions one might draw about the effects of aid. Panel F shows the results of a regression analysis in which (unweighted) effect size was regressed on various study characteristics, for studies comparing aid recipients with nonrecipients.

Analysis 1 in Panel A, the most comprehensive of the analyses comparing average effect sizes, has already been discussed. Analysis 2 in Panel A includes only those studies that control for academic ability. As the data indicate, aid recipients do not persist quite as well as nonrecipients when the treatment and the control groups are matched on academic ability, but the difference is not statistically significant. The regression analysis confirms that sampling procedure has an important influence on the variance of the effect size across samples. Using a matched sample is associated with a statistically significant, substantial decrease of .246 in the predicted effect size. The matched sample results are an important qualification on the findings from the first analysis, which suggested that aid tips the balance slightly in favor of recipients. The matched samples strongly suggest that aid achieves parity but not superiority in retention. This qualification needs to be kept in mind in considering the other subanalyses, because they typically include studies that do not control for academic ability. In any event, the critical finding is that aid recipients persist about as well as nonrecipients. Therefore, it would seem that student aid is succeeding insofar as persistence is concerned.

Analysis 3 suggests that aid is more likely to have a positive influence on persistence if to persist means to remain enrolled through graduation rather than simply to reappear as a second-term or second-year student or at some other period of time prior to graduation. However, when this phenomenon was examined in the multiple regression equation, the persistence specification was not statistically significant, although its coefficient had a positive sign. The difference in the aid effect that is related to the form of the persistence measure is apparently quite modest.

Additional perspectives on the time dimension are provided by analysis 4, in which persistence between 2-year and 4-year institutions is compared. The results suggest that aid has a greater effect on persistence among students at 2-year colleges. The small number of studies at 2-year colleges did not allow this comparison to be evaluated through the regression analysis. The fact that 2-year college students tend to be older than students in 4-year colleges could be a factor. Another finding was that the previously mentioned correlation between longer persistence measures and larger positive effect sizes apparently does not hold at 2-year institutions.

Another variable related to time, the year(s) when the data were gathered, does have a statistically significant relationship with effect size. In the regression model, each year adds .01 to the effect size; in other words, a study using 1980 data would be expected to have an effect size .15 larger than a study using 1965 data, other things being equal. Presumably, the data-year variable is a proxy for changes in student aid, student characteristics and mores, study methods, and whatever else might be evolving over time and affecting persistence behavior or its assessment.

As the results in Panel B indicate, the difference in persistence behavior between male and female aid recipients is mixed. Males are the treatment group for presentation purposes. The positive mean effect sizes indicate that they

Table 8.6

SUMMARY OF META-ANALYSIS RESULTS FOR THE IMPACT OF STUDENT FINANCIAL AID ON PERSISTENCE IN COLLEGE

Analysis	Number of Samples	Unweighted Effect Size	Weighted Effect Size
A. Recipients vs. Nonrecipients			
1. All studies	46	.132***	.063***
2. Controlling for academic ability	14	−.006	−.038
3. Varying the measure of persistence			
Less than graduation	36	.110***	.055**
Graduation in 4 or 2 years	25	.147***	.151***
Graduation in 5+ years	10	.217***	.288***
4. 2-Year versus 4-year institutions			
4-Year/Less than graduation	28	.086***	.106***
2-Year/Less than graduation	6	.221***	.189***
4-Year/Graduation	15	.101**	.069*
2-Year/Graduation	9	.192**	.253**
B. Male recipients versus female recipients			
All studies	27	.071**	.076*
Less than graduation	24	.092**	.083**
Graduation	9	−.066	−.005
C. Nonwhite recipients versus white recipients	6	−.221***	−.282***
D. Recipients of larger amounts of aid versus those receiving lesser amounts	7	.218***	.158*
E. Type of aid versus all other types of aid			
Grants	15	.071	.005
Loans	16	−.093*	−.015
Workstudy	10	−.047	.027
Loans and workstudy	5	−.017	.012
Grants and workstudy	7	.068	.028
Grants, loans, and workstudy	6	.038	.037
Grants and loans	8	.109	.043
Scholarships	8	.139*	.128*

Table 8.6 (Continued)

SUMMARY OF META-ANALYSIS RESULTS FOR THE IMPACT OF STUDENT FINANCIAL AID ON PERSISTENCE IN COLLEGE

Analysis	Number of Samples	Unweighted Effect Size	Weighted Effect Size
F. Multiple regression results: Impact of study characteristics on effect size			
N = 64; R-Squared = .42		B	*t*-score
Data year		.010	2.57*
Persistence measured as graduation		.024	.53
Matched samples		−.246	−2.66**
Random samples		−.031	−.46
Statistical rather than descriptive method		−.083	−1.37
Transfers & stopouts treated as persisters		.199	2.47*
Part-Time students included in sample		−.132	−2.05*
Full-Time students only in sample		.094	1.36

$*p < .05$; $**p < .01$; $***p < .001$.

persist longer overall and when the less-than-graduation measure of persistence is used. The differences are statistically significant but materially small. Females may have a slight edge when graduation is the persistence measure.

A disturbing finding is shown in Panel C, a comparison of the effects of aid on nonwhite versus white students. Nonwhite aid recipients have a lower persistence rate than do white recipients. The average effect size is statistically significant, and the individual effect sizes for nonwhites are negative in all six studies. The results mean that the average nonwhite recipient has a persistence rate greater than only 41 percent of white recipients. Since academic ability was not controlled for in these studies, interpreting this finding is not entirely straightforward. Nonetheless, the finding at least suggests that student aid does not overcome some of the handicaps faced by needy nonwhite students as well as it does for needy white students.

The positive effect size in Panel D indicates that the amount of financial aid has a positive impact on persistence; individuals receiving more aid tend to persist longer. It was not possible to interpret the effect size in terms of dollar amounts. Additional, but implicit, confirmation of the positive effect on persistence of larger amounts of aid comes from five studies of recipient versus nonrecipient persistence rates at private colleges. The average effect size (not tabled) at the private institutions, where aid awards typically are larger than at public institutions, was .211, or considerably higher than the .132 recorded for all samples of recipient versus nonrecipient behavior.

Panel E shows the aggregate results for studies that examine the relative effects of the form in which student aid is received. For each type of aid shown, recipients of that type are considered the treatment group, while recipients of all other forms of aid become the control group. Thus, a form of aid with a positive effect size has been shown to be relatively effective in promoting persistence. One would expect grants and scholarships to have a relatively large impact on persistence in that they are the most obvious form of subsidy (when awarded, the amount of the subsidy in a grant is clear, whereas for loans the subsidy can only be estimated on the basis of future interest and inflation rates). As the data indicate, it does appear to turn out that way, although the effect sizes are quite modest and generally not statistically significant. The relatively large effect size associated with scholarship recipients cannot be taken at face value given that only one of the eight studies controlled for academic ability. The negative effect for loans suggests that loans are less effective in contributing to persistence, although the weighted results are not statistically significant. (It should be kept in mind that the effect sizes in Panel E are not indicators of relative cost effectiveness.) Loan–grant combinations, which occur with great frequency, do not appear to be less effective in promoting persistence than other forms of aid. Interpreting the latter result is not straightforward, however, for it is conceivable, if not likely, that combinations of loans and grants would typically be for larger amounts than loans separately, in which case we might be seeing the positive effects of greater aid amounts rather than that of a particular form of aid package. Or it may be that the positive impact of receiving some grant aid outweighs the relatively negative impact of a loan.

It is worth noting that the majority of the studies reviewed take a conservative, institutional view of what it means to persist, in that they treat both transfers and stopouts (those who are absent for 1 or more terms) as dropouts, that is, as nonpersisters. In those studies that take a more student-oriented view, the average effect sizes are larger than they are for the full range of studies. For studies in which both stopouts and transfers are treated as persisters, the mean effect size is .273, which means that the typical aid recipient would have a persistence likelihood greater than 61 percent of the nonrecipient group. When transfers are treated as persisters and stopouts as nonpersisters the effect size is .283, and when transfers are treated as nonpersisters and stopouts as persisters the mean effect size is .226. The regression model predicts that treating both transfers and stopouts as persisters will add .20 to the effect size, *ceteris paribus*. Apparently, student aid has a salutary effect on student mobility and on student willingness to return to school after a period of absence.

Finally, in the regression analysis there is support for the proposition that effect sizes will be smaller in those studies that include part-time students in the sample populations and larger in those studies that examine the behavior of full-time students only. This result may be related to the fact that part-time students receive smaller aid awards than do full-time students. In any event, given that the majority of studies did not report on student status, these results must be viewed with caution. Similarly, caution is needed in interpreting the negative coefficient on the statistical method variable, which hints that more sophisticated procedures can be associated with lower effect sizes. The multiplicity of statistical procedures among the various studies made coding for this variable difficult. The regression analysis included 64 cases rather than the 46 in analysis 1 of Panel A because the latter analysis included only the sample with the shortest measure of persistence in studies that examined persistence at different points in time, while the regression analysis included all samples regardless of the persistence measure, so long as they compared the behavior of aid recipients to the behavior of students who did not receive aid. One study, that by Haggerty (1985), was excluded from the regression analysis because of its extraordinarily large effect size.

Summary for Persistence

The effect of student aid on persistence in college can be summarized as follows. One, the overall effect is to permit aid recipients to persist about as well as nonrecipients. Two, the effect differs along several dimensions, the most important of which would seem to be that (1) the size of the effect has grown in a positive direction in recent years; (2) nonwhite aid recipients do not persist as well as white aid recipients; (3) persistence is enhanced by larger amounts of aid; and (4) when aid forms are compared to one another, grant and scholarship aid have a more positive effect on persistence than do loans.

The conventional wisdom among those who have examined attrition in higher education is that students typically do not drop out of school because of financial problems (for example, see Noel, 1985). The predominant paradigm for the study of attrition, formulated by Tinto in 1975, models a student's chances of remaining in school as a function of the degree of social and intellectual integration he or she achieves. The paradigm does not include any explicit reference to student aid or student financial status. At a later point (1982), Tinto does cite the lack of attention to a student's financial condition as a weakness of the current approach to studying attrition. The findings we have presented neither confirm nor deny either the conventional wisdom or the research paradigm, but these findings do suggest the reason why both were so dominant during the 1970s and into the 1980s. The meta-analysis results indicate that aid allows recipients to hold their own when compared to students who "officially" have no need, that is, do not qualify for aid. In a word, student aid has apparently worked well enough that those concerned about attrition could legitimately focus on noneconomic dimensions of student life. A substantial decline in aid, particularly in the form of grants, might well require a change in the conventional outlook and in the research paradigm.

Conclusion

Student financial aid has become a major tool for social policy. The evidence assembled and presented in this chapter shows that it is an effective tool. Student aid does work on behalf of the equal opportunity goal. Because of aid, more low-income individuals have been able to study at the college level, attend relatively costly and prestigious institutions, and stay in school longer than would otherwise have been the case. Having said that, it must also be said that aid clearly is not all powerful. It has not removed all of the effects that are associated with variations in income and other aspects of a person's upbringing and overall environment. To put it another way, as a tool for social policy, student aid is not a viable substitute for a nurturing home life and a solid primary and secondary education. Still, at the margin, student aid is helping very considerable numbers of students.

It will have been obvious in reading through the chapter that we know much more about the effect of student aid in the form of grants than in the form of loans. Virtually everything about which we could be definite in the integrative review had to do with grant aid. Yet loans have become an increasingly important part of the overall aid picture. More must be learned soon about their effect on access, choice, and persistence. The long-term, socioeconomic effects of greater reliance on loans must also be examined.

Finally, there is the matter of the cost effectiveness of student aid. We have said nothing at all about it in the chapter. A few studies touch on it, but essentially this is fallow ground. We are not referring to the broader question of student aid versus, say, health care or national defense, but rather to the less value-laden issue of how best to ensure equal higher education opportunities. Presuming that student aid is part of the answer, the relative cost effectiveness of different forms of aid, particularly grants versus loans, is an issue that deserves more attention than it has thus far received.

9

The Economic Value of Higher Education: Formulating Private and Public Policy

What, then, do the foregoing chapters tell us about personal and collective higher education decision making? To return to our questions of Chapters 1 and 3, should we spend more on higher education or less? Should the form of public expenditures be altered or remain the same? The findings of the book are summarized thoroughly in Chapter 1. Therefore, we will provide only highlights of findings here. We suspect that the evidence presented will be used to support diverse personal viewpoints.

This result is to be expected because our chief purpose in writing the book was to assemble and synthesize the evidence, rather than to marshall evidence in support of a particular viewpoint. Nonetheless, in this closing chapter, we will offer conclusions that seem to us to be clearly justified, and then explore the more debatable issue of whether the individual or society should pay more of the costs of higher education. Although we offer our own views in regard to this vital question, we emphasize that the arguments are several on both sides.

Let us begin with the conclusions that are less debatable. For most people, private investment in higher education is a good decision. In many, probably most cases, it is an outstanding decision. In a few cases it may be a questionable choice, at least as measured in purely monetary terms. Direct, monetary yields on investment for most college graduates surpass benchmark yields on alternatives. Nonmonetary investment and consumption benefits add greatly to this already high monetary return. For those in such "helping" professions as teaching and the ministry, monetary returns may be limited, nonexistent, or even negative, but nonmonetary benefits will be adequately compensatory for some individuals. For all, the obtaining of any subsidies, even small ones, will substantially enhance total rates of return, which are already significant on an average basis. As a private policy decision, investment in higher education most likely will pay very handsome dividends, which will be greatly enhanced for those who value certain psychological and other nonmonetary benefits. For those who value less intellectually demanding and rewarding work and leisure activities, and are able to find well-paying jobs that do not require a college degree, the decision may be more problematic.

A second clear conclusion concerns the economic value of colleges to local communities. Communities already possessing postsecondary institutions and those fortunate few communities likely to obtain them in the near future should guard these precious resources jealously. It is more than local pride that has protected local colleges from closure during the past and present years of fiscal stress. Colleges and universities are important economic resources. Collegiate institutions pay handsome returns to their communities; indeed, many communities may possess no more valuable local industry. Loss of a college means more than direct loss of jobs. It means also loss of student earnings and local sales, the export of local wealth to support those students directly in *other* communities, and foregone tax expenditures that are instead allocated to other localities.

The scattering of the nation's 3300-odd collegiate institutions across perhaps almost one-half that many large and small cities and towns of America is a most fortuitous happenstance arising from earlier population distributions. What significant national industry today could be parceled out to small communities essentially lacking in natural resources, skilled labor pools, convenient accesses to markets, and, perhaps most significantly, a population adequate to assure the necessary political influence for obtaining the resource? The industry of higher learning alone may be suitable to communities lacking in these characteristics.

The third and final of the less debatable policy decisions is the support of student aid—at least on the grounds of promoting equal opportunity and thus furthering social mobility of low-income and minority groups. Clearly, student grant aid promotes these social goals. Whether the amounts required are justified by the results achieved is less clear-cut; however, student grant aid is successful, and of all income transfer programs attempted by government, few are viewed more favorably by the electorate than provision of the *opportunity* for upward mobility. Student aid programs have raised low-income college participation rates (or prevented declines), they have enabled enrollment in more expensive institutions, and they have contributed to collegiate persistence.

All the remaining major issues addressed in the content chapters of the book can be captured in the single question of who should pay a larger share of the costs of higher education—society or the individual? Even the less debatable conclusions already reached may be amended or even altered based upon the answer to this question.

In pursuit of the answer, let us first enumerate the principal findings of each research review chapter. Chapter 4 found that private rates of return to higher education are higher than benchmark rates. The immediate suggestion is that students can legitimately be expected to pay a larger share of higher education costs. The corresponding part of Chapter 5 found that social rates of return, as conventionally measured, are slightly lower. This, too, suggests the immediate conclusion that it would be equitable for students to pay a larger share. The major finding of the second part of Chapter 5, however, was that education, including higher education, contributes importantly to national income. This finding suggests, principally, that higher education be further encouraged by raising social investment and encouraging private investment through low prices. Chapter 6 revealed that the poor do *not* subsidize the higher education of the rich, as is commonly perceived in policy arenas, but that there is some modest-to-moderate progressivity represented in the way higher education is financed, given current attendance patterns of students by income class, across institutional types. The immediate conclusion of this finding is that the present system is satisfactory, on equity grounds, but, of course, can always be improved through charging students (who are relatively wealthy, on average, in comparison to nonstudents) more and society (the reference point) less. Chapter 7 reported that potential students do respond to price. This tells us (1) that charging students more, other factors equal, will reduce enrollments, and (2) that price reductions through student aid likely will result in expanded opportunity for targeted students. Again, Chapter 8 informs us that student aid promotes opportunity. In addition, because student aid reduces the student's cost, other factors equal, it indirectly raises society's share of costs and reduces the private share.

In summary, changes in private and social shares of costs can be and are altered through tuition and other price changes. Such changes alter consumption of higher education, affect private and social rates of return to higher education, and presumably impact economic growth. Student aid subsidies to some degree compensate for higher tuitions while promoting another social goal: equality of opportunity. In short, the policy issues are captured in the question of whether the individual or society should pay more. If the former conclusion is reached, tuition should be raised. In this case, however, student aid should be raised, too, if the price increases would reduce opportunity below target levels. The conclusion that society should pay more suggests that public subsidies to institutions be increased so that tuition levels need not rise; student aid levels would again be evaluated against equal opportunity criteria.

We do not believe it possible from existing data to answer definitively this fundamental question as to whether society or the individual should pay more.

What is possible is to carry the analysis a step or two farther—and we shall do that—but in the end answers probably will depend upon the reader's own values.

Charging Students More: The Pros

There are several findings that can be cited in support of the argument for charging students more.

1. For most graduates, private rates of return are sufficiently high to permit higher student charges. The resilience of enrollments to large price increases in the 1980s demonstrates that most students can and will pay more. The most fundamental principle of public finance is that public resources should not be spent when private expenditures will adequately serve the public need, that is, when public expenditures are mere substitutes for private ones.
2. Higher student charges permit government to target its resources on low-income and minority individuals, thus improving efficiency in resource allocation (low-income students being more responsive to price) and promoting the emergent social goal of equal opportunity.
3. Conventionally calculated social rates of return are somewhat less than private rates, suggesting that individuals should pay more. Even if there were some enrollment loss, little if any economic damage would be done to the nation, as evidenced by underemployment of many college graduates.
4. Given that enrollment rates are positively associated with family income, higher student charges would improve upon progressivity of the higher education system.
5. Although higher prices do impact enrollment, especially of lower-income persons, higher tuition prices can be offset with student aid for those who are most needy.

Charging Students More: The Cons

Findings in support of the position against charging students more also are several.

1. Public investments should be increased where social returns are greatest (marginal analysis). Higher education returns to both society and the individual are very high. Reduced public investments, which will cause

price increases and thereby reduce higher education consumption, will reduce national income. Higher education accounts for substantial shares of national income growth. The "yields" from high private rates of return are enjoyed by society overall. Separation of private and social benefits creates a false dichotomy, as evidenced by the fact that the only social benefits counted in social rate of return analysis are earnings received by college graduates. In reality, "a rising tide raises all boats."

2. Social rate of return analysis is too flawed conceptually to be taken seriously. We really have very little idea whether society or the individual receives greater returns on investment.

3. Equity takes not one but several forms. Should individuals be charged more when private returns may well be no greater than social returns? Is it equitable to charge private individuals more merely because they *will* pay more? Higher education costs are shared approximately equally between the public and private individuals (Brinkman and Leslie, 1983). Unless private individuals in fact benefit more, they should not be charged more.

4. Higher education does not have a regressive impact upon resource allocation in society. If greater progressivity is desired, it should be achieved through the tax system, rather than through increased user fees (tuition, etc.).

5. If it is to be argued that private individuals should pay more because of high private benefits, then increased student aid, a subsidy to private individuals, cannot be justified—at least not on these grounds.

Governments are likely merely to substitute tuition revenues for public money. There is little evidence that government subsidies saved through tuition increases are passed along to students in the form of need-based aid. Instead, the savings likely will be allocated to other public functions, where returns probably will be less.

Conclusion

We are not satisfied that we know whether the amount of higher education produced in the United States is at, beyond, or below the optimum level. One thing does appear certain: The present system is yielding high economic returns. We subscribe to the first principle of parsimony: If it isn't broken, don't fix it. Indeed, larger public expenditures are suggested by the high return rates. There may be dangers in raising student charges unless the revenues are returned, dollar-for-dollar, in the form of need-based student aid. With ever-increasing pressures for public dollars for other public purposes, we are less than sanguine that such transfers will occur. Nevertheless, we recognize that institutions have been and are likely to continue to be under financial pressure. The fact is that by several measures, public support of higher education is being reduced. The temptations to raise tuitions are irresistible and perhaps unavoidable. We are convinced, however, that governments will not rush into resuming their former financial commitments, now lightened by higher charges paid by students.

The combination of these factors and our own values leads us to believe that societal support for higher education should be raised and that students, proportionately, should be charged less. This could be done by holding tuition prices constant for some years, or raising tuitions at a lower rate than public subsidies are raised. The two primary reasons for our beliefs involve (1) equity and (2) marginal analysis.

During the past two decades, equity considerations in higher education policy have concerned equity among students and their families: The richer should pay more and the poorer less. If it is assumed that tax systems supporting higher education are regressive or insufficiently progressive, this focus of public attention is appropriate. Besides that, targetting subsidies on the poor increases the efficiency of the public subsidy. Hence, tuitions generally have been raised as a means of freeing up resources for aid to low-income students.

However, there is also the matter of equity between society and the individual. Should students be charged more and society less merely because the former *will* pay more? Our strong sense from the evidence is that society receives at least as large a return on investment as do individuals. Is it equitable to charge individuals proportionately more under such circumstances? We think not. Hence, we hold that public subsidies should be increased or at worst held at present share levels. Specifically, we urge some continuing increases in need-based student aid programs and a slowing of tuition increases for all. Among independent institutions the former would relieve pressure on institutional funds.

The marginal analysis approach to public finance further argues for increased spending on higher education. True rates of return on investment in higher education have been seen to be very high. We doubt that very many public expenditures would yield greater returns from additional public spending than would increased spending for higher education. We believe, on marginal analysis grounds, that higher education should be the beneficiary of proportionately greater public expenditures in the future.

In part what is suggested by the evidence presented here is a more finely tuned system of student charges and subsidies. Differentiated tuition and income-contingent loans come to mind as more sensitive public policy devices. If more money for equity enhancement is desired, why not target price increases on those who are likely to earn more, such as those studying in high-paying fields? Or assess higher charges *ex post facto* upon those who in fact earn more after college? Such strategies would be far more equitable than increasing prices for all, including those of modest means and those who will toil in low-paying public service occupations.

We close, as we began this chapter, with the observation that there is probably something here for everyone. Policymakers in search of a rationale likely will find it between the covers of this book. Does higher education contribute to individual, community, and national economic growth? Yes. Does the evidence support more money for higher education? Yes. Does the evidence support low student charges? Yes. Can tuitions be safely raised? Probably yes. Will higher charges impact enrollments? Yes. Does higher education contribute regressively to wealth distribution? No. Should student aid continue to be supported? Yes. Is more money for higher education a wise public investment? Yes.

For our part, we see no evidence that policy decisions encouraging higher education consumption will be anything but positive for the public welfare.

Appendix

Table 1
RATES OF RETURN

(1) ID No.	(2) Author(s), Year	(3/4) Years of Data/ Population	(5/6) Publication Source/ TS or CS	(7/8) Data Source/ Grade Levels	(9) Cost Specification	(10) Controls, Adjustments
01	Ashenfelter and Mooney, 1968	1966 & "1st year" of earnings/ Woodrow Wilson Fellows (Males)	J/CS	Woodrow Wilson Files/M.A., Ph.D.	FI-($1000 + $1500 stipend)	Discipline, experience, A, Ta
02	Bailey & Schotta, 1972	1966/Academicians	J/CS	Cal., AAUP/Ph.D.	DC = UCLA & UC Berkeley ave. cost. FI from B.A. salaries in Cal. − $2500. Soc = U.C. costs	
03	Becker, 1975	1939, 1949, 1956, 1958/Native born, urban, employed, white males	B/CS	Census/High school and college	Pvt. = .75 FI + DC Soc = Before tax FI + institutional costs of ed. activities + pvt. costs (net of T)	M, S, Ta, A
04	Becker and Cheswick, 1966	1959/White males	J/CS	Census/0–8, 8–12, >12, 16	FI + DC (?)	A, luck, personal traits
05	Borland & Yett, 1967	1949, 1959/Men	J/CS	Census/4 yrs or more	T, Fees, other direct (not room, board, clothing) FI = ¾ of I	
06	Butter, 1966	1964 & earlier/ Ph.Ds in zoology, physics, sociology, English in 12 u's	R/CS	NSF (1964)/ Ph.D.	Instructional, research, facilities, administration, library & FI	M
07	Carnoy and Marenbach, 1975	1939, 1949, 1959, 1969/Whites	J/CS	Census/ Elementary, high school, college graduates	Pvt. = 75% of Post tax FI; Soc. = Gross Exp. - Aux. Enterprises - capital outlay - foregone rents & depreciation + FI"	Ta (Fed, income, men only), M, U, S, A

Symbols, by Column:

(4) J = journal, B = book, R = report, S = secondary source, U = unpublished

(5) CPS = current population surveys, NBER-TH = National Bureau of Economic Research—Thorndike

(6) CS = cross section, meaning one or more cross sections was taken, each at one point in time
L = longitudinal, meaning that one or more cohorts (panel) was followed over time

(7, 10) DC = direct costs, FI = foregone income, Pvt. = private cost, Soc. = social cost
E & G = educational and general, T = tuition

(9) A = ability, H = hours worked, M = mortality, S = secular growth, Ta = taxes, U = unemployment
α = % of earnings attributed to education, NA = not applicable

(10) IRR = internal rate of return

(14) No U. = excludes unemployed

ID No.	(11/12) Dependent Variable Specification/ Includes Psychic?	(13) Special Notes	(14) RESULTS % Private		Social
01	Annual earnings/ No	Early earnings; high ability; prestige colleges; fellowships; Soc. Sci. & Hum. ¾ of total; Apparently no DC; key, years in school	6.5 8.8	M.A. Ph.D.	
02	Coll/univ. salaries/ No	Academicians in 829 highest paying coll.; 2–6 yrs. study; Ph.D. v. B.A.; Soc RR assumes no dropouts. No "outside" earnings.	Neg. to 20.3 neg. to 11.6 for 4 yrs. Ph.D. study .8 (best est.)		Neg. to 14.0 neg. to 7.8 for 4 yrs. Ph.D. study. 0 or <1% best est.
03	Earnings/Somewhat	Results after all adjustments	12.5 11.5 10.9 13.0	1939 1949 1956 1958	11.4 11.0
04	Earnings/No	Average IRR to all college years, high regression controls	8.5		
05	Annual income/No	Includes nonearners, four years or more	12.7 14.8	1949 1959	
06	Median annual salaries/No	Books & misc. cost omitted; student records for cost data; IRR marginal to B.A.; downward biased results (author); Physics, Zoology, English, Sociology			.1–8.0
07	Annual income & earnings/No	No DC, whites only (others available), including unemployed	21.4, 16.3 (no U) 13.2 17.6 15.4, 16.2 (earnings)	1939 1949 1959 1969	10.7, 9.0 (no U) 10.6 11.3 10.9, 11.0 (earnings)

(continued)

Table 1 (Continued)
RATES OF RETURN

(1) ID No.	(2) Author(s), Year	(3/4) Years of Data/ Population	(5/6) Publication Source/ TS or CS	(7/8) Data Source/Grade Levels	(9) Cost Specification	(10) Controls, Adjustments
08	Carroll & Ihnen, 1967	1957–1964/White male grads of N.C. Tech School	J/L	Coll. records, Student Surveys, Census/2 years	Soc. = Books & Supplies, tuitions, public support costs, net FI; pvt = soc-public support costs	Ability, motiv., SES, residence, H.S. size, S, M
09	Danielson, 1969–1970	1956–1966/Males	J/CS, L	(1) CPS 1956–1966 (2) Ga. Survey (3) Woodrow Wilson Files/B.A.-Ph.D.	(2) Perceived FI + DC	M, S, Ta
10	Duncan, 1976	1970–1971, 1973/ Working white nonfarm males	J/CS	Quality of Employment Survey, Panel Study of Income Dynamics/All	None	A, motivation, family background, etc.
11	Eckaus, 1973	1959/White males, 14–64	B/CS	Census/ Elementary - year 17	FI + Tuition and other costs	H, Ta, M, U, S
12	Freeman, 1975	1959, 1969, 1972, 1974/Males	J/CS	Census & CPS/ 4 years college	Soc. = Educational and General Income, + FI; Pvt. = .75 FI + T - scholarships	T
13	Freeman, 1977	1968, 1973/White men & women	J/CS	CPS/4 years college	Pvt. = Books, transp., T net FI; Soc. = Pvt. + E&G - aid	Bus. cycle, S
14	Greer, 1976	1959, 1969/All persons, subcategories	J/CS	Census/4 years college	FI, T	T, M, S
15	Hanoch, 1967	1959/Northern, white males	J/CS	Census/K-17	Total Cost = Gross FI (DC = Student Earnings)	Residence, origin, mobility, marital status, family size
16	Hansen, 1963	1949/Males	J/CS	Census/1–16	Soc. = Schultz method = institutional + pretax FI + incidentals. Pvt. = same except T for institutional	M, T

ID No.	(11/12) Dependent Variable Specification/ Includes Psychic?	(13) Special Notes	(14) RESULTS % Private		Social
08	Earnings per month/Leisure	45 Tech. School grads in N.C., matched control students, regression, net tax effect ~0, actual earnings differences (+ projected)	~20	including leisure value	16.5
			25.9	including leisure value	20.1
09	Annual Income (2) Earnings (3)/No	B.A. expected IRR for GA; M.A. & Ph.D. from Ashenfelter and Moody	14.8 (2)	B.A.	
			6.2 (3)	M.A.	
			8.5 (3)	Ph.D.	
10	Hourly wage, fringe benefits, work conditions, consumption benefits/Yes	Nonpecuniary and pecuniary items, incl. fringe benefits; regression	Rates increase as fringe & nonpecuniary benefits added. 11.3–25.7% (unadjusted)		
11	Hourly wage/No	Full adjustments except ability, poor early earnings data	11.5	4 years	
			4.0	5th yr.	
12	Annual income/No	E & G, 10% discount rate	11.0	1959	10.5
			11.5	1969	11.1
			10.5	1972	9.5
			8.5	1974	7.5
13	Annual & weekly earnings	Full-time workers, regression, E & G	11.0–12.5	1968	12.0–13.0
			7.5–10.0	1973	8.5–10.5
14	Net annual earnings/No	Low cost estimate, unemployed excluded	*All*		
			15.2	1959	
			17.0	1969	
			Unmarried Males		
			13.4		
			15.3		
15	Annual earnings/ No	Regression; coll. grad. earnings start at age 27; poor cost and early earnings data, under-reporting of earnings, student earnings ignored	9.6	16 yrs.	
			7.0	17 yrs.	
16	Annual income/No	Excludes unemployed; overstates costs; few controls	10.1		10.2

(continued)

Table 1 (Continued)
RATES OF RETURN

(1) ID No.	(2) Author(s), Year	(3/4) Years of Data/ Population	(5/6) Publication Source/ TS or CS	(7/8) Data Source/Grade Levels	(9) Cost Specification	(10) Controls, Adjustments
17	Hines, et al., 1970	1959/All	J/CS	Census/16 years	Soc. = "Current expend." incl. 10% of plant, land and eqpt. (book value) Pvt. = FI; Assumes DC = student earnings	Full adjustment
18	Hunt, 1963	1947/College graduates	J/L	Time Magazine 1947, national survey of college graduates/College	"Expense/pupil"	A, SES, occup., Residence, Mortality
19	Johnson & Stafford, 1973	1965/White male, urban employed	J/CS	Survey Research Center/12, 16	"Soc. Cost" = .75 FI + Exp./Student	Residence, SES
20	Koch, 1978	1968–1969/Illinois State University graduates; NSF Science (income)	J/CS	Illinois State cost, NSF Income/ Undergraduate	Undergraduate student cost at Illinois State	Unknown
21	Liberman, 1979	1958–1976	S/CS	CPS/8, 12, 16		
22	Mattila, 1982	1956–1979/Males	J/CS	CPS/High school, some college, continuing college	.75 × wages of high school graduates + T − Aid	Business cycle, unemployment
23	McMahon & Wagner, 1982	1969, 1976/B.A. Graduates, Nat. Sample	B/CS	ACT College Investment Decision Study, CPS, Coll. Placement Council/B.A., Graduate	Pvt. = net FI, books, net of aid; Soc. = pvt. & instructional cost	A, S, T + others, earnings differentials reduced by 34%
24	Mincer, 1962	1939, 1949, 1958/ Males	J/CS	Census/College	.75 FI + DC	A correction factor
25	Mincer, 1974	1959/White non-farm men	B/CS	Census/16, 17	Omits DC & student earnings	Experience, weeks worked

ID No.	(11/12) Dependent Variable Specification/ Includes Psychic?	(13) Special Notes	(14) RESULTS % Private		Social
17	Annual earnings/ No	Full adjustments for A, U, occupation, SES, etc; Poor data for younger	13.2 ~12.0	White Males Overall	9.7 ~7.6
18	Earnings	Admittedly downward biased, questionable sample, overcontrolled, 50% adjustment for controls; regression, both sexes		Unadjusted Adjusted	12 6
19	Hourly earnings/No	Unemployed excluded, regression, select sample (biases downward)			8.8
20	Annual income by discipline	Illinois State, 17 disciplines; poor data documentation, adjustments unknown; very questionable study (documentation)	6.5		
21	Pre-tax income/No	Regression, fitted to Mincer model, calc. at overtaking age (e.g., 1976 data for 1968 grads)		1958 1959 1974 1976	14.2 14.1 13.8 15.2
22	Annual income/No	IRR are averages per year for "starting college"; author "downplays" estimate precision	10–13		
23	Net annual earnings/No	Pvt. = expected IRR, calc. at overtaking age; Soc. = "realized" RR from 1969 census data	17 17 −.7 to 12.7 −1.8 to 19.3	White males Overall M.A. Ph.D.	13.3 13.0
24	Pre-tax earnings, income/No	Downward biased, pretax earnings (1939) & income (1949, 1958), costs-Schultz method, *values include OJT, IRR*	11 10.6 11.5	1939 1949 1958	
25	Annual earnings/ No	Marginal rates calculated at 8 years after graduation; regression	12.8 12.2	4 yrs coll. 17th yr.	

(continued)

Table 1 (Continued)
RATES OF RETURN

(1) ID No.	(2) Author(s), Year	(3/4) Years of Data/ Population	(5/6) Publication Source/ TS or CS	(7/8) Data Source/Grade Levels	(9) Cost Specification	(10) Controls, Adjustments
26	Morgan & David, 1963	1960/Mostly men	J/CS	Survey Research Center/All	Cost Data Lacking	Maximum
27	Raymond and Sesnowitz, 1975	1969/Males	J/CS	Census/College	Pvt. = .75 FI net of taxes, T, books and supplies ($150); Soc. = Pvt. + all subsidies (tax adjusted)	A, S, T, PT workers
28	Rogers, 1969	1935–1965/1935 Male 8th–9th graders, New England	J/L	Author Surveys/4 years, 2nd degree	T & Fees + FI	Maximum
29	Solmon, 1975	1955, 1969/WWII white, high ability male air cadets	J/CS-L	NBER-TH/Some college	FI-$100/mo.	A, college quality, occupation, health, SES, etc.
30	Taubman & Wales, 1973	1955, 1969/WWII white, high ability air cadets	J/CS-L	NBER-TH/High school and B.A., Masters, Ph.D., others	Pvt. = T+FI + incidental Soc. = 71% of E & G + FI + plant	A, health, SES, teaching occup., marital status, + others
31	Tomaske, 1974	1966/Bailey & Schotta data & 1963 supplemental income data	J/CS	USOE Survey/ Ph.D.	Bailey & Schotta data	See Study (#02)
32	Wachtel, 1976	1955, 1969/White, male high ability male air cadets	J/CS-L	NBER-TH/High school, some college, college, graduate	School expenditures	A, SES, α factor, health, unemployment, high earnings

ID No.	(11/12) Dependent Variable Specification/ Includes Psychic?	(13) Special Notes	(14) RESULTS % Private		Social
26	Hourly earnings	Income taxes excluded; multi-variate method removes earnings effects shared by education. Example: control for occupation	4–6%		
27	Annual income/No	Ability adjustment of 25% includes unemployed, Ave. IRR	15.7		14.3
28	Lifetime earnings/ No	Longitudinal, heavily private, over controlled, before tax	*Unadjusted* 4% high cost coll. 15% low cost coll. *Adjusted* 8% high cost coll. 9% low cost coll		*2nd Degree* 1, 2% (hi, low cost) 8, 10% (if 50% subsidy)
29	Annual earnings/ No	Regression, subsidies were $100/mo. + tuition; high FI for vets; 1969 IRR for 1 yr. coll or more, teachers over represented, coll. qual. controlled (omission raises IRR to 12%), unique pop., only "some college"	9.7		
30	Deflated, before tax monthly earnings/ Adjustment for teachers	See Solmon, regression, FI is from sample, no adj. for GI Bill; pvt IRR not CPI deflated, but omission of self employed balances. 1955–1969 data used.	11 8 4	 Masters Ph.D.	8 6 2
	Annual earnings/ No	Incl. summer & term-time earnings	9%	Ph.D.	
32	Annual salary for main job/No	IRR to school expenditures for school attended (expend. composition unknown); adjustments for unemployment, health and high earnings; regression; IRRs for 1969 data (1955 IRR smaller)			10 14 for >16 years

(continued)

Table 1 (Continued)
RATES OF RETURN

(1)	(2)	(3/4)	(5/6)	(7/8)	(9)	(10)
ID No.	Author(s), Year	Years of Data/ Population	Publication Source/ TS or CS	Data Source/Grade Levels	Cost Specification	Controls, Adjustments
33	Weiss, 1971	1966/NSF scientific and technical personnel	J/CS	NSF/Graduate	NET FI and academic expenses	Type employment, region, unemployment, sex, origin
34	Witmer, 1983	1961–1982/Men and women	U/CS	Census/12, 16	Pvt. = net FI, net tuition. Soc. = instructional expend., share of plant, tax exemptions, all net of student aid and consumption benefits	A, M, Ta, U, and other
35	Witmer, 1980	1961–1972/Men and women	J/CS	CPS/College	E&G net of research and public service	α coefficient approach

ID No.	(11/12) Dependent Variable Specification/ Includes Psychic?	(13) Special Notes	(14) RESULTS % Private		Social
33	Annual Income/ Implicitly (See Col. 14*)	Student registered time; sample is heavy in hard sciences (16% social sciences); *holding work type (e.g., academic/ industry) constant raises IRR; student earnings substantial, great IRR variability by field; secular growth inclusion would raise IRR by 4.7%, annual income	10.6 M.A. 12.9 M.A. completed in prescribed time 8.7 Ph.D. 8.9 Ph.D. completed in prescribed time		
34	Annual income/ Implicit consumption benefit	Weighted average per year IRR for men & women, most accurate cost data, complete controls & adjustments, uses earnings estimates	15.0 15.6 16.5 16.5	1961–1962 1971–1972 1979–1980 1981–1982	13.8 12.4 13.4 13.5
35	Annual income/No	See study 34		1961 1969 1973 1975	14.2 13.4 13.9 15.1

Table 2
UNDERGRADUATE PRIVATE RATES OF RETURN, RESULTS ONLY

ID No.*	Author, Year	Data Year	Private IRR
03	Becker, 1975	1939	12.5
		1949	11.5
		1956	10.9
		1958	13.0
04	Becker & Cheswick, 1966	1959	8.5 (all college years)
05	Borland & Yett, 1967	1949	12.7[a]
		1959	14.8
07	Carnoy & Marenbach, 1975	1939	21.4, 16.3[b]
		1949	13.2
		1959	17.6
		1969	15.4, 16.2[c]
08	Carroll & Ihnen, 1967	1957–1964	~20, 25.9[d]
09	Danielson, 1969–70	1956–1966	14.8
10	Duncan, 1976	1970–1973	11.3 to 25.7[e]
11	Eckaus, 1973	1959	11.5
12	Freeman, 1975	1959	11.0
		1969	11.5
		1972	10.5
		1974	8.5
13	Freeman, 1977	1968	11.0 to 12.5
		1973	7.5 to 10.0
14	Greer, 1976	1959	13.4[f], 15.2[g]
		1969	15.3[f], 17.0[g]
15	Hanoch, 1967	1969	9.6
16	Hansen, 1963	1949	10.1
17	Hines, et al., 1970	1959	13.2,~12.0[g]
18	Hunt, 1963	1947	6, 12[h]
20	Koch, 1978	1968–1969	6.5
22	Mattila, 1982	1956–1979	10 to 13
23	McMahon & Wagner, 1982	1969, 1976	17
24	Mincer, 1962	1939	11
		1949	10.6
		1958	11.5
25	Mincer, 1974	1959	12.8
26	Morgan & David, 1963	1960	4 to 6
27	Raymond & Sesnowitz, 1975	1969	15.7
28	Rogers, 1969	1935–1965	8 to 9, 14 to 15[h]
29	Solmon, 1975	1959, 1969	9.7[i]
30	Taubman & Wales, 1973	1955, 1969	11
34	Witmer, 1983	1961–1962	15.0
		1971–1972	15.6
		1979–1980	16.5
		1981–1982	16.5

*I.D. numbers are from meta-analysis matrix, Table 1.
[a]4 years or more
[b]Excluding unemployed
[c]IRR for earnings
[d]Includes value of leisure, 2 yr. tech. school
[e]Rates increase with nonpecuniary benefits
[f]Unmarried males
[g]All persons
[h]Unadjusted
[i]Some college

Table 3
UNDERGRADUATE SOCIAL RATES OF RETURN, RESULTS ONLY

ID No.*	Author, Year	Data Year	Social Rate
03	Becker, 1975	1939	11.4
		1949	11.0
07	Carnoy & Marenbach, 1975	1939	10.7, 9.0[a]
		1969	10.9, 11.0[b]
08	Carroll & Ihnen, 1967	1957–1964	16.5, 20.1[c]
12	Freeman, 1975	1959	10.5
		1969	11.1
		1972	9.5
		1974	7.5
13	Freeman, 1977	1968	12.0 to 13.0
		1973	8.5 to 10.5
16	Hansen, 1963	1949	10.2
17	Hines, et al., 1970	1959	9.7, ~ 7.6[d]
19	Johnson & Stafford, 1973	1965	8.8
21	Liberman, 1979	1958	14.2
		1959	14.2
		1974	13.8
		1976	15.2
23	McMahon & Wagner, 1982	1969, 1976	13.3, 13.0[d]
27	Raymond & Sesnowitz, 1975	1969	14.3
30	Taubman & Wales, 1973	1955, 1969	8
32	Wachtel, 1976	1955, 1969	10
34	Witmer, 1983	1961–1962	13.8
		1971–1972	12.4
		1979–1980	13.4
		1981–1982	13.5
35	Witmer, 1980	1961	14.2
		1964	13.4
		1973	13.9
		1975	15.1

*I.D. numbers are from meta-analysis matrix. See Appendix Table 1.
[a]Excluding unemployed
[b]IRR for earnings
[c]Includes value of leisure, 2 yr. tech. school
[c]All persons

Table 4
ECONOMIC IMPACT STUDIES

(1) Authors(s), Pub. Date / Data Year	(2) Analysis Method	(3) College(s) Type	(4) "Community"	(5) Surveys Collected?	(6) % Local Expend-itures	(7) Multipliers: Spending / Jobs	(8) Business Volume/ College Budget
1. Altman[1], 1985 1984	ACE	Pub. Coll.	Southeast, IN	Yes	NA	1.8 2.8	2.5
2. Baum[1], 1978 1978–1979	ACE	C.C.	Trenton, NJ	No	.30	1.4 1.7	.5
3. Bess, et al., 1980 1977–1978	ACE	C.C.	6 mixed, IL communities	Yes	NA	1.8 3.2	3.0
4. Breslin[1], 1979 1977–1978	ACE	Pub. Coll.	Trenton, NJ	Yes	NA	1.9 2.2	.9
5. Butler[1], 1980 1978, 1979	ACE	C.C.	Hampton, VA	No	.23	1.3 1.3	.4
6. Campbell & Linthicum, 1982 1980–1981	ACE	C.C.	Washington, DC Suburb	No	.37	1.4 1.4	.4

ABBREVIATIONS
General:
NA = Not Applicable or Not Available
NC = Not Calculated
Col. 2:
ACE = American Council on Education. Employs a specific economic base model.
EB = Economic Base, generically
I/O = Input/Output Analysis
Col. 3:
All = All Colleges
C.C. = Community College
Pub. = Public
Pvt. = Private
U. = University
Coll. = College
Col. 14:
PT = Part-time
FT = Full-time
FTE = Full Time Equivalent

(9) Jobs / College Budget ($Million)	(10) Corrected Jobs Multiplier	(11) Corrected Business Volume / College Budget	(12) Corrected Jobs Budget ($Million)	(13) Validity, Comparability	(14) Special Notes/Data Omissions (0)
1. 86	2.9	NC	80	1	Adjustments for induced student migration;* student expenditures high;* FT employees only.
3. 72	1.9	1.0	51	2	Student expenditures (except aid) & visitors* (0); no survey;* includes work study students in jobs data.
3. 178	2.4	NC	84	3	Poorly documented;* key, "college expenditures" term undefined;* values appear inflated.
4. 105	1.8	.9	39	1	Visitors (0); jobs are "positions".
5. 56	1.6	.7	47	2	Student Expenditures, visitors & PT employees* (0); no survey;* low multipliers and low local expenditure shares used.*
6. 42	1.7	.7	44	2	Student expenditures, visitors & PT employees* (0); no survey.*

(continued)

NOTES

Col. 1: 1 = Economics/Business faculty author or advisor

Col. 5: No survey means that data were estimated

Col. 6: % local expenditure is for nonsalary, noninternal and nontax expenditures by the college.

Col. 8: The sum of local college, employee, student, and visitor spending, including multiplier impact, divided by Education and General Expenditures (see col. 14 for exceptions). 1 = Considers only dollars from other states. 2 = Assumes "No college hypothesis."

Col. 9: Number of jobs created. . . . 1 = Considers only dollars from other states.

Col. 10: Jobs multiplier corrected for inflation and to render comparable. Where PT employees omitted, FTE of PT imputed from 1 FTE = 8 PT.

Col. 11: Business volume corrected to standardize roughly, different treatment of student expenditures (see col. 14).

Col. 12: Jobs created when correction of col. 10 applied; expressed in 1985–6 dollars.

Col. 13: 1 = Most valid/comparable studies. 2 = Less valid/comparable but acceptable studies. 3 = Invalid or noncomparable studies.

Col. 14: This column highlights study characteristics important to interpretation. Items marked (*) are most important to interpretation and often explain relatively high or low results unless effects tend to cancel out. (0) = Omitted by study author. Comments as to hi or low values are relative judgments based usually on identification of a questionable value in calculations. "Netting out" = reductions or adjustments.

Table 4 (Continued)
ECONOMIC IMPACT STUDIES

(1) Authors(s), Pub. Date / Data Year	(2) Analysis Method	(3) College(s) Type	(4) "Community"	(5) Surveys Collected?	(6) % Local Expend-itures	(7) Multipliers: Spending / Jobs	(8) Business Volume/ College Budget
7. California Postsecondary Commission, 1984 1981–1982	ACE	*All*	CA				
		a. State U			.50	2.4	NA
		b. U. CA.			NA	2.8	2.1
		c. C.C.			NA	2.5	3.8
		d. Pvt.			NA	2.5	1.4
8. Chestnut, 1983 1981–1982	ACE	C.C.	Schenectady, NY	Yes	NA	1.6 / 3.0	1.5
9. Cosgrove, 1984 1983(?)	ACE	C.C.	St. Louis, MO	employees only	.70	2.5 / NA	3.7
10. Council of Community Colleges of NJ, 1983 1981–1982	ACE	C.C.	NJ	Yes	NA	2.5 / 4.4	NA
11. Eade, 1977 1975–1976	EB	All Pub.	WA	Yes	NA	1.3 / NA	NA
12. Engler, et al.[1], 1980 1978–1979	EB	Pub. U.	LA	No	NA	1.7 / 2.1	NC
13. Gay & Weintraub, 1978 1976–1977	EB	Private	NY	No	NA	2.0 / 2.0	3.5
14. Hargrave & Buford, 1973 NA	I/O	"Education"	LA	Yes	NA	1.5 / NA	NC
15. Hogan & McPheters, 1979 1977–1978	ACE	Pub U.	AZ	Yes	1.00	1.9 / 1.9	3.9
16. Jackson, et al., 1978 1975–1976	EB	C.C.	WA	?	NA	NA / NA	1.5
17. Jeacock, 1983 1982–1983	ACE	C.C.	Rural British Columbia	Yes	.48	1.3 / 2.2	.8

(9) Jobs / College Budget ($Million)	(10) Corrected Jobs Multiplier	(11) Corrected Business Volume / College Budget	(12) Corrected Jobs / Budget ($Million)	(13) Validity, Comparability	(14) Special Notes/Data Omissions (0)
7.				3	Inadequate documentation.*
a.					Very liberal estimates.
b.					Student expenditures & visitors (0).
c. 75					Student expenditures appear low.
d. 107					
8. 111	2.0	1.5	64	1	Col. 8 value reflects "no college hypothesis";* visitors (0).
9. NA	NA	2.0	NA	3	Multiplier high;* student budget data used;* visitors (0); poor documentation.*
10. NA	NC	NA	NC	3	Overstated student expenditures.*
11. NA	NA	NA	NA	1	Perhaps most accurate study but form of results not comparable; dissertation.
12. 95	NC	NC	NC	?	Econometric design.*
13. 120	NC	2.4	NC	3	Very questionable data;* poor documentation; includes PT persons as FT; no survey.*
14. NC	NC	NC	NC	?	Input/output analysis.
15. 162	NC	NC	NC	3	Uses 100% of student and employee spending in measuring *state* impact.*
16. 168	NC	NC	NC	3	Budget amount is state dollars only; not comparable;* student expenditures?*
17. 41	2.3	.8	37	2	British Columbia study; visitors & PT employees (0).

(continued)

Table 4 (Continued)
ECONOMIC IMPACT STUDIES

(1) Authors(s), Pub. Date / Data Year	(2) Analysis Method	(3) College(s) Type	(4) "Community"	(5) Surveys Collected?	(6) % Local Expend-itures	(7) Multipliers: Spending / Jobs	(8) Business Volume/ College Budget
18. Kincaid & Tippett, 1984 1982–1983	EB	C.C.	Lenoir, NC	Yes	.24	1.5 2.1	2.5[2]
19. Lange[1], 1980 1979	ACE	Pub. Coll.	St. Cloud, MN	Yes	NA	2.1 4.0	2.3
20. Linthicum, 1978 1976–1977	ACE	C.C.	MD	No	.68	2.0 1.5	1.2
21. Littlefield[1], 1982 1980–1981	ACE	C.C.	Long Beach, CA	Yes	NA	1.8 2.7	.7
22. Lucas, 1982 1980–1981	ACE	C.C.	Palatine, IL	No(?)	.92	1.8 3.8	2.2
23. Mahon, 1979 1978–1979	ACE	C.C.	Trenton, NJ Suburb	No	.10	1.4 2.0	.6
24. McEnany[1], 1979 1977–1978	ACE	Pvt. U.	Providence, RI & State	Yes	NA	1.9 2.1	.9/1.5
25. Olson, 1981 1980–1981	EB	All Pvt.	MA	Yes	NA	1.4? (Income) 2.4?	1.6
26. Pennsylvania Economy League[1], 1981 1979–1980	ACE	All	PA	Yes	.83	1.7 1.7	2.0
27. Philadelphia Community College, 1982 1980–1981	ACE	C.C.	Philadelphia, PA	Yes	NA	1.8 4.6	2.8
28. Poris & Eskow, 1978 1976–1977	ACE	C.C.	Surburban New York City	Yes	.38	1.9 NA	2.0

(9) Jobs / College Budget ($Million)	(10) Corrected Jobs Multiplier	(11) Corrected Business Volume / College Budget	(12) Corrected Jobs / Budget ($Million)	(13) Validity, Comparability	(14) Special Notes/Data Omissions (0)
18. 84	2.4	NA	97	2	Visitors (0); poor documentation.*
19. 97	2.7	NC	65	2	Hi multipliers;* all employees (PT) included; expenditure values high.*
20. 64	NC	NC	NC	2	Student expenditures & Fed student aid* (0); no survey;* problem of above for C.C. impact on *State*.
21. 69	2.4	1.4	55	3 (2 corrected)	Student expenditures (except aid) & PT employees* (0); calculations not compatible.*
22. 127	2.4	NA	63	2	No survey* (?); poor documentation;* 92% local expenditure figure; visitors (0).
23. 70	1.8	.7	43	2	Student expenditures (except aid) & visitors* (0); no survey.*
24. 61	1.8	.9/1.5	38	1	89% of students from out-of-state; first values are for impact upon the city.
25. 80	NC	NC	NC	1	Objective analysis; Includes pub. expenditure saved and received; considers migration.
26. 93	NC	NC	NC	1	PT students, nonresident employees (0);* student expenditures low;* budget uncertain.*
27. 131	3.5	NA	78	2	Visitors & PT students and employees (very large in CCs) (0);* hi jobs multiplier.*
28. NA	NA	NC	NC	1	Proper "netting out" of dollar values; loss of college would raise Col. 8 to 2.7.

(continued)

Table 4 (Continued)
ECONOMIC IMPACT STUDIES

(1) Authors(s), Pub. Date / Data Year	(2) Analysis Method	(3) College(s) Type	(4) "Community"	(5) Surveys Collected?	(6) % Local Expend-itures	(7) Multipliers: Spending / Jobs	(8) Business Volume/ College Budget
29. Posey[1], 1983 1982–1983	EB	Pub. U.	Atlanta, GA	Yes	1.00	1.6 2.4	2.5
30. Romano, 1985 1975–1976	ACE	C.C.	Binghamton, NY	Yes	.49	1.9 2.3	1.8
31. Rosen[1], 1985 1983–1984	EB	Pub. U.	Madison, WI	Yes	.85	2.2 1.8	2.8
32. Ryan, 1983 1981–1982(?)	ACE	C.C.	Brookdale, NJ	No	.54	2.0 NA	4.1
33. Salley[1], 1976 1975–1976	EB	Pub. U.	Atlanta, GA	Yes	1.00	1.5 2.6	2.9
34. Salley[1], 1979 1978–1979	EB	Pub. U.	Atlanta, GA	Yes	1.00	1.5 3.1	2.6
35. Schimmelpfennig, 1983 1981	ACE	C.C.	Bismarck, ND	Yes	.76	1.8 NA	2.0
36. Selgas, et al.[1], 1979 1978–1979	ACE	C.C.	Harrisburg, PA	Yes	.29	1.5 NA	1.5
37. Stevenson, 1982 1980–1981	ACE	C.C.	OR/ Local	Yes	NA	1.8 NC	NA

(9) Jobs / College Budget ($Million)	(10) Corrected Jobs Multiplier	(11) Corrected Business Volume / College Budget	(12) Corrected Jobs / Budget ($Million)	(13) Validity, Comparability	(14) Special Notes/Data Omissions (0)
29. 87	3.1	NC	78	2	Hi local expenditure ratio;* visitors & PT employees & (most) PT students (0); very hi student spending.*
30. 134	2.1	NA	66	1	PT students (0); loss of college would raise col. 8 value.
31. 69	3.5	NC	64	2	Values not comparable;* hi jobs multiplier.*
32. NC	1.9	1.8	65	3	Visitors (0); corrected values may be OK;* uncorrected reflect student "budgets".* No surveys;* may include all spending in-state;* poorly documented.*
33. 176	3.5	NC	96	2	Hi student & local spending values;* hi jobs multipliers;* PT employees & (most) PT students & visitors (0).
34. 137	3.2	NC	91	2	Hi student & local spending values;* hi jobs multipliers;* PT employees & (most) PT students & visitors (0).
35. NA	NA	NC	NA	1	Low student spending.
36. NA	NA	NC	NA	1	Study also contains full "netting out" values; Col. 8 nets out local tax support, all PT student & employees spending;* budget excludes auxiliaries.*
37. NA	NC	NA	NA	3	Local values used;* visitors (0); data not comparable.

(continued)

Table 4 (Continued)
ECONOMIC IMPACT STUDIES

(1) Authors(s), Pub. Date / Data Year	(2) Analysis Method	(3) College(s) Type	(4) "Community"	(5) Surveys Collected?	(6) % Local Expend-itures	(7) Multipliers: Spending / Jobs	(8) Business Volume/ College Budget
38. Taylor & Byrden[1], 1973 1972–1973	ACE	Pvt. U.	CO	Yes	NA	1.9 2.6	2.4
39. Wellsfry[1], 1976 1973–1974	ACE	C.C.	VA	No?	.75	1.2 3.0	1.7 .7[1]

(9) Jobs / College Budget ($Million)	(10) Corrected Jobs Multiplier	(11) Corrected Business Volume / College Budget	(12) Corrected Jobs / Budget ($Million)	(13) Validity, Comparability	(14) Special Notes/Data Omissions (0)
38. 128	2.4	NA	56	1	PT students (0); appears objectively done; hi jobs multiplier;* hi student spending.*
39. 191 128	NC	NC	NC	2	Low spending multiplier; probably no survey;* student spending (except aid) (0); not compatible.

Table 5
REDISTRIBUTION OF WEALTH

(1) ID No.	(2) Author(s), Year	(3/4) Year of Data/ Publication Source	(5/6) Population/Data Source	(7/8) Progressive or Regressive/Special Notes
01	Crean, 1975	1961–1962/J	Canadian universities/ Canadian government	Progressive
02	Hansen, 1970	1964–1965/J	University of Wisconsin and Wisconsin State Universities/WI universities and government data	Progressive*/Same data and method limitations as in Hansen and Weisbrod, 1969
03	Hansen and Weisbrod, 1969	1964/J	CA undergraduates/ Coordinating Council for Higher Education (CA)	Indeterminate/ Compared only averages, numerous methodological problems
04	Hartman, 1970	1970 $/J	CA/Secondary analysis of Hansen and Weisbrod and Pechman data	Progressive*
05	Hight and Pollock, 1973	1968/J	CA, FL, HI/ Secondary analyses of data from other authors	CA: Progressive FL and HI: neutral to slightly regressive/ Tax share and university enrollment rates assessed
06	Jencks, 1968	1965/J	U.S.: Census	Progressive/Taxes paid versus B.A.s received
07	Judy, 1970	1961/B	Canadian universities; Dominion Bureau of Statistics, Canada	Progressive
08	Machlis, 1973	1968 $/J	18–24 year olds CUNY, Census	Progressive

*Judgment by the authors from data provided

Symbols, by Column

(3) $ = year of $, not year of data

(4) J = journal, B = book

Table 5 (Continued)
REDISTRIBUTION OF WEALTH

(1) ID No.	(2) Author(s), Year	(3/4) Year of Data/ Publication Source	(5/6) Population/Data Source	(7/8) Progressive or Regressive/Special Notes
09	Machovec, 1972	1970/J	CO 2-year, 4-year, and universities; Census	Progressive
10	McGuire, 1976	Inflated to 1971 $/J	Undergraduates and graduates; Census, CA government	Progressive/ Families whose head was 35–60, student aid included, costs unconsidered
11	Moore, 1982	1974 $/J	SUNY/Census	Progressive; Families whose head was 35–59, student aid considered
12	Pechman, 1970	1964/J	CA undergraduates/ Secondary analysis of Hansen and Weisbrod data	Progressive
13	Windham, 1970	1960–1961; 1967–1978/J	Florida/Florida government, Federal tax data	Regressive/ Thorough methods, Florida taxes regressive
14	Zimmerman, 1973	1969/J	St. Louis area/St. Louis County Junior College	Slightly progressive or neutral*/ Community college only

Table 6
STUDENT DEMAND META-ANALYSIS MATRIX

(1) ID No.	(2) Author(s), Year	(3) Year of Data	(4) Population	(5) Publication Source	(6) TS or CS	(7) Price Specification	(8) Degree of Control*	(9) Statistics	(10) Individual Students (v. Aggregate Data)
01	AASCU, 1977	1973	WI	R	CS	Tuition	Low	Descriptive	No
02	AASCU, 1977	1976	WI	R	CS	Tuition	Low	Descriptive	No
03	Barnes, 1975	1970	NC	S	CS	Tuition	High	Linear probability	Yes
04	Berne, 1980	1975	NY	J	CS	Student Aid	High	Regression	Yes
05	Bishop, 1977	1960	Project Talent, U.S.	J	CS	Tuition, room and board, travel	High	Logit	Yes
06	Campbell and Siegel, 1967	1927–1963	U.S.	J	TS	Tuition	Low	Regression	Yes
07	Clotfelter, 1976	1970	U.S.	J	CS	Tuition	High	Regression	Yes
08	Corrazzini et al., 1972	1963	Project Talent, U.S.	J	CS	Tuition	High	Regression	Yes
09	Funk, 1972	1959–1970	Creighton, U.	J	TS	Tuition	Low	Regression	No
10	Ghali, et al., 1977	1970	Hawaii	J	CS	Tuition, Total Cost	High	Logit	Yes
11	Hight, 1975	1927–1972	U.S.	J	TS	Tuition	Middle	Regression	No
12	Hoenack, 1968	1967	U. CA	R	CS	Commute Cost	High	Regression	No
13	Hoenack and Feldman, 1969	1963	Project Talent, U.S.	R	CS	Tuition	High	Regression	Yes
14	Hoenack and Weiler, 1975	1958–1972	MN	J	CS, TS	Commute Cost	High	Regression	No
15	Hopkins, 1974	1963–1964	49 states	J	CS	Net Tuition	High	Regression	No
16	Jackson, 1978	1972	U.S.	J	CS	Student Aid	High	Discriminate, Regression	Yes
17	Knudsen and Servelle, 1978	1970	U.S.	J	CS	Tuition, net tuition	Middle	Regression	Yes

*Degree of control is a subjective matter referring to number and importance of variables controlled. For example, at one end of the continuum, the AASCU studies are descriptive studies that do not control statistically for any variables although qualifying statements are made regarding the student population and which students were affected. In contrast, most econometric analyses control for a more or less consistent set of important variables, such as family income, student ability, high school curriculum, sex, residence, number of siblings, and religion. Such studies are deemed to have a high degree of control.

Symbols, by Column:

(5) Publication Source: D = dissertation, J = journal, R = report, S = secondary source

(6) TS = time series, CS = cross section

(7) Denotes the form of the price variable.

ID No.	(11) Financial Aid Considered	(12) Institutional Type	(13) Special Notes	(14) SPRC (a) 18–24 year old Enrollment Rate Change/$100	(14) SPRC (b) Institutional Enrollment Change/$100
01	No	2-year	Experiment	+1.3	+4.1
02	No	2-year	Experiment	−1.0	−3.0
03	Yes	All		−0.6	−1.8
04	Yes	2-year	Applicants only	+0.5	+1.5
05	Yes	All	11th graders, minimum cost college	−0.4	−1.2
06	No	4-year		−0.6	−1.7
07	No	Public		−0.5	−1.5
08	No	All	10th graders	−0.5	−1.5
09	No	4-year private	Average SPRC, over time	−0.2	−0.5
10	Yes	Public	Hawaii	−0.6	−1.8
11	Yes	Public and private	Identification problem	−1.1	−3.3
12	Yes	4-year public	12th graders, total cost	−0.6	−1.8
13	No	All	10th graders, "indifferent"	−1.0	−3.0
14	No	4-year public	Own price response only	−1.3	−4.1
15	Yes	Public, private	Rate = % of enrollment to H.S. grads in 4 years	−0.6	−1.8
16	Yes	All	Aid is dependent variable	−0.2	−0.6
17	No	Private	Mid-Selective privates, Average weighted values	−0.6	−1.9

(continued)

Table 6 (Continued)
STUDENT DEMAND META-ANALYSIS MATRIX

(1) ID No.	(2) Author(s), Year	(3) Year of Data	(4) Population	(5) Publication Source	(6) TS or CS	(7) Price Specification	(8) Degree of Control*	(9) Statistics	(10) Individual Students (v. Aggregate Data)
18	Kohn, et al., 1976	1966	IL, NC	J	CS	Tuition, room and board, commute cost	High	Logit	Yes
19	Lehr and Newton, 1978	1960–1974	OR	J	TS	Tuition	Middle	Regression, Discriminate	No
20	Orvis, 1975	1970	MN	D	CS	Commute Cost	High	Regression	No
21	Radner and Miller, 1970	1966	IL, CA	J	CS	Cost income ratio	High	Logit, Regression	Yes
22	Sulock, 1982	1969	U.S.	J	CS	Tuition	Middle	Regression	No
23	Tannen, 1978	1959, 1969	Census	J	CS	Foregone income, net tuition, room and board	High	Regression	No
24	Tauchar, 1969	1966	CA	J	CS	Cost	NA	Descriptive	Yes
25	Wilson, 1977	1972	MN	D	CS	Commute Cost	High	Regression, Logit	No

	(11)	(12)	(13)	(14) SPRC	
ID No.	Financial Aid Considered	Institutional Type	Special Notes	(a) 18–24 year old Enrollment Rate Change/$100	(b) Institutional Enrollment Change/$100
18	No	All	Estimates calculated, Average, 12th graders	−0.6	−1.8
19	Yes	All	Oregon	−0.7	−2.2
20	No	Public	11th graders	−1.1	−3.3
21	No	All	Average	−0.3	−0.9
22	Yes	Community College	Community Colleges	−2.4	−7.4
23	Yes	All	14–24 age rates, males only	−0.8	−2.5
24	No	Roman Catholic	Catholic High Schools	−0.3	−0.8
25	No	All	Distance is dependent variable	−0.8	−2.5

Table 7
STUDENT AID

(1)	(2)	(3)	(4)	(5)
ID No.	Author, Year	Year of Data/ Population	Source/ Publication	Statistics/ Control
A. ACCESS				
Econometric Analyses:				
01	Berne, 1980	1975/Applicants to two 2-year colleges	Own survey/J	Regression/High
02	Blakemore & Low, 1985	1972/N, 10385	NLS/J	Probit/High
03	Carlson, 1975	Early 1970s/Various	Various/R	Regression/Low
04	Crawford, 1966	1959/N, 7300 Merit finalists	Own survey/R	Descriptive/ Moderate
05	Carroll et al., 1977	1972/N, 14131 freshmen	NLS/R	Bayesian/High
06	Jackson, 1978	1972, 1973/N, 2133 college applicants	NLS/J	Regression/High

Symbols, by Column:

(3) N = national sample, L = local sample, HS = high school, FT = full-time, PT = part-time, D = dependent, NR = not reported.

(4) J = journal, R = report, M = monograph, B = book, D = dissertation, NLS = National Longitudinal Study of the High School Class of 1972, HSB = High School and Beyond, CPS = Current Population Survey, CIRP = Cooperative Institutional Research Program, ACT = American College Testing service, ETS = Educational Testing Service, HEGIS = Higher Education General Information Survey, SAT = Scholastic Aptitude Test, PSAT = Preliminary SAT, NCES = National Center for Education Statistics, CEEB = College Entrance Examination Board, PHEAA = Pennsylvania Higher Education Assistance Authority

(5) High = a considerable number of variables are controlled for, typically including parents, education, race, sex, academic ability, and when appropriate, high school and college character-

ID No.	(6) Type of Aid/ Persistence Measure	(7) Results	(8) Remarks
		Estimated Enrollment Dependent on Grant Aid, by Family Income:	
01	Change in net price/NA	Low/Middle: 30.8%	Figure is based on average total grant award (1982–1983) of $1400; 2.2% per $100.
02	Scholarships & Grants/NA	$11,000: 32.1% $34,000: 19.5% $57,000: 3.0%	Figures are extrapolations (to all aid) of results for effects of 30% of aid.
03	Grants, Loans, & Work Study/NA	<$13,000: 34.4% $13–25,000: 12.4%	Figure is based on average total grant award (1982–1983) of $1400; 2.5% per $100 for low income.
04	All/NA	Needy: 37.0%	Reported 14.8% for very high ability students adjusted for average students using Carroll and Blakemore & Low.
05	BEOG/NA	<$14,000: 20.6% $14–23,000: 7.4%	Mean results from 10 simulations of the effects of different BEOG award policies.
06	All/NA	Low SES: 19.5%	The effect on applicants of the award of some aid.

(continued)

istics; Moderate = a smaller set of control variables; Low = a small or sometimes nonexistent set of control variables; Matched = study employs experimental and control groups matched on academic ability; Random = samples were chosen randomly

EOG = Educational Opportunity Grant; BEOG = Basic Educational Opportunity Grant, SEOG = Supplementary Educational Opportunity Grant, SSIG = State Student Incentive Grant, NDSL = National Defense Student Loan, CWS = college work study, HS = high school, G = graduation, G−4 = graduation in four years (g−6, etc.), G/E−5 = graduation or still enrolled after five years, # = number of, T = transfer, S = stopout, DO = dropout, P = persister, NI = not included in the study, NR = not reported.

PRU = public research university, PCC = public comprehensive college, HCP = high cost private college or university

Table 7 (Continued)
STUDENT AID

(1) ID No.	(2) Author, Year	(3) Year of Data/ Population	(4) Source/ Publication	(5) Statistics/ Control
07	Manski & Wise, 1983	1972/N, 4000 respondents	NLS/B	Logit/High
Student Opinion Surveys:				
08	Fenske et al., 1979	1976, 1973, 1970, 1967/L, Illinois aid recipients	Own surveys/J	Descriptive/Low
09	Fife & Leslie, 1976	1972–1973/L, 3000 aid recipients across 4 states	Own surveys/J	Descriptive/ High
10	Springer, 1976	1973/N, Social Security beneficiaries	Own survey/J	Descriptive/Low
Participation Rate Calculations:				
11	Clowes et al., 1986	1961, 1972, 1982/N, recent HS graduates	Project Talent, NLS, HSB/J	Descriptive/Low
12	Davis & Johns, 1982	1966, 1971, 1976, 1980/N, first-time FT freshman	CIRP/J	Descriptive/Low
13	Frances, 1982	1974, 1980/N, families with FT 18–24 yr old D	CPS/R	Descriptive/Low
14	Frances, 1980	1967–1977/N, 18–24 yr old D	CPS/R	Descriptive/Low
15	Hansen, 1983	1971/1972, 1979/ 1980/N, 18–24 yr old D	CPS/J	Descriptive/Low
16	Lee, 1986	1978, 1981, 1983/N, coll. eligible 18–24 yr old D	CPS/P	Descriptive/Low
17	Lee & Others, 1984	1969, 1974, 1981/N, coll. eligible 18–24 yr old D	CPS/R	Descriptive/Low

ID No.	(6) Type of Aid/ Persistence Measure	(7) Results			(8) Remarks
07	BEOG	<$23,000: $23–30,000: >$30,000:	37.3% 11.1% 2.4%	41.5% 14.1% 3.5%	Lesser figures based on BEOGs as substitutes for other aid; greater on BEOGs as complementary.
		Aid Recipient Enrollment Dependent on Grant Aid:			
08	Scholarships & Grants/NA	Grants: (Needy)	50.5% 45.8% 37.5% 15.8%	Scholarships: (Needy & Able)	32.8% 26.9% 23.7% 11.0%
09	Scholarships & Grants/NA		<13,700	$13,700– $22,800	$22,800– $34,200
		CA Scholarship:	46.5%	36.5%	22.5%
		NJ Grant:	50.9%	44.6%	44.9%
		NJ Scholarship:	67.1%	50.3%	43.7%
		NY Grant:	65.3%	50.4%	37.1%
		PA Grant:	53.8%	43.4%	27.5%
10	Grants/NA	All:	36.0%		would not continue; another 16% were unsure of their ability to continue
		Changes in Participation Rates:			
11	All/NA	See Table 8.3.			
12	All/NA	See Table 8.3.			
13	All/NA	See Table 8.3.			
14	All/NA	See Table 8.3.			
15	All/NA	See Table 8.3.			
16	All/NA	See Table 8.3.			
17	All/NA	See Table 8.3.			

(continued)

Table 7 (Continued)
STUDENT AID

(1) ID No.	(2) Author, Year	(3) Year of Data/ Population	(4) Source/ Publication	(5) Statistics/ Control
18	Lee et al., 1985	1970, 1975, 1981/N, coll. eligible 18–24 yr old D	CPS/R	Descriptive/Low
19	Leslie, 1977	1967–1975/N, families with FT 18–24 yr olds	CPS/M	Descriptive/Low
20	Longanecker, 1980	1968, 1974, 1978/N, 17–22 yr. old D with HS diploma	CPS/R	Descriptive/Low
21	Peng, 1979	1967–1976/N, 18–24 yr. old D	CPS/P	Descriptive/Low
22	Sutter, 1977	1970, 1976/N, 18–24 yr. old D	CPS/R	Descriptive/Low
23	Tierney, 1982	1973, 1979/N, 18–34 yr. olds	CPS/R	Descriptive/Low
B. CHOICE				
Econometric Analyses, Set One (Standardized):				
24	Berne, 1980	1975/Applicants to two 2-year colleges	Own survey/J	Regression/High
25	Tierney, 1982	1975/N, college freshmen	CIRP, ACT, ETS, HEGIS/J	Logit/High
26	Tierney, 1980	1975/N, college freshmen	CIRP, ACT, ETS, HEGIS/J	Regression/High
27	Tierney & Davis, 1985	1979, 1981/ Pennsylvania HS seniors	CEEB, PHEAA/J	Regression/ Moderate
Econometric Analyses, Set One (Additional):				
28	Astin, Christian, & Henson, 1980	1973–1975/N, various, large	CIRP, PSAT, SAT/R	Regression/High
29	Fields & LeMay, 1973	1969, 1970/L, admitted applicants	Oregon St. U./ J	Discriminant/ Moderate
30	Hoenack & Weiler, 1979	1948–1976/L, HS grads in Minnesota	Various/J	Regression/High

ID No.	(6) Type of Aid/ Persistence Measure	(7) Results	(8) Remarks
18	All/NA	See Table 8.3.	
19	All/NA	See Table 8.3.	
20	All/NA	See Table 8.3.	
21	All/NA	See Table 8.3.	
22	All/NA	See Table 8.3.	
23	All/NA	See Table 8.3.	
	Enrollment increase at higher cost institution for $100 grant award in 1982 dollars, for students from low-income families:		
24	Change in net price/NA	1.7% metro community college 0.8% non-metro community college (t-score = 1.1)	
25	Change in net price/NA	1.1% medium cost institution 1.1% high cost institution	
26	BEOG, Loans, & CWS/NA	2.0% for students prefering public 2.4% for students prefering private.	
27	BEOG, PA awards, loan subsidies/NA	2.6% whites, 1981, PRU vs. PCC 2.7% non-whites, 1981, PRU vs. PCC 3.6% whites, 1979, PRU vs. PCC 3.0% non-whites, 1979, PRU vs. PCC 1.1% whites, 1981, HCP vs. PRU 1.3% non-whites, 1981, HCP vs. PRU	
28	BEOG, SEOG, Loans, CWS/NA	Extensive study with multiple samples and multiple issues; many more findings than those reported in text.	
29	Grants, loans, workstudy/NA	Award of some aid increased the enrollment rate an average of 33 percentage points across two years.	
30	Grants & loans, per HS grad/NA	An enrollment forecasting model for the U. of Minnesota based on rate of return theory; partial derivatives with respect to financial aid are positive.	

(continued)

Table 7 (Continued)
STUDENT AID

(1) ID No.	(2) Author, Year	(3) Year of Data/ Population	(4) Source/ Publication	(5) Statistics/ Control
31	Jackson, 1977	1972, 1973/N, 1681 accepted at more than one institution	NLS/D	Discriminant, Regression/High
32	Miller, 1981	1971/L, freshmen applicants	Stanford U./J	Regression, Probit/ Moderate
33	Weinschrott, 1978	1972/N, 14131 freshmen and non-students	NLS/D	Logit/High
Econometric Analyses, Set Two:				
34	Carlson, 1980	1968–1974/N, 50 states	NCES/R	Regression/Low
35	Carroll et al., 1977	1972/N, 14131 freshmen	NLS/R	Bayesian/High
36	Kehoe, 1981	NR/L, 26903 HS seniors	Own survey/J	Discriminant/ High
37	Manski & Wise, 1983	1972–1976/N, 4000 college students	NLS/B	Logit/High
38	Schwartz, 1985, 1986	1980/N, 11500 HS seniors	HSB/J	Logit, Tobit/ High
39	Zollinger, 1984	1980/L, Illinois scholarship winners	Own survey/J	t-tests/Moderate

ID No.	(6) Type of Aid/ Persistence Measure	(7) Results	(8) Remarks
31	All/NA	A college offering aid is 30 percent more likely to be chosen than colleges offering no aid—for students applying to two or more colleges; 44 percent of students offered aid at one college are offered aid at one or more other colleges, implying importance of specific aid awards.	
32	Grants, loans, CWS, wages/NA	Loans offered instead of grants repelled admitted applicants, when controlling for race, academic ability, and scholastic achievement.	
33	Grants, loans/NA	Grants useful anywhere induce low-income enrollment at both low-cost and high-cost four-year colleges; some evidence that grants useful only at specific colleges can influence choices of low-income students.	
34	All federal/NA	Enrollment at public four-year schools is enhanced by increases in the amount of federal aid available per FTE undergraduate and by increases in the percent of total federal aid available in the form of grants.	
35	BEOG/NA	Various choice effects of BEOG program are examined; BEOGs are associated with modest shifts of nonwhite males from public two-year to public four-year institutions and with slight shifts of white males from public two-year to private colleges; technical schools are considered non-collegiate.	
36	All/NA	Examined the ability of many student and institutional characteristics to discriminate between choice patterns. State grants were more influential than BEOGs on choices between in-state and out-state institutions.	
37	BEOG/NA	Used NLS to simulate effects of BEOGs in late 1970s. Two-year colleges and vocational-technical schools were virtually the only institutions gaining enrollment because of BEOGs.	
38	Public & private grants and loans/ NA	Effects of student aid on enrollment in four-year colleges are examined in two journal articles reporting on the same study; public grants promote enrollment, but private grants and the interest subsidy on loans do not.	
39	Pell, Illinois & Institutional aid/N	Hypothetical choice sets are used to examine the effects of student aid on choice; a large proportion of aid recipients enjoy enhanced choices, but 56 percent of students could not afford the least expensive colleges in their assigned choice sets.	

(continued)

Table 7 (Continued)
STUDENT AID

(1) ID No.	(2) Author, Year	(3) Year of Data/ Population	(4) Source/ Publication	(5) Statistics/ Control
Econometric Analyses, Set Three:				
40	Baird, 1984	1981/N, 3200 HS graduates who took SAT	CEEB/J	Descriptive/Low
41	Leslie, 1978	1965–1975/N, students in private institutions	NCES/M	Regression/Low
42	Mullen, 1982	1972, 1974/L, college students in NY	NY State Educ. Dept./J	Descriptive/Low
43	Munday, 1976	1976/N, 2384 aid applicants	ACT/R	Descriptive/ Moderate
44	Shaut & Rizzo, 1980	1973/L, 1100 TAP recipients	NY State Educ. Dept./J	Chi-square, t-test/Low
45	Spies, 1973, 1978	1971, 1976/N, 2545 college students who took PSAT	ETS, Own survey/R	Regression, Logit/High
A. ACCESS **Student Opinion Surveys:**				
46	Astin et al., 1985, 1982, 1979, 1976	1985, 1982, 1979, 1976/N, freshman, very large	CIRP/R	Descriptive/Low
47	Carnegie, 1986	1984/N	Own survey/J	Descriptive/NR
48	Fenske et al., 1979	1976, 1973, 1970, 1967/Illinois aid recipients	Own surveys/J	Descriptive/Low

ID No.	(6) Type of Aid/ Persistence Measure	(7) Results	(8) Remarks
40	All (by implication)/NA	Effect of aid was examined indirectly by analyzing the college-going behavior of individuals who took the SAT test; income was unrelated to ability to enroll in first choice institution but was related to enrollment in four-year colleges.	
41	All/NA	In one analysis, the share of degree credit enrollment in the private sector is regressed on changes in the sum of federal and state student aid from 1965 through 1975 (the resulting r-squared value was .51). On the basis of several methods, the author concluded that student aid lead to the enrollment of an additional 250,000 students in the private collegiate sector in 1975.	
42	NY Tuition Assistance/NA	Primarily an examination of how higher education subsidies are distributed in New York State as a result of the TAP program; some movement of students among sectors is recorded, but much confounding due to other aid.	
43	All/NA	No correlation found between average family income of aid applicants and average family income at college attented; more low-income aid applicants than low-income students generally attend high-cost institutions.	
44	NY Tuition Assistance/NA	Examined effects of TAP for one year's recipients; the impact of income on enrollment choices seemed to be neutralized, but little control exerted over possible intervening variables.	
45	All/NA	Enrollment behavior of high ability students is studied; the effect of family income is smaller in 1976 than in 1971; probability of applying to high-cost college goes up as income increases, but modestly.	
		Aid Recipient Choices Dependent on Grant Aid: Family Income; Effect; Remarks	
46	All/NA	See Table 8.3, Panel B.	
47	Grants, loans/NA	All: 40.0% "any worthwhile"college 20.0% first choice institution	
48	Scholarships & Grants/NA	Grants: 10.2% (Needy) 8.4% 13.0% 11.6%	Scholarships: 23.0% (1976) (Needy & Able) 21.1% (1973) 31.3% (1970) 33.0% (1967)

(continued)

Table 7 (Continued)
STUDENT AID

(1) ID No.	(2) Author, Year	(3) Year of Data/ Population	(4) Source/ Publication	(5) Statistics/ Control
49	Foreman et al., 1984	1982/L, applicants for KY aid	Own survey/R	Chi-square, Discriminant/ High
50	Leslie et al., 1977	1974/L, HS seniors in portions of PA and NY	Own survey/J	Descriptive/Low
51	Litton, 1983	1979/L, HS seniors in 6 urban areas	Own survey/J	Descriptive/ Moderate
52	NY HESC, 1984	1981/L, 1788 FT undergraduates in NY State	Own survey/R	Descriptive/Low
53	Schwartz & Chronister, 1978	1977/L, 430 VA state grant recipients in private colleges	Own surveys/J	Chi-square/Low
Enrollment Shares:				
54	Astin, 1985	1966–1983/N, first-time FT freshmen	CIRP/B	Descriptive/Low
55	Davis & Johns, 1982	1966, 1971, 1976, 1980/N, first time FT freshman	CIRP/J	Descriptive/Low
56	Leslie, 1977	1967–1975/N, first time FT freshman	CIRP/M	Descriptive/Low
57	Fife & Leslie, 1976	1972–1973/Aid recipients in 4 states	Own surveys/J	Descriptive/ High
C. PERSISTENCE				
58	Astin, 1964	1957–1961/N, 6660	Merit Sch. Program/J	Chi-square/Low

ID No.	(6) Type of Aid/ Persistence Measure	(7) Results		(8) Remarks
49	SSİG & Ky Grants/Na	Needy:	56.6%	students at private colleges
			39.5%	students at public colleges
50	All/NA	Low:	42.2%	present college
		Middle:	32.2%	present college
		High:	21.2%	present college
51	All (net price)/NA	All:	45.0%	overall
			68.0%	blacks (19 respondents)
			51.0%	Asians (44 respondents)
			44.0%	whites (1178 respondents)
52	All/NA		51.0%	present college; aid somewhat more important to minority than to white students
53	VA Tuition Assistance/NA	Low:	22.6%	present college
		Middle:	15.4%	present college
		High:	4.9%	present college
54	All/NA	See Table 8.5.		
55	All/NA	See Table 8.5.		
56	All/NA	See Table 8.5.		
57	Scholarships & Grants/NA	See Table 8.5.		
		Effect Size:		
58	Scholarships/G/ E−4; T=P; S=P	.08		Graduation.

(continued)

Table 7 (Continued)
STUDENT AID

(1) ID No.	(2) Author, Year	(3) Year of Data/ Population	(4) Source/ Publication	(5) Statistics/ Control
59	Astin & Cross, 1979	1975–1977/N, PT/ FT, 14604	CIRP/R	Regression/ Moderate
60	Baber, 1974	1966–1972/L, PT/FT, 402	U. Missouri/D	z-ratio/Matched
61	Baber, 1974	1967–1972/L, PT/FT, 706	U. Missouri/D	z-ratio/Matched
62	Baber, 1974	1968–1972/L, PT/FT, 590	U. Missouri/D	z-ratio/Matched
63	Baber, 1974	1969–1970/L, PT/FT, 510	U. Missouri/D	z-ratio/Matched
64	Baber, 1974	1970–1971/L, PT/FT, 484	U. Missouri/D	z-ratio/Matched
65	Baber, 1974	1971–1972/L, PT/FT, 544	U. Missouri/D	z-ratio/Matched
66	Baber & Caple, 1970	1966–1967/L, FT, 243	U. Missouri/J	t-test/Low

ID No.	(6) Type of Aid/ Persistence Measure	(7) Results	(8) Remarks
59	All/2+ years T=P; S=P	−.06	Less than graduation.
		−.06	Grants vs. other.
		.01	Loans vs. other.
		−.03	Workstudy vs. other.
		−.05	Loans and workstudy vs. other.
		.02	Grants and workstudy vs. other.
		.04	Grants, loans, and workstudy vs. other.
		.06	Grants and loans vs. other.
		.14	Scholarships vs. other.
60	EOG/1+ years; G−4; G−6+; T=DO; S=P	−.04	Less than graduation.
		.25	Graduation.
		.20	Graduation in 5 or more years.
		−.02	Males vs. females.
		−.11	Males vs. females; graduation.
61	EOG/1+ years; G−4; G−5+; T=DO; S=P	−.13	Less than graduation.
		−.20	Graduation.
		−.17	Graduation in 5 or more years.
		−.04	Males vs. females.
		−.08	Males vs. females; graduation.
62	EOG/1+ years; G−4; T=DO; S=P	−.11	Less than graduation.
		−.15	Graduation.
		.21	Males vs. females.
		.32	Males vs. females; graduation.
63	EOG/1+ years; T=DO; S=P	−.14	Less than graduation.
		−.21	Males vs. females.
64	EOG/1+ years; T=DO; S=P	−.15	Less than graduation.
		.29	Males vs. females.
65	EOG/1+ years; T=DO; S=P	−.04	Less than graduation.
		.03	Males vs. females.
66	EOG/1+years; T=DO; S=DO	0.2	Large vs. small amount of aid.

(continued)

Table 7 (Continued)
STUDENT AID

(1) ID No.	(2) Author, Year	(3) Year of Data/ Population	(4) Source/ Publication	(5) Statistics/ Control
67	Beyer, 1971	1967–1970/L, PT/FT, 502	Southwest Union C./D	Factor analysis/ Moderate
68	Brooks, 1980	1977–1979/L, FT, 641	Indiana U./D	Chi-square/Low
69	Burnham, 1971	1966–1967/L, FT, 90	U. Arkansas/ D	Descriptive/Low
70	Burnham, 1971	1967–1968/L, FT, 99	U. Arkansas/ D	Descriptive/Low
71	Burnham, 1971	1968–1969/L, FT, 84	U. Arkansas/ D	Descriptive/Low
72	Burnham, 1971	1969–1970/L, FT, 90	U. Arkansas/ D	Descriptive/Low
73	Cameron et al., 1978	1976–1977/L, PT/FT, 200	A Michigan/ Comm. C./R	NR/Low
74	Cesa, 1980	1977–1979/L, 176	U. Calif., Berkeley/R	Descriptive/Low

ID No.	(6) Type of Aid/ Persistence Measure	(7) Results	(8) Remarks
67	All/1 + years; T = DO; S = DO	−.14	Private; 1967–69 in transition from 2-year to 4-year college; less than graduation.
68	NDSL, CWS/ 2 + years; T = DO; S = P	−.03	Males vs. females.
		−.11	Nonwhite vs. white.
		−.09	Loans vs other.
		.09	Workstudy vs. other.
69	EOG/1 + years; T = DO; S = DO	.05	Males vs. females.
		−.36	Males vs. females; graduation.
70	EOG/1 + years; T = DO; S = DO	.74	Males vs. females
71	EOG/1 + years; T = DO; S = DO	.05	Males vs. females.
72	EOG/1 + years; T = DO; S = DO	.11	Males vs. females.
73	BEOG/1 + years; T = DO; S = DO	.19	Less than graduation.
74	All/1 + years; T = DO; S = DO	.20	Less than graduation.
		.12	Grants vs. other.
		−.19	Loans vs. other.
		.30	Grants and loans vs. other.
		−.34	Scholarships vs. other. Freshmen and junior college transfer students.

(continued)

Table 7 (Continued)
STUDENT AID

(1) ID No.	(2) Author, Year	(3) Year of Data/ Population	(4) Source/ Publication	(5) Statistics/ Control
75	Cihak, 1983	1975–1981/L, 266	Oregon St. U./ D	Chi-square/ Matched
76	Clark, 1971	1966–1968/L, 182	U. Miss./D	Chi-square/Low
77	Crawford, 1966	1959–1961/N, 1291	Merit Sch./ Program R	Descriptive/Low
78	Davis, 1978	1976–1977/L, PT/FT, 13029	Montgomery C./D	t-test/Low
79	Fields, 1973	1969–1970/L, FT, 1321	Oregon St. U./ D/J	Chi-square, Discriminant/ Random
80	Fields, 1973	1970–1971/L, FT, 1252	Oregon St. U./ D/J	Chi-square, Discriminant/ Random

ID No.	(6) Type of Aid/ Persistence Measure	(7) Results	(8) Remarks
75	All/1 + years; G−4; G−6; T=DO; S=P	.20	Less than graduation.
		.00	Graduation.
		.12	Graduation in 5 or more years.
		−.35	Grants vs. other.
		.03	Loans vs. other.
		−.43	Workstudy vs. other.
		.13	Loans and workstudy vs. other.
		−.05	Grants and workstudy vs. other.
		.35	Grants, loans, and workstudy vs. other.
		.28	Grants and loans vs. other.
			Junior college transfer students.
76	EOG/1 + years; T=DO; S=DO	−.11	Males vs. females.
		−.07	Nonwhites vs. whites.
		.15	Large vs. small amount of aid.
		.10	Grants vs. other.
		−.06	Grants and workstudy vs. other.
		.11	Grants and loans vs. other.
77	All/2 + years; T=P; S=P	.25	Less than graduation.
		−.26	Loans vs. other.
		.05	Scholarships vs. other.
78	All/1 + semester; T=DO; S=DO	.16	Less than graduation.
79	All/1 + years; T=DO; S=DO	.13	Less than graduation.
		.17	Males vs. females.
		.03	Large vs. small amount of aid.
80	All/1 + years; T=DO; S=DO	−.10	Less than graduation.
		.28	Males vs. females.
		−.05	Large vs. small amount of aid.

(continued)

Table 7 (Continued)
STUDENT AID

(1) ID No.	(2) Author, Year	(3) Year of Data/ Population	(4) Source/ Publication	(5) Statistics/ Control
81	Flynn, 1980	1968–1976/L, 399	Dominican C./D	Discriminant/ Moderate
82	Haggerty, 1985	1975–1984/L, PT/FT, 724	Youngstown/ St. U./D	Chi-square, Discriminant/ Moderate
83	Herndon, 1981	1975–1980/L, PT/FT, 226	California St. Bakersfield/ D/J	Discriminant/ Moderate
84	Higgins, 1983	1980–1981/L, 3733	Ball St. U./J	Descriptive/Low
85	Hochstein & Butler, 1983	1981–1982/L, 655	U. Nebraska, Omaha/J	Descriptive/ Random
86	Iwai & Churchill, 1982	1975–1976/L, 1849	Arizona St. U./J	ANOVA, Chi-square/Low
87	Jensen, 1984	1970–1975/L, 475	Washington St. U./J	ANOVA/ Moderate
88	Jensen, 1981	1970–1974/L, 655	Washington St. U./J	ANOVA/ Moderate
89	Karmas, 1974	1966–1967/N, 547	U.S. Dept. of Labor/D/J	Regression/ Moderate

ID No.	(6) Type of Aid/ Persistence Measure	(7) Results	(8) Remarks
81	All/2+years; T=NI; S=DO	.35	Private; males vs. females.
		.10	Grants vs. other.
		.50	Loans vs. other.
		−.20	Workstudy vs. other.
82	All/G–8; T=DO; S=P	.91	Graduation in 5 or more years. Students over 24 years of age; graduation includes A.A. degrees.
83	All/2+years; T=P; S=P	.00	Males vs. females.
		−.11	Nonwhites vs. whites.
		−.01	Grants vs. other.
		−.08	Loans vs. other.
		.39	Workstudy vs. other.
		.33	Scholarships vs. other.
84	All/1+years; T=DO; S=DO	.17	Less than graduation.
85	All/1 semester; T=DO; S=DO	−.31	Males vs. females.
		.09	Grants vs. other.
		−.79	Loans vs. other.
		−.01	Workstudy vs. other.
		−.01	Loans and workstudy vs. other.
		.25	Grants and workstudy vs. other.
		−.08	Grants, loans, and workstudy vs. other.
		.16	Grants and loans vs. other.
		.54	Scholarships vs. other.
86	All/1+semester; T=DO; S=DO	.16	Grants vs. other.
		.18	Loans vs. other.
87	All/G−5; T=NI; S=DO	−.15	Graduation in 5 or more years.
88	All/# semesters; T=NI; S=DO	−.10	Less than graduation.
89	Scholarships/ 1+years; T=P; S=DO	.28	Males students only; 2-year and 4-year college students.

(continued)

Table 7 (Continued)
STUDENT AID

(1) ID No.	(2) Author, Year	(3) Year of Data/ Population	(4) Source/ Publication	(5) Statistics/ Control
90	Kinney, 1970	1967–1970/L, FT, 162	Washington St. U./D	Sign test/ Matched
91	Kreiger, 1980	1974–1979/L, 542	Troy St. U./D	Regression/ Random
92	McCreight & LeMay, 1982	1975–1981/L, FT, 300	Oregon St. U./ J	NR/Matched

ID No.	(6) Type of Aid/ Persistence Measure	(7) Results	(8) Remarks
90	Scholarships/3 years; T=DO; S=DO	−.03	Reenrolled sophomores; less than graduation.
		.49	Males vs. females.
91	All/# semesters, G−5; T=DO; S=P	.45	Less than graduation.
		.08	Graduation in 5 or more years; includes A.A. degrees.
		.82	Large vs. small amount of aid.
		.26	Grants vs. other.
		−.57	Loans vs. other.
		−.25	Workstudy vs. other
		−.18	Loans and workstudy vs. other.
		.10	Grants and workstudy vs. other.
		.20	Grants, loans, and workstudy vs. other.
		.08	Grants and loans vs. other.
92	BEOG/1+years; T=DO; S=P	.10	Less than graduation.
		.09	Graduation.
		.17	Graduation in 5 or more years.
		.41	Males vs. females; graduation.
		.22	Grants vs. other.
		.18	Grants and workstudy vs. other.
		−.31	Grants, loans, and workstudy vs. other.
		−.01	Grants and loans vs. other.
		.18	Scholarships vs. other.

(continued)

Table 7 (Continued)
STUDENT AID

(1) ID No.	(2) Author, Year	(3) Year of Data/ Population	(4) Source/ Publication	(5) Statistics/ Control
93	Nelson, 1983	1977–1981/L, FT, 2569	U. Connecticut/D	Discriminant/ Moderate
94	Odutola, 1983	1974–1975/L, FT, 615	Florida St. U./ D	Regression/High
95	Parker, 1974	1969–1973/L, 100	Chicago St. U./D	t-test, ANOVA/ Random
96	Peng & Fetters, 1978	1972–1974/N, 4539	NLS/J	Regression/ Moderate
97	Peng & Fetters, 1978	1972–1974/N, 1378	NLS/J	Regression/ Moderate
98	Riccobono & Dunteman, 1975	1972–1973/N, 6128	NLS/R	Descriptive/Low
99	Riccobono & Dunteman, 1975	1972–1973/N, 3047	NLS/R	Descriptive/Low
100	Selby, 1973	1968–1969/L, 101	U. Missouri, Columbia/J	Point biserial/ Matched

ID No.	(6) Type of Aid/ Persistence Measure	(7) Results	(8) Remarks
93	All/1 + years; T = DO; S = DO	.06	Males vs. females.
		−.32	Nonwhites vs. whites.
		−.08	Grants vs. other.
		−.11	Loans vs. other.
		.09	Workstudy vs. other.
		.02	Loans and workstudy vs. other.
		.05	Grants and workstudy vs. other.
		.04	Grants, loans, and workstudy vs. other.
		−.11	Grants and loans vs. other.
94	All/1 year; T = DO; S = DO	.28	Large vs. small amount of aid.
95	All/G − 4; T = DO; S = DO	.05	Graduation. Minority junior students.
97	All/2 years; T = P; S = DO	.09	Grants vs. other.
		−.09	Loans vs. other. Four-year college students enrolled in degree programs.
97	All/2 years; T = P; S = DO	.19	Grants vs. other.
		−.19	Loans vs. other. Two-year college students in transfer degree programs.
98	All/1 + years; T = P; S = NR	.07	Four-year college students; less than graduation.
99	All/1 + years; T = P; S = NR	.16	Two-year college students; vo-tech students excluded; less than graduation.
100	All/1 + years; T = P; S = DO	.28	Matched black students with white students; large vs. small amount of aid.

(continued)

Table 7 (Continued)
STUDENT AID

(1) ID No.	(2) Author, Year	(3) Year of Data/ Population	(4) Source/ Publication	(5) Statistics/ Control
101	Sheddan, 1976	1963–1973/L, 291	Bryan C./D	Discriminant/ Moderate
102	Silver, 1978	1975–1977/L, FT, 252	N. Greenville College/D	Descriptive/Low
103	Snyder, 1971	1967–1970/L, FT, 306	Four Penn. Comm. Col's/ D	Chi-square/Low
104	Snyder & Klien, 1969	1967–1969/L, 193	Harrisburg Comm. C./R	Chi-square/Low
105	Stampen & Cabrera, 1986	1979–1982/L, 4980	U. Wisconsin System/J	Logit/High
106	Stephenson & Eisele, 1982	1968–1972/N, 140	U.S. Dept. of Labor/J	Regression/ Moderate
107	Stephenson & Eisele, 1982	1972–1976/N, 101	U.S. Dept. of Labor/J	Regression/ Moderate
108	Taylor & Rafetto, 1983	1973–1974/L, 92	Temple J.C./J	Chi-square/ Random
109	Taylor & Rafetto, 1983	1974–1975/L, 96	Temple J.C./J	Chi-square/ Random
110	Taylor & Rafetto, 1983	1975–1976/L, 96	Temple J.C./J	Chi-square/ Random
111	Taylor & Rafetto, 1983	1976–1977/L, 99	Temple J.C./J	Chi-square/ Random
112	Taylor & Rafetto, 1983	1977–1978/L, 93	Temple J.C./J	Chi-square/ Random

ID No.	(6) Type of Aid/ Persistence Measure	(7) Results	(8) Remarks
101	All/2+years; T=NI; S=DO	.28	Private; males vs. females.
		.18	Grants vs. other.
		.00	Loans vs. other.
		.02	Workstudy vs. other.
102	All/2-years; G−2 T=DO; S=DO	.52	Less than graduation.
		.50	Graduation.
			Private college
103	All/2-years; G−3 T= DO; S=DO	.29	Less than graduation.
		.15	Graduation.
		−.15	Males vs. females.
		−.07	Males vs. females; graduation.
104	All/G/E−2; T= DO; S=DO	.44	Graduation.
		−.29	Males vs. females; graduation.
105	All/1 year; T= DO; S=NI	.03	Excludes nondegree students; less than graduation.
		.07	Loans vs. other.
		.12	Scholarships vs. other.
106	All/# semesters; G−5; T=P; S=P	.48	Female students only; less than graduation.
		.41	Graduation in 5 or more years.
107	All/# semesters; G−5; T=P; S=P	.46	Female students only; less than graduation.
		.17	Graduation in 5 or more years.
108	BEOG/G; T= DO; S=NR	.03	Graduation.
109	BEOG/G; T=DO; S=NR	.12	Graduation.
110	BEOG/G; T=DO; S=NR	.07	Graduation.
111	BEOG/G; T=DO; S=NR	−.15	Graduation.
112	BEOG/G; T=DO; S=NR	.36	Graduation.

(continued)

Table 7 (Continued)
STUDENT AID

(1) ID No.	(2) Author, Year	(3) Year of Data/ Population	(4) Source/ Publication	(5) Statistics/ Control
113	Taylor & Rafetto, 1983	1978–1979/L, 94	Temple J.C./J	Chi-square/ Random
114	Terkla, 1985	1972–1979/N, 4448	NLS/J	Path Analysis/ High
115	Thompson, 1971	1966–1970/L, FT, 384	U. Wyoming/ D	Descriptive/ Matched
116	Thompson, 1971	1967–1970/L, FT, 240	U. Wyoming/ D	Descriptive/ Matched
117	Thompson, 1971	1968–1970/L, FT, 204	U. Wyoming/ D	Descriptive/ Matched
118	Van Eaton, 1970	1970/L, FT, 135	U. Missouri, C. of Agric./D	Chi-square/ Random
119	Voorhees, 1985	1980–1981/L, 343	A Southwest U./D/J	LISREL/High
120	Williams, 1975	1969–1973/L, 195	U. Oregon/D	Chi-square/Low
121	Williamson & Feder, 1953	1947–1951/L, FT, 566	U. Denver/J	Descriptive/Low
122	Winder, 1972	1970–1971/L, FT, 200	Austin C./D	Chi-square/ Random
123	Yuker, et al., 1972	1970–1971/L, FT, 5883	Hofstra U./R	Descriptive/Low
124	Zielke, 1977	1973–1978/L, 204	U. Wyoming/ D	Chi-square/ Matched

ID No.	(6) Type of Aid/ Persistence Measure	(7) Results	(8) Remarks
113	BEOG/G; T=DO; S=NR	.20	Graduation.
114	All/G−7; T=P; S=NI	.43	Students in occupational programs; graduation in 5 or more years.
115	EOG/G−4; T=DO; S=P	.07	Graduation.
		.01	Males vs. females; graduation.
116	EOG/3 years; T=DO; S=P	.00	Less than graduation.
		−.15	Males vs. females.
117	EOG/2 years; T=DO; S=P	.02	Less than graduation.
		−.11	Males vs. females.
118	Scholarship/1 semester; T= DO; S=DO	.00	Less than graduation.
119	All/ 1+years; T=DO; S=DO	.14	Males vs. females.
		−.02	Nonwhites vs. whites.
120	EOG/# semesters; T=DO; S=DO	.00	Less than graduation.
		−.65	Nonwhites vs. whites.
121	Scholarship/1 year; G−4; T=DO; S=DO	−.11	Private; less than graduation.
		.00	Graduation.
		−.42	Males vs. females.
122	All/1 year; T=DO; S=DO	.50	Private college; less than graduation.
123	All/1+years; T=DO; S=DO	.29	Private; less than graduation.
		.05	Grants vs. other.
		.08	Loans vs. other.
		−.13	Workstudy vs. other.
		.09	Scholarships vs. other.
124	BEOG/1+years; G-4; T=DO; S=P	.16	Less than graduation.
		−.11	Graduation.

References

ALEXANDER, K. (1976). "The Value of an Education." *Journal of Education Finance*, 1 (Spring), pp. 429–467.

ALTMANN, J. L. (1985). *Indiana University Southeast's Impact on the Local Economy*. (ERIC Document Reproduction Service No. ED 254 180).

AMERICAN ASSOCIATION OF STATE COLLEGES AND UNIVERSITIES (1977). "Wisconsin Low Tuition Experiment Ends: Tuition Up; Enrollments Down." [Special report Nos. 1 and 2, August 31] Washington, DC: Author.

ANDERSON, C. J. (1986). *Student Financial Aid to Full-Time Undergraduates, Fall 1984*. Higher Education Panel Report No. 68. Washington, DC: American Council on Education.

ASHENFELTER, O., AND HAM, J. (1979). "Education, Unemployment, and Earnings." *Journal of Political Economy*, 87, pp. S99–S116.

ASHENFELTER, O., AND MOONEY, J. (1968). "Graduate Education, Ability, and Earnings." *Review of Economics and Statistics*, 50, pp. 78–86.

ASTIN, A. W. (1964). "Personal and Environmental Factors Associated with College Dropouts Among High Aptitude Students." *Journal of Educational Psychology*, 55 (August), pp. 219–227.

ASTIN, A. W. (1985). *Achieving Educational Excellence*. San Francisco: Jossey-Bass.

ASTIN, A. W., CHRISTIAN, C. E., AND HENSON, J. W. (1980). *The Impact of Student Financial Aid Programs on Student Choice*. Final Report to the U.S. Office of Education. Los Angeles: Higher Education Research Institute, University of California at Los Angeles.

ASTIN, H. S., AND CROSS, P. H. (1979). "Student Financial Aid and Persistence in College." Washington, DC: Office of the Assistant Secretary of Planning and Budget, U.S. Department of Education.

ASTIN, A. W., GREEN, K. C., KORN, W. S., AND SCHALIT, M. (1985). *The American Freshman: National Norms for Fall 1985.* Los Angeles: Higher Education Research Institute, University of California at Los Angeles.

ASTIN, A. W., KING, M. R., AND RICHARDSON, G. T. (1976). *The American Freshman: National Norms for Fall 1976.* Los Angeles: Higher Education Research Institute, University of California at Los Angeles.

ASTIN, A. W., KING, M. R., AND RICHARDSON, G. T. (1979). *The American Freshman: National Norms for Fall 1979.* Los Angeles: Higher Education Research Institute, University of California at Los Angeles.

ASTIN, A. W., HEMOND, M. K., AND RICHARDSON, G. T. (1982). *The American Freshman: National Norms for Fall 1982.* Los Angeles: Higher Education Research Institute, University of California at Los Angeles.

BABER, B. (1974). "Educational Progress of Educational Opportunity Grant Recipients Compared to Non-Recipients." Doctoral dissertation, University of Missouri, Columbia.

BABER, B. B., AND CAPLE, R. B. (1970). "Educational Opportunity Grant Studies: Persisters and Non-Persisters." *Journal of College Student Personnel,* 11 (March), 115–119.

BAILEY, D., AND SCHOTTA, C. (1972). "Private and Social Rates of Return to Education of Academicians." *American Economic Review,* 62, pp. 19–31.

BAIRD, L. L. (1984). "Relationships Between Ability, College Attendance, and Family Income." *Research in Higher Education,* 21, 4, 373–396.

BARBER, W. J. (1981). *The United States: Economists in a Pluralistic Polity.* History of Economy. Durham, NC: Duke University Press.

BARNES, G. W. (1975, June). Extension of the college-going/college-choice model to the NLS class of 1972 data. Washington, DC: Inner City Fund, Inc., HEW-ASPE Contract OS-74-154. 71–79.

BARTLETT, S. (1978). "Education, Experience and Wage Inequality: 1939–1969." *Journal of Human Resources,* 13, pp. 349–365.

BAUM, S. (1978). *The Economic Impact of Mercer County Community College on the Local Community.* Advanced Institutional Development Program Two-Year College Consortium. (ERIC Document Reproduction Service No. ED 160 178).

BEATON, A. (1975). The Influence of Education and Ability on Salary and Attitudes. In F. T. Juster (Ed.), *Education, Income and Human Behavior,* pp. 365–404. New York: McGraw-Hill.

BECKER, G. S. (1964). *Human Capital: A Theoretical and Empirical Analysis, with Special Reference to Education.* New York: National Bureau of Economic Research and Columbia University Press.

BECKER, G. S. (1975). *Human Capital: A Theoretical and Empirical Analysis, with Special Reference to Education* (2nd ed.). New York: National Bureau of Economic Research.

BEN-PORATH, Y. (1970). The Production of Human Capital Over Time. In W. L. Hansen (Ed.), *Education, Income, and Human Capital.* New York: Columbia University Press and the National Bureau of Economic Research.

BERGEN, M. B., AND ZIELKE, D. D. (1979). "Educational Progress of Basic Educational Opportunity Grant Recipients." *Journal of Student Financial Aid,* 9 (February), pp. 19–22.

BERGER, M. D. (1983). "Changes in Labor Force Composition and Male Earnings: A Production Approach." *Journal of Human Resources,* 18, pp. 177–196.

BERNE, R. (1980). "Net Price Effects on Two-year College Attendance Decisions." *Journal of Education Finance,* 5, 4, pp. 391–414.

BESS, R. (1980). *A Study of the Economic Impact of Six Community Colleges in Illinois.* Springfield: Illinois Community College Board. (ERIC Document Reproduction Service No. ED 191 516).

BEYER, D. E. (1971). "Analysis of Selected Intellectual and Non-Intellectual Characteristics of Dropouts and Survivors in a Private College." Doctoral dissertation, Baylor University.

BIRD, C. (1975). *The Case Against College.* New York: D. McKay.

BISHOP, J. (1977). "The Effect of Public Policies on the Demand for Higher Education." *Journal of Human Resources,* 12, pp. 285–307.

BLACKWELL, G. W. (1978). *Impact Study of Postsecondary Financial Aid in South Carolina.* Technical Report No. 4. Greenville, SC: South Carolina College Council.

BLAKEMORE, A. E., AND LOW, S. A. (1983). "Scholarship Policy and Race–Sex Differences in the Demand for Higher Education." *Economic Inquiry,* 21, pp. 504–519.

BLAKEMORE, A. E., AND LOW, S. A. (1985). "Public Expenditures on Higher Education and Their Impact on Enrollment Patterns." *Applied Economics,* 17, pp. 331–340.

BLAUG, M. (Ed.) (1968). *Economics of Education I.* New York: Penguin Books.

BLAUG, M. (1985). "Where Are We Now in the Economics of Education?" *Economics of Education Review,* 4, pp. 17–28.

BORUS, M. E., AND CARPENTER, S. A. (1984). "Factors Associated with College Attendance of High-School Seniors." *Economics of Education Review,* 3, 3, pp. 169–176.

BOWEN, H. R. (1977). *Investment in Learning: The Individual and Social Value of American Higher Education.* San Francisco: Jossey-Bass.

BRESLIN, T. P. (1979). *The Economic Impact of Trenton State College on the Local Community.* Trenton, NJ: Trenton State College. (ERIC Document Reproduction Service No. ED 185 911).

BRINKMAN, P. T., AND LESLIE, L. L. (1983). *Higher Education Financing: 1973–1980.* Boulder, CO: National Center for Higher Education Management Systems.

BROOKS, J. W. (1980). "Academic Performance and Retention Rates of Participants in the College Work Study Program and Recipients of National Direct Student Loans." Doctoral dissertation, Indiana University.

BURNHAM, J. E. (1971). "The Effectiveness of the Educational Opportunity Grant Program at the University of Arkansas as Measured by Student Persistence." Doctoral dissertation, University of Arkansas.

BUTLER, T. E. (1980). *An Estimate of the Economic Impacts of Thomas Nelson Community College.* Hampton, VA: Thomas Nelson Community College. (ERIC Document Reproduction Service No. ED 180 559).

BUTTER, I. H. (1966). *Economics of Graduate Education: An Exploratory Study.* Ann Arbor: The University of Michigan Department of Economics. (ERIC Document Reproduction Service No. ED 010 639).

CAFFREY, J., AND ISAACS, H. (1971). *Estimating the Impact of a College or University on the Local Economy.* Washington, DC: American Council on Education.

CALIFORNIA STATE POSTSECONDARY EDUCATION COMMISSION. (1984). *The Wealth of Knowledge: Higher Education's Impact on California's Economy.* Commission Report 84-1. Sacramento, CA. (ERIC Document Reproduction Service No. ED 248 833).

CAMERON, S. M., HAMILTON, B. E., AND HULL, A. L. (1978). "A Study of Community College BEOG Recipients." (ERIC Document Reproduction Service No. ED 194 126).

CAMPBELL, R., AND SIEGEL, B. N. (1967). "The Demand for Higher Education in the United States 1919–1964." *American Economic Review,* 57, pp. 482–494.

CAMPBELL, W. E., AND LINTHICUM, D. S. (1982). *Montgomery College Economic Impact Study, FY 1981.* Rockville, MD: Montgomery College Office of Institutional Research. (ERIC Document Reproduction Service No. ED 223 303).

CARLSON, D. E. (1975). *A Flow of Funds Model for Assessing the Impact of Alternative Student Aid Programs.* Menlo Park, CA: Stanford Research Institute.

CARLSON, D. E. (1976). *Access and Choice in Higher Education: Alternative Measures and Implications for Planning.* Davis, CA: Department of Agriculture, University of California at Davis.

CARLSON, D. E. (1980). *Student Access to Postsecondary Education: Comparative Analysis of Federal and State Aid Programs.* Summary of SISFAP Study D. Washington, DC: Office of Education, HEW.

CARNEGIE FOUNDATION FOR THE ADVANCEMENT OF TEACHING. (1986). "The Price of College Shaping Students' Choices." *Change,* 18, 3, pp. 27–30.

CARNEVALE, A. P. (1982). Cooperation for What? In J. C. Hoy and M. H. Bernstein (Eds.), *Financing Higher Education: The Public Investment.* Boston: Auburn House.

CARNOY, M., AND MARENBACH, D. (1975). "The Return to Schooling in the United States, 1939 to 1969." *Journal of Human Resources,* 10, pp. 312–331.

CARROLL, C. D. (1984). "Packaging of Grants, Loans, and Earnings for Financing Postsecondary Education." *Bulletin* (February). Washington, DC: National Center for Education Statistics.

CARROLL, S. J., MORI, B. M., RELLES, D. A., AND WEINSCHROTT, D. J. (1977). *The Enrollment Effects of Federal Student Aid Policies.* Rand Report R-2192. Santa Monica, CA: Rand Corporation.

CESA, T. A. (1980). *Undergraduate Leavers and Persisters at Berkeley: Results of a Telephone Survey Conducted in Spring, 1979.* Berkeley: University of California.

CHAPMAN, R. G. (1979). "Pricing Policy and the College Choice Process." *Research in Higher Education,* 10, 1, pp. 37–57.

CHESTNUT, E. R. (1983). *The Economic Impact of Schenectady County Community College on Schenectady County, 1981–1982.* Schenectady, NY: Schenectady County Community College. (ERIC Document Reproduction Service No. ED 241 078).

CHINLOY, P. (1980). "Sources of Quality Change in Labor Input." *American Economic Review,* 70 (March), 1, pp. 108–119.

CHISHOLM, M., & COHEN, B. (1982). *A Review and Introduction to Higher Education Price Response Studies.* Boulder, CO: National Center for Higher Education Management Systems.

CIHAK, M. R. (1983). "A Longitudinal Study of Oregon Community College Transfer Financial Aid Recipients at Oregon State University, 1975–81." Doctoral dissertation, Oregon State University.

CLARK, G. H. (1971). "Characteristics of Students Who Received Educational Opportunity Grants at the University of Mississippi." Doctoral dissertation, University of Mississippi.

CLINE, H. (1982). "The Measurement of Change in the Rate of Return to Education: 1967–75." *Economics of Education Review,* 2, pp. 275–293.

CLOTFELTER, C. T. (1976). "Public Spending for Higher Education: An Empirical Test of Two Hypotheses." *Public Finance,* 31, pp. 177–195.

CLOWES, D. A., HINKLE, D. E., AND SMART, J. C. (1986). "Enrollment Patterns in Postsecondary Education: 1961–1982." *Journal of Higher Education,* 57, 2, 121–133.

COHEN, J. (1977). *Statistical Power Analysis for the Behavioral Sciences* (rev. ed.). New York: Academy Press.

COHN, E. (1972). "Investment Criteria and the Ranking of Educational Investments." *Public Finance,* 27, pp. 355–360.

COHN, E., AND GESKE, T. G. (1986). *Benefit-cost Analysis of Investment in Higher Education.* Paper prepared for the Seventh Annual Yearbook of the American Education Finance Association.

COMMITTEE FOR ECONOMIC DEVELOPMENT. (1973). *The Management and Financing of Colleges.* New York: Author.

CONLISK, J. (1977). "A Further Look at the Hansen-Weisbrod–Pechman Debate." *Journal of Human Resources,* 12, pp. 147–163.

CORAZZINI, A. J., DUGAN, D. J., AND GRABOWSKI, H. G. (1972). "Determinants and Distributional Aspects of Enrollment in U.S. Higher Education." *Journal of Human Resources,* 7, pp. 39–59.

COSGROVE, J. J. (1984). *St. Louis Community College and the Local Economy: An Estimate of the College's Economic Impact.* St. Louis, MO: St. Louis Community College. (ERIC Document Reproduction Service No. ED 257 528).

CRARY, L. J., AND LESLIE, L. L. (1978). "The Private Costs of Post-secondary Education." *Journal of Education Finance,* 4, pp. 14–28.

CRAWFORD, N. C. (1966). *Effects of Offers of Financial Assistance on the College-Going Decisions of Talented Students with Limited Financial Means.* (ED 017000). Evanston, IL: National Merit Scholarship Corporation.

CREAN, J. (1975). "The Income Redistributive Effects of Public Spending on Higher Education." *Journal of Human Resources,* 10, pp. 116–123.

CURTIS, T. D., AND CAMPBELL, J. M., JR. (1978). "Investment in Graduate Human Capital: An Evaluation of the Rate of Return Approach." *Review of Business and Economic Research*, 14, pp. 74–89.

DANIELSON, A. (1969–70). "Some Evidence on the Private Returns to Graduate Education: Comment." *Southern Economic Journal*, 36, pp. 334–338.

DAVIS, H. L. (1978). "A Study Regarding Student Financial Aid Packaging and Academic Progress in a Community College." Doctoral dissertation, George Washington University.

DAVIS, J. S., AND JOHNS, K., JR. (1982). "Low Family Income: A Continuing Barrier to College Enrollment?" *Journal of Student Financial Aid*, 12, pp. 5–10.

DEAN, E. (1984). *Education and Economic Productivity*. Cambridge, MA: Ballinger.

DENISON, E. F. (1962). *The Source of Economic Growth in the United States and the Alternates before us*. (Supplementary Paper No. 13). New York: Committee for Economic Development.

DENISON, E. F. (1964). *Measuring the Contribution of Education, and the Residual, to Economic Growth. The Residual Factor and Economic Growth*. Paris: Organization for Economic Cooperation and Development.

DENISON, F. F. (1984). Accounting for Slower Growth: An Update. In J. Kendrick (Ed.), *International Comparisons of Productivity and Courses of Slowdowns*. Cambridge, MA: Ballinger.

DOUGLASS, GORDON K. (1977). Economic Returns on Investments in Higher Education. In H. R. Bowen, *Investment in Learning: The Individual and Social Value of American Higher Education*. San Francisco: Jossey-Bass.

DUNCAN, G. J. (1976). "Earnings Function and Nonpecuniary Benefits." *Journal of Human Resources*, 11, pp. 462–483.

DYE, R. F. (1980). "Contributions to Volunteer Time: Some Evidence on Income Tax Effect." *National Tax Journal*, 33, pp. 89–93.

EADE, T. I. (1977). "A Statewide Economic Impact Model for Public Institutions of Higher Education." Doctoral dissertation, University of Washington.

ECKAUS, R. S. (1973). *Estimating the Returns to Education: A Disaggregated Approach*. Berkeley, CA: The Carnegie Commission on Higher Education.

ECKAUS, R. S., EL SAFTY, A., AND NORMAN, V. (1974). An Appraisal of the Calculation of Rates of Return to Higher Education. In M. S. Gordon (Ed.), *Higher Education and the Labor Market*, pp. 333–371. New York: McGraw-Hill.

EL-KHAWAS, E. (1986). *Campus Trends, 1985*. Washington, DC: American Council on Education.

ENGLER, S. D., FIRNBERG, J. W., AND KUHN, L. R., JR. (1980, April). *The Economic Impact of the Louisiana State University System on the Louisiana State Economy*. Paper presented at the Annual Forum of the Association for Institutional Research, Atlanta, Georgia. (ERIC Document Reproduction Service No. ED 189 924).

ERLICH, I. (1975). On the Relation Between Education and Crime. In F. T. Juster (Ed.), *Education, Income and Human Behavior*, pp. 313–338. New York: McGraw-Hill.

FELDMAN, J. A., AND NEWCOMB, T. M. (1969). *The Impact of College on Students*. San Francisco: Jossey-Bass.

FELDSTEIN, P. J. (1979). *Health Care Economics.* New York: John Wiley.

FENSKE, R. H., BOYD, J. D., AND MAXEY, E. J. (1979). "State Financial Aid to Students: A Trend Analysis of Access and Choice of Public and or Private Colleges." *College and University,* 54, pp. 139–155.

FIELDS, C. R., AND LEMAY, M. L. (1973). "Student Financial Aid: Effects on Educational Decisions and Academic Achievement." *Journal of College Student Personnel,* 14 (February), pp. 425–429.

FIFE, J. D., AND LESLIE, L. L. (1976). "The College Student Grant Study: The Effectiveness of Student Grant and Scholarship Programs in Promoting Equal Educational Opportunity." *Research in Higher Education,* 4, pp. 317–333.

FLYNN, M. M. (1980). "Predictive Effectiveness of Financial Aid and Other Variables for Persistence of Baccalaureate Degree Students." Doctoral dissertation, Fordham University.

FOREMAN, D. W., LUNCEFORD, B. E., AND ELTON, C. F. (1984). *The Kentucky Grant Study: The Effect of State Grants on Access and Choice in Higher Education.* Frankfort, KY: Kentucky Higher Education Assistance Authority.

FRANCES, C. (1980). *College Enrollment Trends: Testing the Conventional Wisdom Against the Facts.* Washington, DC: American Council on Education.

FRANCES, C. (1982). *Basic Facts on College-Going Rates by Income, Race, Sex, and Age, 1970 to 1980.* Washington, DC: National Commission on Student Financial Assistance.

FREEMAN, R. B. (1975). "Overinvestment in College Training." *The Journal of Human Resources,* 10, pp. 287–311.

FREEMAN, R. B. (1976). *The Declining Economic Value of Higher Education and The American Social System.* [Occasional Paper] Palo Alto, CA: Aspen Institution for Humanistic Studies, Program of Education for a Changing Society.

FREEMAN, R. B. (1978). *The Effect of Trade Unionism on Fringe Benefits.* Working Paper No. 292. New York: National Bureau of Economic Research.

FREIDEN, A., AND LEIMER, D. (1981). "The Earnings of College Students." *Journal of Human Resources,* 16, pp. 152–156.

FUNK, H. J. (1972). "Price Elasticity of Demand for Education at a Private University." *Journal of Educational Research,* 66, pp. 130–134.

GARFINKEL, I., AND HAVEMAN, R. (1977). *Earnings Capacity, Poverty, and Inequality.* Institute for Research on Poverty Monograph. New York: Academic Press.

GAY, D., AND WEINTRAUB, F. (1978). *The Economic Impact of Independent Higher Education in New York State.* New York: Commission on Independent Colleges and Universities of the State of New York. (ERIC Document Reproduction Service No. ED 162 561).

GHALI, M., MIKLIUS, W., AND WADA, R. (1977). "The Demand for Higher Education Facing an Individual Institution." *Higher Education,* 6, pp. 477–487.

GILLESPIE, D. A., AND CARLSON, N. (1983). *Trends in Student Aid: 1963–1983.* Washington, DC: Washington Office of the College Board.

GLASS, G. V. (1976). "Primary, Secondary, and Meta-analysis of Research." *Educational Researcher,* 5, 3–8.

GLASS, G. V., MCGAW, B., AND SMITH, M. L. (1981). *Meta-analysis in Social Research.* Beverly Hills, CA: Sage Publications.

GOURMAN, J. (1967). *The Gourman Report.* Phoenix, AZ: The Continuing Education Institute.

GRILICHES, Z. (1958). "Research Costs and Social Returns: Hybrid Corn and Related Innovations." *Journal of Political Economy,* 66, pp. 419–431.

GRILICHES, Z. (1970). Notes on the Role of Education in Production Functions and Growth Accounting. In L. Hansen (Ed.), *Education and Income: Studies in Income and Wealth,* p. 35. New York: National Bureau of Economic Research.

GRILICHES, Z. (1977). "Estimating the Returns to Schooling: Some Econometric Problems." *Econometrica,* 45, pp. 1–22.

GRILICHES, Z. (1979). "Sibling Models and Data in Economics: Beginnings of Survey." *Journal of Political Economy,* 84, pp. S37–S64.

GROSSMAN, M. (1976). The Correlation Between Health and Schooling. In N. Terleckyj (Ed.), *Household Production and Consumption,* pp. 147–211. New York: Columbia University Press and the National Bureau of Economic Research.

GROSSMAN, M. (1982). *Determinants of Children's Health.* Report PHS 81-3309, NTIS P380-163603. Washington, DC: National Center for Health Services.

GUTHRIE-MORSE, B. (1979). "The Utilization of Part-Time Faculty." *Community College Frontiers,* 7, 3, pp. 8–17.

HAGGERTY, M. (1985). "A Comparison of Selected Variables of Adult Persisters and Nonpersisters over Age 24 at an Urban Commuter University." Doctoral dissertation, University of Pittsburgh.

HAMBRY, A. L. (1973). *Beyond The New Deal: Harry S. Truman and American Liberalism.* New York: Columbia University Press.

HANOCH, G. (1967). "An Economic Analysis of Earnings and Schooling." *Journal of Human Resources,* 2, pp. 310–329.

HANSEN, W. L. (1963). "Total and Private Rates of Return to Investment in Schooling." *Journal of Political Economy,* 71, pp. 128–140.

HANSEN, W. L. (1970). "Income Distribution Effects of Higher Education." *American Economic Review,* 60, pp. 335–340.

HANSEN, W. L. (1983). Impact of Student Financial Aid on Access. In J. Froomkin (Ed.), *The Crises in Higher Education.* New York: Academy of Political Science.

HANSEN, W. L., AND STAMPEN, J. (1986). Independent Students at Two-Year Institutions and the Future of Student Aid. In L. S. Zerling (Ed.), *The Community College and Its Critics.* New Directions for Community Colleges, No. 54. San Francisco: Jossey-Bass.

HANSEN, W. L., AND WEISBROD, B. A. (1969). "The Distribution of Costs and Direct Benefits of Public Higher Education: The Case of California." *Journal of Human Resources,* 4, pp. 176–191.

HARGRAVE, C. H., AND BURFORD, R. L. (1973). "An Input-Output Study of the Louisiana Economy." Occasional Paper No. 16. Division of Research, College of Business Administration, Louisiana State University.

HARTMAN, R. W. (1970). "A Comment on the Pechman–Hansen-Weisbrod Controversy." *Journal of Human Resources,* 5, pp. 519–523.

HARTMAN, R. W. (1972). "Equity Implications of State Tuition Policy and Student Loans." *Journal of Political Economy*, 80, pp. S142–S171.

HAVEMAN, R. H., AND WOLFE, B. L. (1984). "Schooling and Economic Well-Being: The Role of Nonmarket Effects." *Journal of Human Resources*, 19, 3, pp. 377–407.

HEARN, J. C. (1980). "Effects on Enrollment of Changes in Student Aid Policies and Programs." In J. B. Henry (Ed.), *The Impact of Student Financial Aid on Institutions*. New Directions for Institutional Research, No. 25. San Francisco: Jossey-Bass.

HELLER, W. W. (1966). *New Dimensions in Political Economy*. Cambridge, MA: Harvard University Press.

HERNDON, S. (1981). "A Longitudinal Study of Financial Aid Persisters, Dropouts, and Stopouts: A Discriminant Analysis." Doctoral dissertation, University of California, Los Angeles.

HETTIC, W. (1972). Consumption Benefits from Education. In S. Ostry (Ed.), *Canadian Higher Education in the Seventies*. Ottawa: Economic Council of Canada.

HIGGINS, S. A. (1983). "Student Financial Aid and Equal Opportunity in Higher Education." *College and University*, 58 (Summer), pp. 341–361.

HIGHT, J. E. (1975). "The Demand for Higher Education in the United States 1927–1972; the Public and Private Institutions." *Journal of Human Resources*, 10, pp. 512–520.

HIGHT, J. E., AND POLLOCK, R. (1973). "Income Distribution Effects of Higher Education Expenditures in California, Florida, and Hawaii." *Journal of Human Resources*, 8, pp. 318–330.

HILL, C. R., AND STAFFORD, F. P. (1974). "Allocation of Time to Preschool Children and Educational Opportunity." *Journal of Human Resources*, 9, pp. 323–341.

HILL, C. R., AND STAFFORD, F. P. (1980). "Parental Care of Children; Time Diary Estimate of Quantity, Predictability & Variety." *Journal of Human Resources*, 15, pp. 219–239.

HINES, F., TWEETEN, L., AND REDFERN, M. (1970). "Social and Private Rates of Return to Investment in Schooling by Race–Sex Groups and Regions." *Journal of Human Resources*, 5, pp. 318–340.

HOCHSTEIN, S. K., AND BUTLER, R. R. (1983). "The Effects of the Composition of a Financial Aids Package on Student Retention." *Journal of Student Financial Aid*, 13 (February), pp. 21–26.

HOENACK, S. A. (1968). "Private Demand for Higher Education in California." Doctoral dissertation, University of California, Berkeley, 1967. *Dissertation Abstracts International*, 29, p. 18A.

HOENACK, S. A., AND FELDMAN, P. (1969). *Private Demand for Higher Education in the United States*. Research Paper P-649. Arlington, VA: Institute for Defense Analyses.

HOENACK, S., AND WEILER, W. (1975). "Cost-related Tuition Policies and University Enrollments." *Journal of Human Resources*, 10, pp. 332–360.

HOENACK, S. A., AND WEILER, W. C. (1979). "The Demand for Higher Education and Institutional Enrollment Forecasting." *Economic Inquiry*, 17 (January), 89–113.

HOGAN, T. D. AND MCPHETERS, L. R. (1979). *The Economic Impact of Arizona State University*. Report to Arizona State University, College of Business Administration, Bureau of Business and Economic Research. Phoenix: Arizona State University.

HOPKINS, T. D. (1974). "Higher Education Enrollment Demand." *Economic Inquiry*, 12, pp. 53–65.

HOSSLER, D. (1984). *Enrollment Management: An Integrated Approach*. New York: College Entrance Examination Board.

HUFFMAN, W. E. (1974). "Decision-Making: The Role of Education." *American Journal of Agricultural Economics*, 56, pp. 85–97.

HUFFMAN, W. E. (1977). "Allocative Efficiency: The Role of Human Capital." *Quarterly Journal of Economics*, 91, pp. 59–80.

HUNT, S. J. (1963). "Income Determinants for College Graduates and the Return to Educational Investment." *Yale Economic Essays*, 3, pp. 305–358.

HUNTER, J. E., SCHMIDT, F. L., AND JACKSON, G. B. (1982). *Meta-Analysis: Cumulating Research Findings Across Studies*. Beverly Hills, CA: Sage Publications.

HYDE, W. D., JR. (1978). *The Effect of Tuition and Financial Aid on Access and Choice in Postsecondary Education*. Papers in Education Finance, No. 1. Denver: Education Commission of the States.

IWAI, S. I., AND CHURCHILL, W. D. "College Attrition and the Financial Support Systems of Students." *Research in Higher Education*, 17, 2, 105–113.

JACKSON, G. A. (1977). "Financial Aid to Students and the Demand for Postsecondary Education." Doctoral dissertation, Harvard University.

JACKSON, G. A. (1978). "Financial Aid and Student Enrollment." *Journal of Higher Education*, 49, 6, pp. 548–574.

JACKSON, G. A. (1980). "How Students Pay for College: Temporal and Individual Variation." *Higher Education*, 9, pp. 619–632.

JACKSON, G. A., AND WEATHERSBY, G. B. (1975). "Individual Demand for Higher Education." *Journal of Higher Education*, 46, pp. 623–652.

JACKSON, G. B. (1978). *Methods for Reviewing and Integrating Research in the Social Sciences*. Final report to the National Science Foundation for Grant No. DIS 76-20309. Washington, DC: George Washington University, Social Research Group.

JACKSON, G. B. (1980). "Methods for Integrative Reviews." *Review of Educational Research*, 50, pp. 438–460.

JACKSON, S., WALES, C., AND MONTI, G. (1978). *Washington State Community Colleges: Impact on the Economy of the State*. Seattle: Washington State Board for Community College Education, Research and Planning Office. (ERIC Document Reproduction Service No. ED 156 250).

JAMES, E. (1978). "Product Mix and Cost Disaggregation: A Reinterpretation of the Economics of Higher Education." *Journal of Human Resources*, 13, pp. 157–186.

JEACOCK, R. L. (1983). *The Impact of Malaspina College on the Local Economy*. (ERIC Document Reproduction Service No. ED 251 024).

JENSEN, E. L. (1981). "Student Financial Aid and Persistence in College." *Journal of Higher Education*, 52, pp. 280–294.

JENSEN, E. L. (1984). "Student Financial Aid and Degree Attainment." *Research in Higher Education*, 20, 117–127.

JOHNSON, G. E., AND STAFFORD, F. P. (1973). "Social Returns to Quantity and Quality of Schooling." *Journal of Human Resources,* 8, pp. 139–155.

JOHNSON, W. R. (1978). "A Further Look at the Hansen-Weisbrod–Pechman Debate: Comment." *The Journal of Human Resources,* 13, pp. 566–567.

JORGENSON, D. W. (1984). The Contribution of Education to U.S. Economic Growth, 1948–1973. In E. Dean (Ed.), *Education and Economic Productivity.* Cambridge, MA: Ballinger.

JUDY, R. W. (1970). The Income-Redistributive Effects of Aid to Higher Education. In L. H. Officer & L. B. Smith (Eds.), *Canadian Economic Problems and Policies,* pp. 302–317. Toronto: McGraw-Hill.

KARMAS, C. (1974). "Progress Through College: Determinants of Successful Completion of Each Undergraduate Year. Doctoral dissertation, Ohio State University.

KEHOE, J. J. (1981). "Migrational Choice Patterns in Financial Aid Policy Making." *Research in Higher Education,* 14, 1, 57–69.

KENDRICK, J. (1981). International Comparison of Recent Productivity Trends. In W. Fellner (Ed.), *Essays in Contemporary Economic Problems: Demand, Productivity, and Population—1981–1982 edition,* pp. 125–170. Washington, DC: American Enterprise Institute.

KENDRICK, J. W. (1983). *Interindustry Differences in Productivity Growth.* Washington, DC: American Enterprise Institute.

KINCAID, C., AND TIPPETT, C. (1984). *Caldwell Community College and Technical Institute Spending Patterns and the Caldwell County Economy: An Economic Impact Study.* Lenoir, NC: Caldwell Community College and Technical Institution, Office of Research and Planning.

KINNEY, R. G. (1970). "The Effect of Scholarship Aid Upon the Academic Achievement and Persistence of Washington State University Undergraduates." Doctoral dissertation, Washington State University.

KNUDSEN, O. K., AND SERVELLE, P. J. (1978). "The Demand for Higher Education at Private Institutions of Moderate Selectivity." *American Economist,* 22, pp. 30–34.

KOHN, M., MANSKI, C., AND MUNDEL, D. (1976). "An Empirical Investigation of Factors Which Influence College-Going Behavior." *Annals of Economic and Social Measures,* 5, pp. 391–419.

KREIGER, T. B. (1980). "A Longitudinal Study of the Relationship Between Federal Financial Aid Packaging and Retention for the Members of the Freshman Class of 1974–1975 at Troy State University." Doctoral dissertation, Florida State University.

LANDO, M. (1975). The Interaction Between Health and Education. *Social Security Bulletin,* 38, pp. 16–22.

LANGE, M. D. (1980). *St. Cloud State University's Impact on the Local Economy.* Report No. *HE 0134.91.* St. Cloud, MN: St. Cloud State College. (ERIC Document Reproduction Service No. ED 197 696).

LAZEAR, E. P. (1977). "Education: Consumption or Production?" *Journal of Political Economy,* 85 (June), pp. 569–598.

LEE, J. B. (1986, May). *Changes in Student Participation Rates.* Paper presented at the NASGGP/NCHELP Research Conference in Chicago, Illinois.

LEE, J. B., AND ASSOCIATES. (1984). *Rates of College Participation: 1969, 1974, and 1981.* Washington, DC: American Council on Education.

LEE, J. B., ROTERMUND, M. K., AND BERTSCHMAN, J. (1985). *Student Aid and Minority Enrollment in Higher Education.* Washington, DC: Applied Systems Institute, Inc.

LEE, L. (1982). "Health and Wage: A Simultaneous Equation Model with Multiple Discrete Indicators." *International Economic Review,* 23, pp. 199–222.

LEHR, D., AND NEWTON, J. (1978). "Time Series and Cross-sectional Investigations of the Demand for Higher Education." *Economic Inquiry,* 16, pp. 411–422.

LEIBOWITZ, A. (1974). "Home Investments in Children." *Journal of Political Economy,* 82, pp. S111–S131.

LEIBOWITZ, A. (1975). Education and the Allocation of Women's Time. In F. T. Juster (Ed.), *Education, Income, and Human Behavior,* pp. 171–198. New York: McGraw-Hill.

LEONTIEF, W. (1936). "Quantitative Input-output Study of the Louisiana Economy." *Review of Economics and Statistics,* 18, pp. 105–125.

LESLIE, L. L. (1977). *Higher Education Opportunity: A Decade of Progress.* ERIC Higher Education Research Report No. 3. Washington, DC: American Association for Higher Education.

LESLIE, L. L. (1978). *The Role of Public Student Aid in Financing Private Higher Education.* Topical Paper No. 10. Tucson, AZ: Higher Education Program, University of Arizona.

LESLIE, L. L. (1984). "Changing Patterns in Student Financing of Higher Education." *Journal of Higher Education,* 55, pp. 313–346.

LESLIE, L. L., AND FIFE, J. D. (1974). "The College Student Grant Study: The Effects of Student Grant and Scholarship Programs upon Higher Education Enrollment and Patterns of Attendance." *Journal of Higher Education,* 45, pp. 651–671.

LESLIE, L. L., JOHNSON, G. P., AND CARLSON, J. (1977). "The Impact of Need-Based Student Aid Upon the College Attendance Decision." *Journal of Education Finance,* 2, pp. 269–285.

LIBERMAN, J. (1979). *The Rate of Return to Schooling: 1958–1976.* Faculty Working Paper. Urbana: University of Illinois, Department of Finance.

LINK, C. R., AND RATLEDGE, E. C. (1975). "Social Returns to Quantity and Quality of Education: A Further Statement." *Journal of Human Resources,* 10, pp. 78–89.

LINTHICUM, D. S. (1978). *Economic Impacts of Maryland Community Colleges: A Closer Look.* Report No. *JC 780 533.* Annapolis: Maryland State Board of Community Colleges. (ERIC Document Reproduction Service No. ED 160 170).

LITTLEFIELD, W. N. (1982). *The Economic Impact of the Long Beach Community College District, Fiscal 1981.* Research/Technical Report 143. Long Beach, CA: Long Beach City College. (ERIC Document Reproduction Service No. ED 227 919).

LITTON, L. H. (1983). "Different Strokes in the Applicant Pool." *Journal of Higher Education,* 53, pp. 383–402.

LONGANECKER, D. (1980). *Federal Student Assistance: Issues and Options.* Washington, DC: Congressional Budget Office.

LUCAS, R. E. B. (1977). "Hedonic Wage Equations and Psychic Wages in the Returns to Schooling." *American Economic Review,* 67, pp. 549–558.

MACHLIS, P. D. (1973). "The Distributional Effects of Public Higher Education in New York City." *Public Finance Quarterly,* 1, pp. 35–57.

MACHOVEC, F. M. (1972). "Public Higher Education in Colorado: Who Pays the Costs? Who Receives the Benefits?" *Intermountain Economic Review*, 3, pp. 24–35.

MAHON, J. (1979). *The Economic Impact of Bucks County Community College on the Local Economy During Fiscal Year 1978–1979*. Report No. *JC B00 02B*. Newton, PA: Bucks County Community College, Office of Institutional Research. (ERIC Document Reproduction Service, No. ED 179 276).

MANSFIELD, E. (1982). *Education, R & D, and Productivity Growth*. Paper prepared for the National Institute of Education, Washington, D.C.

MANSKI, C. F., AND WISE, D. A. (1983). *College Choice in America*. Cambridge, MA: Harvard University Press.

MARKS, J. L. (1985). *The Enrollment of Black Students in Higher Education: Can Declines be Prevented?* Atlanta: Southern Regional Education Board.

MARRIS, R. (1982). *Economic Growth in Cross Section*. Birbeck College, Department of Economics. (Mimeograph).

MARSHALL, A. (1927). *Principles of Economics* (8th ed.). London: MacMillan Press.

MATTILA, J. P. (1982). "Determinants of Male School Enrollments: A Time Series Analysis." *Review of Economics and Statistics*, 64, pp. 242–251.

MAXWELL, L. (1970). "Some Evidence on Negative Returns to Graduate Education." *Western Economic Journal*, 8, pp. 186–189.

MCCREIGHT, K., AND LEMAY, M. (1982). "A Longitudinal Study of the Achievement and Persistence of Students Who Received Basic Educational Opportunity Grants." *Journal of Student Financial Aid*, 12 (February), pp. 11–15.

MCDONALD, M. B. (1980). "Educational Equity and the Fiscal Incidence of Public Education." *National Tax Journal*, 13, pp. 45–54.

MCENANY, G. S. (1979, September). *The Economic Impact of Brown University on the City of Providence and on the State of Rhode Island*. Providence, RI: Brown University.

MCGUIRE, J. W. (1976). "The Distribution of Subsidy to Students in California Public Higher Education." *Journal of Human Resources*, 11, pp. 343–353.

MCMAHON, W. W. (1976). "Influences on Investment by Blacks in Higher Education." *American Economic Review*, 2, pp. 320–324.

MCMAHON, W. W. (1981). *Expected Rates of Return to Education*. Faculty Working Paper No. 832. Urbana-Champaign: University of Illinois.

MCMAHON, W. W. (1982). *Externalities in Education*. Faculty Working Paper No. 877. Urbana-Champaign: University of Illinois.

MCMAHON, W. W. (1984). "The Relation of Education and R & D to Productivity Growth." *Economics of Education Review*, 3, pp. 299–313.

MCMAHON, W. W., AND WAGNER, A. P. (1981). "Expected Returns to Investment in Higher Education." *Journal of Human Resources*, 16, pp. 274–285.

MCMAHON, W. W., AND WAGNER, A. P. (1982). The Monetary Returns to Education as Partial Social Efficiency Criteria. In W. W. McMahon & T. G. Geske (Eds.), *Financing Education*. Urbana: University of Illinois Press.

MCPHERSON, M. S. (1982). Higher Education Investment or Expense? In J. C. Hoy & M. H. Bernstein (Eds.), *Financing Higher Education: The Public Investment*. Boston: Auburn House.

MICHAEL, R. T. (1972). *The Effect of Education on Efficiency in Consumption.* New York: National Bureau of Economic Research.

MICHAEL, R. T. (1982). Measuring Nonmonetary Benefits of Education. In W. W. McMahon & T. Geske (Eds.), *Financing Education: Overcoming Inefficiency and Inequity.* Urbana: University of Illinois Press.

MILLER, H. P. (1960). "Annual and Lifetime Income in Relation to Education: 1939–1959." *American Economic Review,* 50, pp. 962–986.

MILLER, L. S. (1981). "College Admissions and Financial Aid Policies as Revealed by Institutional Practices." *Economic Inquiry,* 19 (January), pp. 117–131.

MINCER, J. (1958). "Investment in Human Capital and Personal Income Distribution." *Journal of Political Economy,* 66, pp. 281–302.

MINCER, J. (1974). *Schooling, Experience and Earnings.* New York: Columbia University Press.

MINCER, J. (1984). *Comment: Overeducation or Undereducation?* In E. Dean (Ed.), *Education and Economic Productivity,* pp. 205–212. Cambridge, MA: Ballinger.

MOORE, G. A. (1978). "Equity Effects of Higher Education Finance and Tuition Grants in New York State." *Journal of Human Resources,* 13, pp. 482–501.

MOORE, G. A. (1982). "Income Redistribution From Public Higher Education Finance Within Relevant Age Cohorts." *Economics of Education Review,* 2, pp. 175–187.

MUELLER, M. W. (1978). *An Economic Theory of Volunteer Work.* Middletown, CT: Wesleyan University, Department of Economics.

MULLEN, J. K. (1982). "Implications of Tuition Grants in Higher Education: The Case of a Prior Need-Based Aid Program." *Economics of Education Review,* 2, 1, 49–65.

MUNDAY, L. A. (1976). *Impact of Educational Development, Family Income, College Costs, and Financial Aid in Student Choice and Enrollment in College.* Report No. 7. Iowa City, IA: American College Testing Service.

MURDOCK, T. A. (1986). "The Effect of Financial Aid on Persistence in American Higher Education." Doctoral dissertation, University of Arizona.

NELSON, D. W. (1983). "The Relationship of Race, Sex, Family Income, and Major Types of Financial Aid to Persistence of Freshmen Students at the University of Connecticut." Doctoral dissertation, University of Connecticut.

NEW YORK STATE HIGHER EDUCATION SERVICES CORPORATION. (1984). *Aid & Access: The Role of Financial Aid in Access to Postsecondary Education for Different Ethnic Groups in New York State.* Albany, NY: New York State Higher Education Services Corporation.

NOEL, L. (1985). Increasing Student Retention: New Challenges and Potential. In L. Noel, R. Levitz, D. Saluri, and Associates, *Increasing Student Retention.* San Francisco: Jossey-Bass, pp. 1–27.

NORTH, D. (1955). "Location Theory and Regional Economic Growth." *Journal of Political Economy,* 63, pp. 243–258.

ODUTOLA, A. A. (1983). "A Longitudinal Study of the Effects of Academic, Demographic, and Financial Aid Factors on Retention for the Freshmen Class of 1974 at the Florida State University." Doctoral dissertation, Florida State University.

OLSON, L., AND ROSENFELD, R. (1984). "Parents and the Process of Gaining Access to

Student Financial Aid." *Journal of Higher Education,* 55 (July/August), pp. 455–480.

Olson, L. (1981). *The Economic Impact of Independent Colleges and Universities on Massachusetts in 1979–80 and 1980–81.* Report No. *HE 015 T54.* Washington, DC: Data Resources. (ERIC Document Reproduction Service No. ED 217 776).

O'Neill, D. M., and Sepielli, P. (1985). *Education in the United States: 1940–1983.* U.S. Bureau of the Census, Special Demographic Analysis, CDS-85-1. Washington, DC: U.S. Government Printing Office.

Orvis, C. C. (1975). "The Effects of Distance on College Attendance Rates and a Cost/Benefit Analysis of Closing a Minnesota State College." Doctoral dissertation, University of Minnesota. *Dissertation Abstracts International,* 38, 6244A.

Parker, S. A. (1974). "The Effect of Financial Assistance and Counseling on the Educational Progress of Minority Students in an Urban Public University." Doctoral dissertation, Northwestern University.

Parsons, D. O. (1974). "The Cost of School Time, Foregone Earnings, and Human Capital Formation." *Journal of Political Economy,* 82, pp. 251–266.

Pechman, J. A. (1970). "The Distributional Effects of Public Higher Education in California." *Journal of Human Resources,* 5, pp. 361–370.

Pechman, J. A. (1972). "Notes on the Intergenerational Transfer of Public Higher-Education Benefits." *Journal of Political Economy,* 80, pp. S256–S259.

Peng, S. S. (1979). "Impact of Student Financial Aid Programs on the Achievement of Equal Educational Opportunity in Higher Education." Paper presented at the Annual Conference of the Association for the Study of Higher Education, Chicago.

Peng, S. S., and Fetters, W. B. (1978). "Variables in Withdrawal During the First Two Years of College: Preliminary Findings from the National Longitudinal Study of the High School Class of 1972." *American Educational Research Journal,* 15 (Summer), pp. 361–372.

Pennsylvania Economy League. (1981). *Higher Education and the Economy: A Survey of the Impact on Pennsylvania Economy of Its Colleges and Universities.* Report No. *HE 014 674.* Harrisburg: Pennsylvania Economy League. (ERIC Document Reproduction Service, No. ED 212 204).

Philadelphia Community College. (1982, February). *The Economic Impact of Community College of Philadelphia on the Philadelphia Area.* Report 18. Philadelphia: Philadelphia Community College, Office of Institutional Research.

Plant, M., and Welch F. (1984). Measuring the Impact of Education on Productivity. In E. Dean (Ed.), *Education and Economic Productivity,* pp. 163–194. Cambridge, MA: Ballinger.

Plisko, V. W. (Ed.). (1984). *The Condition of Education.* Washington, DC: National Center for Education Statistics.

Poris, M., and Eskow, S. (1978). *The Impact of Rockland Community College on the Economy of Rockland County.* Report No. *JC 790 056.* Suffern, NY: Rockland Community College. (ERIC Document Reproduction Service No. ED 164 049).

Posey, E. I. (1983). *Georgia State University Spending Patterns and the Atlanta Economy, 1983.* Institutional Research Report No. 84-2, Office of Institutional Planning. Atlanta: Georgia State University. (ERIC Document Reproduction Service No. ED 234 712).

PSACHAROPOULOS, G. (1973). *Returns to Education.* New York: American Elsevier.

PSACHAROPOULOS, G. (1975). *Earnings and Education on OECD Countries.* Paris: Organization for Economic Co-operation and Development.

PSACHAROPOULOS, G. (1981). "Returns to Education: An Updated International Comparison." *Comparative Education,* 17, pp. 321–340.

PSACHAROPOULOS, G. (1984). The Contribution of Education to Economic Growth: International Comparisons. In J. W. Kendrick (Ed.), *International Comparisons of Productivity and Causes of the Slowdown.* Cambridge, MA: Ballinger.

RADNER, R., AND MILLER, L. S. (1970). "Demand and Supply in U.S. Higher Education: A Progress Report." *American Economic Review,* 60, pp. 326–334.

RAYMOND, R., AND SESNOWITZ, M. (1975). "The Returns to Investments in Higher Education: Some New Evidence." *Journal of Human Resources,* 10, pp. 139–154.

REED, R. H., AND MILLER, H. P. (1970). "Some Determinants of the Variation in Earnings for College Men." *Journal of Human Resources,* 5, pp. 177–190.

RIBICH, T. L., AND MURPHY, J. L. (1975). "The Economic Returns to Increased Educational Spending." *Journal of Human Resources,* 10, pp. 56–77.

RICCOBONO, J. A., AND DUNTEMAN, G. H. (1975). *National Longitudinal Study of the High School Class of 1972: Preliminary Analysis of Student Financial Aid.* Washington, DC: National Center for Education Statistics. (ERIC Document Reproduction Service No. ED 170303).

ROGERS, D. (1969). "Private Rates of Return to Education in the United States: A Case Study." *Yale Economic Essays,* 9, pp. 88–134.

ROMANO, R., AND HERBERT, N. (1985, January). *The Economic Impacts of the College on the Local Economy.* Binghamtown, NY: Broome Community College, Institution for Community College Research.

ROSEN, M. I. AND OTHERS. (1985). *The University of Wisconsin-Madison and the Local and State Economies: A Second Look.* Monograph No. 20. Madison: Wisconsin University, Graduate School of Business. (ERIC Document Reproduction Service No. ED 256 199).

ROSEN, S. (1977). Human Capital: A Survey of Empirical Research. In R. G. Ehrenberg (Ed.), *Research in Labor Economics* pp. 3–39. Greenwich, CT: JAI Press.

ROSEN, S., AND TAUBMAN, P. (1982). "Changes in Life Cycle Earnings: What Do Social Security Data Show?" *Journal of Human Resources,* 17, pp. 321–338.

RUMBERGER, R. W. (1980). "The Economic Decline of College Graduates: Fact or Fallacy?" *Journal of Human Resources,* 15, pp. 99–112.

RUMBERGER, R. W. (1984a). "The Changing Economic Benefits of College Graduates." *Economics of Education Review,* 3, pp. 3–11.

RUMBERGER, R. W. (1984b). "The Job Market for College Graduates, 1960–90." *Journal of Higher Education,* 55, pp. 433–454.

RYAN, G. (1983). *The Direct Economic Impact of Brookdale Community College.* Lincroft, NJ: Brookdale Community College, Office of Research and Development.

ST. JOHN, E. P., AND BYCE, C. (1982). "The Changing Federal Role in Student Financial Aid." In M. Kramer (Ed.), *Meeting Student Aid Needs in a Period of Retrenchment.* New Directions for Higher Education, No. 40. San Francisco: Jossey-Bass.

SALLEY, C. D. (1976). *Georgia State University Spending Patterns and the Atlanta Economy.* Institutional Research Report No. 77-8. Atlanta: Georgia State University, Office of Institutional Planning. (ERIC Document Reproduction Service No. ED 135 320).

SALLEY, C. D. (1979). *Georgia State University Spending Patterns and the Atlanta Economy, 1978.* Institutional Research Report No. 79-8. Atlanta: Georgia State University, Office of Institutional Planning. (ERIC Document Reproduction Service No. ED 167 059).

SCHIMMELPFENNIG, H. R. (1983). *A Study of the Economic Impacts of Bismarck Junior College upon the Local Community.* Bismarck, ND: Bismarck Junior College. (ERIC Document Reproduction Service No. ED 229 057).

SCHULTZ, T. W. (1960). "Capital Formation by Education." *Journal of Political Economy,* 86, pp. 571–583.

SCHULTZ, T. W. (1961). Education and Economic Growth. In N. B. Henry (Ed.), *Social Forces Influencing American Education.* Chicago: National Society for the Study of Education.

SCHULTZ, T. W. (1963). *The Economic Value of Education.* New York: Columbia University Press.

SCHULTZ, T. W. (1971). *Investment in Human Capital: The Role of Education and of Research.* New York: The Free Press.

SCHULTZ, T. W. (1975). "The Value of the Ability to Deal with Disequilibria." *Journal of Economic Literature,* 13, pp. 827–846.

SCHULTZ, T. W. (1981). *Investing in People.* Los Angeles: University of California Press.

SCHWARTZ, J. B. (1985). "Student Financial Aid and the College Enrollment Decision: The Effects of Public and Private Grants and Interest Subsidies." *Economics of Education Review,* 4, 7, 129–144.

SCHWARTZ, J. B. (1986). "Wealth Neutrality in Higher Education; The Effects of Student Grants." *Economics of Education Review,* 5, 2, 107–117.

SCHWARTZ, T. A., AND CHRONISTER, J. L. (1978). "Meeting the Intent of a State-Funded Student Aid Program: Test of an Assessment Model." *Journal of Student Financial Aid,* 8, 3, 18–29.

SEEBORG, M. C. (1975). "The Effect of Curricular Choice on Alumni Income." *Journal of Behavioral Economics,* 7, pp. 151–172.

SELBY, J. E. (1973). "Relationships Existing Among Race, Student Financial Aid, and Persistence in College." *Journal of College Student Personnel,* 14 (January), pp. 38–40.

SELGAS, J. W., SAUSSY, J. C., AND BLOCKER, C. E. (1979). *The Impact of the College on the Local Economy.* Research Report No. 1. Harrisburg, PA: Harrisburg Area Community College.

SELOWSKY, M. (1969). "On the Measurement of Education's Contribution to Growth." *Quarterly Journal of Economics,* 83, pp. 449–463.

SHAUT, W. E., AND RIZZO, L. M. (1980). "Impact of a Tuition Assistance Program on Students' Freedom of Choice in College Selection." *Journal of Student Financial Aid,* 10, 1, pp. 34–42.

SHEDDAN, M. K. (1976). "Prediction of Persistence for College Students Receiving Federal Financial Aid: A Multiple Discriminant Function Analysis." Doctoral dissertation, University of Tennessee.

SHEEHAN, J. (1973). *The Economics of Education.* London: George Allen and Unwin.

SIEGFRIED, J. J. (1972–1973). "Rate of Return to the Ph.D. in Economics." *Industrial and Labor Relations Review,* 26, pp. 420–431.

SILVER, J. H. (1978). "The Effect of State and Federal Aid Awards on Persistence, Academic Success and Chances for Graduation Among Freshmen Enrolling at North Greenville College in Fall, 1975." Practicum, Nova University.

SMITH, A. (1776). *The Wealth of Nations.* Dublin: Whitestone.

SMITH, J. P., AND WELCH, F. R. (1978). *Local Labor Markets and Cyclic Components in Demand for College Trained Manpower.* Santa Monica, CA: Rand Corporation.

SOLMON, L. C. (1975). "The Definition of College Quality and Its Impact on Earnings." *Exploring Economic Research,* 2, pp. 537–587.

SOLMON, L. C. (1985). "Quality of Education and Economic Growth." *Economics of Education Review,* 4, pp. 273–290.

SOLOW, R. M. (1957). "Technical Change and the Aggregate Production Function." *Review of Economics and Statistics,* 39, pp. 312–320.

SPIEGLEMAN, R. G. (1968). "A Benefit/Cost Model to Evaluate Educational Programs." *Socio-Economic Planning Sciences,* 1, pp. 443–460.

SPIES, R. R. (1973). *The Future of Private Colleges: The Effect of Rising Costs on College Choice.* Princeton, NJ: Princeton University, Industrial Relations Section.

SPIES, R. R. (1978). *The Effect of Rising Costs on College Choice.* New York: College Entrance Examination Board.

SPRINGER, P. (1976). "Characteristics of Student OASDI Beneficiaries in 1973: An Overview." *Social Security Bulletin, November.* (ERIC Document Reproduction Service No. ED 072 877).

STAMPEN, J. (1980). *The Financing of Public Higher Education: Low Tuition, Student Aid, and the Federal Government.* AAHE-ERIC Higher Education Research Report No. 9. Washington, DC: American Association for Higher Education.

STAMPEN, J. O., AND CABRERA, A. F. (1986). "Exploring the Effects of Student Aid on Attrition." *Journal of Student Financial Aid,* 16 (Spring), pp. 28–40.

STATE UNIVERSITY OF NEW YORK, OFFICE OF COMMUNITY COLLEGES (1982). *The Economic Impact of SUNY Community Colleges.* Analysis Paper No. 823. Albany, NY: Author.

STEPHENSON, S. P., JR., AND EISELE, T. W. (1982). "The Impact of Financial Aid on Women's Demand for Higher Education." *Research in Higher Education,* 17, 4, 345–361.

STEVENSON, M. (1982). *The Impact of Community Colleges on Oregon's 1980–81 Economy.* Gresham, OR: Mount Hood Community College, Office of Research.

SULOCK, J. (1982). "The Demand for Community College Education." *Economics of Education Review,* 2, pp. 351–361.

SUTER, L. E. (1977). *Trends in College Enrollment by Family Income for Regions of the United States.* Washington, DC: U.S. Bureau of the Census.

SYNDER, F. A. (1971). "Financial Assistance in Selected Pennsylvania Community Colleges and Its Relationship to Persistence and Achievement." Doctoral dissertation, University of Maryland.

SYNDER, F. A., AND KLEIN, R. B. (1969). "Does Financial Aid Help? A Study of the Effectiveness of Financial Assistance to Students at Harrisburg Area Community College." (ERIC Document Reproduction Service No. ED 035 389).

TANNEN, M. B. (1978). "The Investment Motive for Attending College." *Industrial and Labor Relations Review,* 31, pp. 489–497.

TAUBMAN, P., AND WALES, T. (1973). "Higher education, mental ability, and screening." *Journal of Political Economy,* 81, pp. 28–55.

TAUBMAN, P., AND WALES, T. (1974). *Higher Education and Earnings.* New York: McGraw-Hill.

TAUCHAR, W. F. (1969). "Cross Elasticities of Collegiate Demand." *Review of Social Economics,* 17, pp. 222–232.

TAYLOR, G. C., AND BYRDEN, J. P. (1973). *The Economic Impact of the University of Denver on the State of Colorado.* Denver: University of Denver, Research Institution, Industrial Economics Divison.

TAYLOR, J. L., AND RAFFETTO, W. (1983). "Comparison of Success Rates of Basic Educational Opportunity Grant (Pell) Recipients with the Success Rates of Non Recipients." *Community College Review,* 11 (Summer), pp. 44–51.

TERKLA, D. G. (1985). "Does Financial Aid Enhance Undergraduate Persistence?" *Journal of Student Financial Aid,* 15 (Fall), pp. 11–18.

THOMPSON, J. R. (1971). "Academic Characteristics of Economically Disadvantaged Students in Educational Opportunity Grants Program. The University of Wyoming, 1966–1970." Doctoral dissertation, University of Wyoming.

THUROW, L. C. (1970). *Investment in Human Capital.* Belmont, CA: Wadsworth.

TIEBOUT, C. M. (1962). *The Community Economic Base Study.* New York: Committee for Economic Development.

TIERNEY, M. L. (1980). "Student Matriculation Decisions and Financial Aid." *Review of Higher Education,* 3, pp. 14–25.

TIERNEY, M. L. (1982a). *Trends in College Participation Rates.* Boulder, CO: National Center for Higher Education Management Systems.

TIERNEY, M. L. (1982b). "The Impact of Institutional Net Price of Student Demand for Public and Private Higher Education." *Economics of Education Review,* 2, 4, pp. 363–384.

TIERNEY, M. L., AND DAVIS, J. S. (1985). "The Impact of Student Financial Aid and Institutional Net Price on the College Choice Decisions of In-State Seniors." *Journal of Student Financial Aid,* 15, 1, pp. 3–20.

TINTO, V. (1975). "Dropout from Higher Education: A Theoretical Synthesis of Recent Research." *Review of Educational Research,* 45, 89–125.

TINTO, V. (1982). "Limits of Theory and Practice in Student Attrition." *Journal of Higher Education,* 53, 6, pp. 687–700.

TOMASKE, J. A. (1974). "Private and Social Rates of Return to Education of Academicians: Note." *American Economic Review,* 64, pp. 220–224.

TRUSHEIM, D., AND CROUSE, J. (1981). "Effects of College Prestige in Men's Occupational Status and Income." *Research in Higher Education*, 14, 4, 283–304.

UNITED STATES BUREAU OF THE CENSUS. (1985). *Income of Families and Persons in the United States*. Current Population Series, p. 60.

UNITED STATES DEPARTMENT OF LABOR. (1986). *Chronicle of Higher Education*, 31, pp. 29, 32.

VAN EATON, E. N. (1970). "The Effects of Financial Reward on Student Performance, Attrition, Attitude, and Work-Study Extracurricular-Leisure Activities." Doctoral dissertation, University of Missouri, Columbia.

VOORHEES, R. A. (1985). "Student Finances and Campus-Based Financial Aid: A Structural Model Analysis of the Persistence of High Need Freshmen." *Research in Higher Education*, 22, 1, pp. 65–92.

WACHTEL, P. (1975). The Returns to Investment in Higher Education: Another View. In F. T. Juster (Ed.), *Education, Income and Human Behavior*, pp. 151–170. New York: McGraw-Hill.

WAGNER, A. P. (1984, October). *An (Almost) Sure Bet: The Payoff to a College Degree*. Paper prepared for presentation at the College Board Annual Meeting, New York, NY.

WALSH, J. R. (1935). "The Capital Concept Applied To Man." *Quarterly Journal of Economics*, 49, pp. 255–285.

WALTERS, P. B., AND RUBINSON, R. (1983). "Educational Expansion and Economic Output in the United States, 1890–1969: A Production Function Analysis." *American Sociological Review*, 48, pp. 480–493.

WEBSTER, D. (1984). "Who is Jack Gourman and Why is He Saying All Those Things About My College?" *Change*, 16, 18, pp. 14–19, 45–56.

WEINSCHROTT, D. J. (1978). "Private Demand for Higher Education: The Effect of Financial Aid and College Location on Enrollment and College Choice." Doctoral dissertation, University of California at Los Angeles.

WEISBROD, B. A. (1962). "Education and Investment in Human Capital." *Journal of Political Economy*, 80, pp. 106–123.

WEISBROD, B. A. (1964). *External Benefits of Public Education*. Princeton, NJ: Industrial Relations Section, Princeton University.

WEISBROD, B. A. (1971). "Costs and Benefits of Medical Research: A Case Study of Poliomyelitis." *Journal of Political Economics*, 79, pp. 527–544.

WEISS, Y. (1971). "Investment in Graduate Education." *American Economic Review*, 61, pp. 833–852.

WELCH, F. (1970). "Education in Production." *Journal of Political Economy*, 78, pp. 35–59.

WELCH, F. (1974). Comment. In T. W. Schultz (Ed.), *Economics of the Family*. Chicago: University of Chicago Press and the National Bureau of Economic Research.

WELCH, F. (1979). "Effects of Cohort Size on Earnings: The Baby Boom Babies' Financial Bust." *Journal of Political Economy*, 87, pp. S65–S98.

WELLSFRY, N. L. (1976). *The Economic Impact of the Virginia Community College System from 1966 to 1974*. (ERIC Document Reproduction Service No. ED 241 098).

WILLIAMS, E. R. (1975). "Comparative Analysis of the Attrition and Retention Rate of Students Who Received the Educational Opportunity Grant at the University of Oregon for the Academic Years 1969–70, 70–71, 71–72, and 72–73." Doctoral dissertation, University of Oregon.

WILLIAMS, J. L. (1977). "A Comparative Analysis of Occupational Basic Educational Opportunity Grant Recipients and Non-Recipients in Two Michigan Community Colleges." Doctoral dissertation, University of Michigan.

WILLIAMSON, B. L., AND FEDER, D. B. (1953). "Scholarship Winners—How They Rate on Campus and in Class." *Personnel and Guidance Journal*, 31, pp. 236–240.

WILSON, F. S. (1977). Regression and Choice Models to Estimate the Enrollment Effects of Campus Closure. Doctoral dissertation, University of Minnesota, 1976. *Dissertation Abstracts International*, 37, 7870A.

WINDER, J. B. (1972). "A Comparison of Certain Factors in Students With and Without Financial Aid at Austin College." Doctoral dissertation, North Texas State University.

WINDHAM, D. M. (1970). *Education, Equality, and Income Redistribution*. Boston: D. C. Heath.

WITMER, D. R. (1980). "Has the Golden Age of American Higher Education Come to an Abrupt End?" *Journal of Human Resources*, 15, pp. 113–120.

WITMER, D. R. (1983). Let's Increase College Quality, Funding and Tuition. La Crosse, WI: Office of the Vice Chancellor, University of Wisconsin–La Crosse.

YUKER, H. E., LECHTENSTEIN, P., AND WITHKEILER, P. (1972). "Who Leaves Hofstra and For What Reason?" Research Report No. 102. Hempstead, NY: Center for the Study of Higher Education, Hofstra University.

ZIMMERMAN, D. (1973). "Expenditure-tax Incidence Studies, Public Higher Education, and Equity." *National Tax Journal*, 26, pp. 65–70.

ZOLLINGER, R. A. (1984). "Financial Aid and Equity of College Choice: The Illinois Experience." *Journal of Education Finance*, 10, 1, pp. 121–131.

Index